ANALYTICAL REVIEW PROCEDURES AND PROCESSES IN AUDITING

by
Stanley F. Biggs,
Theodore J. Mock
and
Paul R. Watkins

The Canadian Certified General Accountants' Research Foundation

La Fondation de recherche de l'Association des comptables généraux licenciés du Canada

Research Monograph Number 14

PUBLISHED CCGA RESEARCH FOUNDATION MONOGRAPHS

No. 1: Historical Cost Accounting and its Rationality, by Yuji Ijiri
No. 2: Accounting for Local Governments in Canada: The State of the Art, by Arthur Beedle
No. 3: Local Government Financial Management and Accounting: A Research Framework, by Katherine Graham
No. 4: Accountants' Roles in Industrial Organizations and Access to Information, by Newman, Smart, Vertinsky and Kanetkar
No. 5: The Financial Reporting of Contingencies and Uncertainties: Theory and Practice, by Daniel Thornton
No. 6: Research in Audit Decision Making: Rationale, Evidence and Implications, by Robert Ashton
No. 7: Modern Accounting Research: History, Survey and Guide, by Richard Mattessich
No. 8: International Conflict of Accounting Standards, by Kenneth Most
No. 9: La compatibilité en périodes de changements de prix, par Daniel Zéghal
No. 10: Risk Assessment in Accounting and Auditing, by Theodore Mock and Ilan Vertinsky
No. 11: The Serviceability of Financial Information: A Survey, by Raymond Chambers and Haim Falk
No. 12: Materiality: An Empirical Study of Actual Auditor Decisions, by Chris Robinson and Len Fertuck
No. 13: Product Differentiation in Auditing: Auditor Choice in the Market for Unseasoned New Issues, by Dan Simunic and Michael Stein
No. 14: Analytical Review Procedures and Processes in Auditing, by Stanley Biggs, Theodore Mock and Paul Watkins
No. 15: Le marché de la vérification au Canada, par Daniel Zéghal

Ordering information is available from:

The CCGA Research Foundation
Suite 740, 1176 West Georgia Street
Vancouver, B.C. Canada
V6E 4A2
Telephone: (604) 669-3555
Facsimile: (604) 689-5845

ISBN 0-920167-10-1

The Canadian Certified General Accountants' Research Foundation was incorporated and registered as a charitable foundation on May 30, 1979. The creation of the Foundation grew from the desire of members of the Certified General Accountants' Association of Canada to make a meaningful contribution to accounting research in Canada by supporting research which would advance the accounting community as a whole. It is our desire to encourage pure and applied research in the areas of auditing, accounting and finance.

This monograph is the fourteenth in a series to be published by The Canadian Certified General Accountants' Research Foundation as part of CGA-Canada's continuing research effort. Each monograph expresses the viewpoint of its authors, and has been neither approved nor disapproved by CGA-Canada. These monographs are intended to stimulate thought, discussion and debate on matters relating to accounting, auditing and finance. The Foundation welcomes comments from readers.

William N. Perrault, FCGA
President
The Canadian Certified General
Accountants' Research Foundation
March 1989

Acknowledgements

The preparation of this monograph was supported by research grants from the Research Opportunities in Auditing Program at Peat, Marwick, Mitchell, and from the Canadian Certified General Accountants' Research Foundation. Derek Yee and his colleagues at The CCGARF were particularly helpful in bringing the project to completion. Support was also provided by the Center for Accounting Research at the University of Southern California, and by the University of Connecticut.

The opinions presented in this monograph are those of the authors, and should not be attributed to any of the supporting organizations. The authors gratefully acknowledge Glen Gray, William Holder, George Klersey, John Wild, and several anonymous independent auditors for assistance in case development and validation, participation in the study, and preliminary data analysis. We also acknowledge helpful comments on preliminary drafts from Al Arens, Jean C. Bedard, Ed Blocker, Jim Heintz and William Wright, and from research workshops at the following Universities: Connecticut, Michigan State, North Carolina, Ohio State, Southern California and Utah. Finally, Ingrid McClendon was very helpful in performing the many clerical duties involved in completing the monograph.

Stanley F. Biggs
Associate Professor
University of Connecticut

Theodore J. Mock
Professor
University of Southern California

Paul R. Watkins
Associate Professor
University of Southern California

March 1989

Abstract

This monograph presents a multi-method study of the effects of auditor analytical review judgments on audit program decisions. The monograph makes the following unique contributions to a better understanding of analytical review:

(1) It is the first study to provide descriptive evidence of the effect of analytical review judgments on changes in tests of detail in a planned audit program. An interesting finding was that auditors did not use analytical review to reduce tests of detail. However, analytical review was used to identify problems and provide guidance for increasing other tests of detail. This asymmetric use of analytical review has important implications for auditing.

(2) Most research in analytical review has been directed at developing statistical models. However, surveys of auditor practice indicate that auditor judgment, not statistical modelling, is predominant. This monograph provides a framework for studying auditor judgment and descriptive evidence of auditor judgment processes in several realistic audit settings. Results contrast judgments of experienced audit managers with less experienced seniors. The results provide evidence of auditor information search, evaluation and reasoning processes during analytical review.

(3) The research employed multiple methods. Both verbal protocol analysis and multidimensional scaling were used to identify and categorize auditor judgmental processes. Two audit settings were investigated, the first involving a case adapted from an actual audit client and the other involving systematic observation of auditors performing both statistical and judgmental analytical review during an actual audit.

Résumé

La présente monographie traite des effets, sur les décisions touchant le programme de vérification, des jugements que le vérificateur porte dans le cadre d'un examen analytique. Fondée sur plusieurs méthodes de recherche, cette étude apporte une contribution exceptionnelle à la documentation actuelle en matière d'examen analytique, comme le démontrent les précisions ci-dessous :

(1) Cette étude est le premier travail du genre à fournir des preuves descriptives sur les modifications que les jugements portés dans le cadre d'un examen analytique permettent d'apporter aux sondages détaillés dans un programme de vérification établi. Fait intéressant, les auteurs de cette monographie ont constaté que les vérificateurs n'avaient pas recours à l'examen analytique pour réduire les sondages détaillés mais plutôt pour déceler les problèmes et déterminer s'il y avait lieu d'augmenter l'étendue des sondages. Cette utilisation de l'examen analytique fondée sur les connaissances personnelles de chaque vérificateur a des répercussions importantes sur le domaine de la vérification.

(2) La plupart des recherches portant sur l'examen analytique sont axées sur l'élaboration de modèles statistiques. Toutefois, une étude des pratiques des vérificateurs révèle que c'est le jugement professionnel, et non pas les modèles statistiques, qui vient au premier rang. La présente monographie fournit un cadre à l'étude du jugement du vérificateur de même que des preuves descriptives illustrant le processus de jugement des vérificateurs dans plusieurs mises en situation réalistes. Les résultats de cette étude font ressortir le contraste entre les jugements de chefs de groupe chevronnés et ceux de premiers vérificateurs moins expérimentés. En outre, ils démontrent comment les vérificateurs obtiennent l'information, comment ils évaluent cette dernière et comment ils raisonnent au cours de l'examen analytique.

(3) Les recherches dont les résultats sont exposés dans la présente monographie reposent sur plusieurs méthodes. En effet, les auteurs ont eu recours à l'analyse de protocoles verbaux et à l'analyse multidimensionnelle pour déterminer et classer les processus de jugement des vérificateurs. Pour ce faire, ils se sont penchés sur deux mises en situation, la première portant sur un cas hypothétique inspiré d'une situation réelle et l'autre reposant sur l'observation systématique de vérificateurs mettant en oeuvre, dans le cadre d'un mandat de vérification réel, des procédés d'examen analytique fondés tant sur le jugement professionnel que sur les méthodes statistiques.

Contents

Chapter 1

INTRODUCTION

Analytical review is an area within auditing that has recently been the focus of considerable research attention. Practitioners hope that analytical review can increase the efficiency of audits, since it is thought to be a relatively inexpensive procedure that seems to have considerable power for identifying errors and guiding audits [Hylas and Ashton (1982); Willingham (1985); Felix and Kinney (1982)]. Researchers have focused mainly on the development of statistical and other formal models for use in the analytical review process in audits [e.g., Kinney (1978); Stringer (1975)].

While this research has been important, the judgmental aspects of analytical review have been largely ignored in the literature except for Kinney and Uecker (1982), Blocher *et al.* (1983), and Biggs and Wild (1985). This lack of attention seems misplaced, in light of two recent studies showing that analytical review, as it is currently practiced, is largely a judgmental process [Biggs and Wild (1984); Biggs, Mock and Watkins (1983)]. Even though analytical review is widely used, auditing firms define analytical review differently, and little is known about how analytical review procedures are actually applied and used in the course of an audit. In addition, a review of the literature reveals no studies of the link between analytical review judgments and audit program planning decisions. Ashton (1983) identifies only one study that has dealt with analytical review as it relates to audit decision-making.

The judgmental processes involved in analytical review are not well understood, and little theory exists to guide the design of judgmental analytical review research. One objective of this monograph is to provide some initial descriptive evidence of how auditors perform analytical review in relatively complex and realistic audit settings. A related objective is to induce theory based on the results of the descriptive study, so that hypotheses can be developed for future research.

This descriptive study investigates how experienced and inexperienced auditors design and conduct analytical review, and revise audit programs in light of their analytical review judgments. Two decision settings are studied, using a multi-method approach that allows the evaluation of analytical review judgments from several research perspectives. The first setting consists of a comprehensive case, containing over 100 pages of audit workpapers based on an actual audit. The content and comprehensiveness of this case was validated through discussions with practicing auditors and several statistical and analytical procedures. The case was administered to four auditors, who were asked to perform an audit planning task while thinking aloud. *Concurrent verbal protocol analysis* was used as one method of data collection and analysis, and *multi-dimensional scaling* was called upon to evaluate the cognitive structure underlying certain information processing activities. *Statistical (time series)* and *ratio analysis* were also performed on the underlying case data, to interpret the resulting analytical review judgments.

In a second task situation, auditors who were conducting an actual audit were asked to verbalize part of their actual analytical review. In this setting, the auditors evaluated client data from both a statistical and unaided judgment perspective, and provided largely *retrospective verbal protocols* for analysis.

The two task settings provided a range of results that are described in the course of the monograph. For example, the results from the first setting show that, based on preliminary analytical review, both managers and seniors identified the crucial audit problems embedded in the case. However, there were important differences in information acquisition and decision behaviour between the managers and seniors. These differences are consistent with differences found in studies of physics experts and novices, and can be attributed to existing theories and constructs in human memory and reasoning research. Surprisingly, there was little evidence that analytical review provided a basis for reducing the nature or extent of planned tests of details. This raises questions about statements such as the following, which is drawn from a recent CICA research monograph [Smith (1983, p. 2)]:

> Analytical review may, however, provide an essential portion of the evidence as to the reliability of the financial statements . . . .

If auditors do not rely on analytical review to reduce other testing, then how is analytical review used within an audit? The multi-method research approach was used to develop a better understanding of auditor behaviour, and to provide insight into auditor analytical review. For example, little evidence of probabilistic reasoning was found in the auditors' reasoning and judgment processes.

The intent of this monograph is to contribute to a better understanding of analytical review by auditors. Major topics include:

(1) A review of the professional and academic literature on analytical review;
(2) Development of a framework that illustrates the application of judgment and expertise in analytical review. Since research indicates that a large portion of analytical review is based on intuitive judgment, the framework is based on current research on human judgment, decision-making and cognitive science;
(3) A critical evaluation of the strengths and limitations of various methods for conducting research in complex accounting and auditing environments;
(4) The results of a descriptive study comparing experienced and inexperienced auditors conducting judgmental and statistical analytical review in realistic audit settings. This empirical research looks at the following issues:
    (a) The use of analytical review in audit planning and identification of critical audit areas;
    (b) The nature of the auditors' information search and reasoning processes in making analytical review decisions;

(c) Use of analytical review evidence in evaluating and adjusting a planned audit program;
(d) Differences between experienced and inexperienced auditors in the quality of analytical review judgments; and
(e) Differences between statistical and judgmental analytical reviews;

(5) Discussion of the implications of the empirical research for audit practice and research, including:

(a) The usefulness of detailed descriptive research for developing decision aids and expert systems;
(b) The usefulness of analytical review for making the audit more effective;
(c) Comparative advantages of statistical and judgmental analytical review procedures; and
(d) Implications for future research in analytical review; and

(6) Demonstration of the potential usefulness of a multi-method approach for studying complex judgment phenomena.

1.1 OVERVIEW OF RESEARCH PHILOSOPHY

In the past few years, there has been a growing dissatisfaction with traditional social science research methods, which tend to focus on the hypothetico-deductive approach to research. McCloskey (1985) in economics, and Mitroff and Kilman (1978) in organizational behaviour and management science, have identified a number of limitations to traditional research methods, and have recommended some alternative approaches. A central theme running through this literature is the need for greater tolerance of different methods, as opposed to narrow reliance on any one approach to the development of scientific knowledge. McCloskey (1985) notes that economists often develop elaborate assumptions about the behaviour of economic decision-makers, rather than simply asking them what they do or observing their behaviour. This literature suggests that a viable discipline should maintain room for a variety of research methods, any one of which may provide an appropriate approach to develop scientific knowledge.

This project attempted to implement some of the suggested alternatives, through the design of a multi-method study of the nature of auditor judgment in analytical review. Given the lack of relevant theory and understanding of auditor judgments related to analytical review, it was appropriate to consider a number of research strategies that differ from more traditional theory-based, hypothesis-testing methods. The selected approach involved the use of descriptive and inductive research methods to investigate auditor judgment.

These methods could be considered controversial, in that trade-offs have been made in favour of external validity, realism, and theory development, at the risk of less internal validity and less certainty that the collected data will apply to specific hypotheses. However, the lack of theory regarding auditor judgment in analytical review strongly suggested that a more inductive approach could make a greater contribution.

Our objective, then, was to gain insight into auditor judgment by applying an inductive, multi-method approach. To better understand the nature of analytical review judgments, the research involved actual auditors conducting a real audit and performing a realistic case. The costs of such an approach include limited sample sizes, and the need to filter and interpret a large of amount of data using coding and analysis methods that are not well established. The benefit is the generation of detailed descriptive evidence of analytical review judgments in complex tasks that was not previously available.

Chapters 2 and 3 of the monograph discuss the existing professional and academic literature on the use of analytical review in auditing, and derive a framework within which the judgmental and analytical aspects of analytical review may be considered. Chapter 4 discusses the research methods, including some general research questions that provide a focus for interpreting the data. Chapters 5 and 6 then describe the results of a process tracing analysis of a comprehensive case study, Pacific Electronics. The discussion includes an investigation of information search and acquisition, and a review of the auditors' detailed evaluation and decision activities. Chapter 7 presents a complementary methodology aimed at identifying the underlying cognitive dimensions of analytical review data obtained in the Pacific Electronics case, using a multi-dimensional scaling analysis of the information requested for use in the analytical review. Chapter 8 presents the results of our investigation of analytical review within an actual audit. The monograph concludes with a summary chapter, and prescriptions for future research.

Chapter 2

NATURE AND STATUS OF ANALYTICAL REVIEW

In this chapter, we will review and synthesize the literature on analytical review, focussing on papers published or received through the middle of 1986, as a basis for identifying the role of auditor judgment in analytical review. The literature originates with three major source categories: authoritative, professional (CPA firm), and academic. The review will show that the authoritative and professional literature provides few specific guidelines for the application of analytical review procedures (ARPs), while the academic literature has concentrated primarily on mathematical and statistical modelling of ARPs. The literature shows that auditor judgment plays an integral role in ARPs, even in cases where quantitative models are appropriately used.

2.1 AUTHORITATIVE LITERATURE

The review covered generally accepted auditing standards in the United States and Canada. In the United States, three statements have been issued: [SAS 23, AICPA (1978); SAS 36, AICPA (1981); and SSARS 1, AICPA (1979)]. The two latter statements apply to "non-audit" services: SAS 36 involves reviews of interim statements, while SSARS 1 covers reviews of financial statements. Although they fall somewhat outside the scope of a review which focuses on audits of financial statements, both documents define analytical review in a manner similar to SAS 23, so that many of the conclusions of this analysis would apply to reviews of interim or annual financial statements. The Auditing Standards Board in the United States recently issued an exposure draft [AICPA (1987)] which would revise auditing standards for analytical review, but as of this writing an official statement has not been issued.

SAS 23 (318.02) states that "analytical review procedures are substantive tests of financial information made by a study and comparison of relationships among data". The statement describes the essential aspect of analytical review as follows:

> A basic premise underlying the application of analytical review procedures is that relationships among data may reasonably be expected by the auditor to exist and continue, in the absence of known conditions to the contrary. The presence of those relationships provides the auditor with evidential matter required by the third standard of field work. The application of analytical review procedures may indicate the need for additional procedures, or may indicate that the extent of other auditing procedures may be reduced [SAS 23, (318.03)].

The Canadian standards view analytical review somewhat differently [CICA *Handbook*, paragraph 5100.02]:

> Sufficient, appropriate audit evidence should be obtained by such means as inspection, observation, inquiry and confirmation, computation and analysis, to afford a reasonable basis to support the content of the report.

This statement does not refer specifically to analytical review, nor does it specifically state that analysis can provide sufficient audit evidence, as does SAS 23. Smith (1983, p. 2) suggests that "the terms 'sufficient', 'appropriate' and 'reasonable' in this paragraph are those that need interpretation by the auditor in determining the nature, extent and timing of audit tests to be performed."

The CICA *Handbook*, paragraphs 5300.30 and .31, explain the term "analysis" as it applies to the third examination standard quoted above, and briefly discusses the concept and technique of analytical review. It states that analytical review alone does not normally provide the auditor with sufficient, appropriate audit evidence, even when the auditor considers the system of internal control to be very effective. However, analytical review can provide essential evidence on the reliability of financial statements which, when combined with other audit evidence, permits the auditor to report.

Thus, on the surface, SAS 23 provides a stronger role for analytical review than the Canadian standards. But in identifying the stages of the audit where analytical review applies, there is considerable similarity between the American and Canadian standards. SAS 23 states that ARPs may be applied:

(a) In the initial planning stages of an audit, to assist in determining the nature, extent, and timing of other audit procedures;
(b) While the examination is underway in conjunction with other procedures applied to individual elements of financial information; and

(c) At or near the conclusion of the examination, as an overall review of the financial information.

It is noteworthy that the exposure draft on analytical procedures [AICPA (1987)] issued by the United States Auditing Standards Board requires the use of analytical review during the planning and final review stages and strongly recommends their inclusion in the substantive testing stage.

While ARPs are applicable to all three major stages in the audit process, Kinney (1981) has suggested that ARPs perform mainly an "attention-directing" function during audit planning and testing. In applying analytical review as an attention-directing tool or as a substantive test, the auditor forms an expectation as to what the unaudited book values should be, based on evidence acquired during analytical review. This expectation may be a point estimate, or may consist of a reasonable range of possible values. The unaudited book value is compared to the expectation, and a materiality standard is applied to judge the significance of any difference.

The authoritative literature does not require the use of any particular type of procedure in an analytical review. However, SAS 23 suggests that auditors consider the following general approaches and factors in applying ARPs:

(a) The nature of the entity;
(b) The scope of the engagement;
(c) The availability of financial information about the entity's financial position, and the results of its operations;
(d) The availability of relevant non-financial information;
(e) The reliability of financial and non-financial information; and
(f) The availability and comparability of financial information for the industry in which the entity operates.

This review shows that the authoritative literature is just beginning to explicitly address issues related to analytical review. The recent monograph by Smith (1983) and the American Auditing Standards Board's reassessment of SAS 23, indicate that this is just the beginning of the profession's efforts on analytical review, rather than the end.

2.2 PROFESSIONAL (FIRM) PRACTICE LITERATURE

Auditors use analytical review procedures in various ways based on a range of techniques, methods, and practices. Based on a survey of audit practice, Esposito (1980) lists some 14 types of ARPs, including:

(a) Trend analysis, involving comparison and extrapolation of operating, budgeted, industry, and other data over time;
(b) Percentage analysis, based on fluctuations in the relative magnitudes of items within income statements, balance sheets, etc.;
(c) Ratio analysis, based on fluctuations in standard financial and operating ratios;
(d) Regression analysis of time series data to identify statistically significant deviations among current unaudited data;
(e) "Red flag" check limits;
(f) Prior-year audit adjustment analysis;
(g) Analysis of client discussions during the audit; and
(h) Reasonableness tests.

With the exception of regression analysis, which is a statistical modelling procedure, these ARPs may all be classified as informal procedures, that rely primarily on auditor judgment.

The results of several recent surveys are remarkably consistent in identifying the types of ARPs that are most commonly used in practice. The informal, judgment-based procedures are used widely, while the more formal statistical procedures that have dominated the academic literature are rarely called upon [see Esposito (1980); Biggs and Wild (1985); Tabor and Willis (1985); Biggs, Mock and Watkins (1984); Kaputz and Lemon (1986)]. In a survey of approximately 120 auditors, from large international accounting firms, all of whom were located in a large midwestern American city, Biggs and Wild (1985) found that over 90 percent used simple analytical review techniques such as scanning of data and ratio analysis. Biggs, Mock and Watkins (1984) surveyed a stratified sample of members of the American Institute of CPAs. Over 200 responses were received from auditors representing firms that ranged in size from small local to large international. Their results were essentially similar to Biggs and Wild, showing that auditors used informal ARPs most frequently, while the more formal statistical techniques were rarely used.

Tabor and Willis (1985) interviewed seven audit managers from one international accounting firm located in a southwestern American city, to determine the types of ARPs used and track changes in usage between 1978 and 1982. They found that ARP usage during the planning stage ranged from zero to over 90 percent of audit time. Usage was consistently high during the detailed substantive phase ranging from 15 to 65 percent of audit time, but was quite limited during the final phase. In general, ARPs were used more extensively in 1982 than in 1978. Only three auditors used statistical ARPs, and this usage was limited to a very small percentage of audit time (from 15 to 26 percent), for only three clients, during the detailed substantive phase. There was no usage of statistical ARPs during the planning or final phases of the audit.

Except for Biggs, Mock and Watkins (1984), the surveys all involved very limited samples of auditors. However, the results are all consistent with respect to the type of ARPs used. There is very little evidence that statistical ARPs such as regression analysis have received significant practical application. Informal techniques, such as scanning of data and ratio analysis, appear to be used extensively in practice.

There is some empirical research evidence to suggest that these procedures are effective in identifying material errors and irregularities in financial statements [Hylas and Ashton (1982)]. This conclusion was confirmed by Biggs and Wild (1985), who found that auditors considered analytical review the most useful procedure in detecting errors in financial statements.

In summary, the current authoritative literature provides some guidelines for ARPs, but allows considerable latitude in deciding how and when ARPs should be applied during an audit. As a result, auditors appear to use many different ARPs, ranging from informal procedures to more formal statistical modelling. Such statistical procedures as regression analysis, while used extensively by some firms [Stringer (1975); Stringer and Stewart (1986)], have not generally been utilized to the same extent as informal measures. Although some auditing firms believe that statistical modelling provides increased objectivity and greater audit efficiency, others believe that more research is necessary to determine whether statistical procedures are cost-effective.

2.3 RESEARCH LITERATURE

Research on ARPs has been directed at developing and testing mathematical and statistical models for ARPs, and at examining auditor judgment during analytical review. Since there has been no research to determine the relative merits of judgmental and statistical approaches, or to assess their combined use, statistical and judgmental research are reviewed separately. However, this distinction should not necessarily be maintained in future research.

2.4 STATISTICAL MODELLING RESEARCH

Since the literature on the uses of statistical models in auditing has already been reviewed in detail [see Kinney (1983); Arrington, Hillison and Icerman (1983); Felix and Kinney (1982)], and since the main purpose of this chapter is to provide a framework for the judgment research performed, this section is limited to a brief discussion of the statistical research, with emphasis on the strengths and limitations of the approach.

Statistical models in ARPs are used primarily to assist the auditor in forming an expectation about the unaudited book value of an account, and to provide an objective test of whether the expectation is significantly different from the unaudited value. The statistical modelling approaches that have been evaluated in the research literature for ARPs may be grouped into regression, time series, and other categories.

Regression analysis

Kinney (1979, 1981), Collins (1980), Kinney and Salamon (1979), and Kaplan (1978) have investigated the use of regression analysis in auditing. Kinney (1979) focused on identification of explanatory (predictor) variables to trace material misstatements in the account balances, and found that the best predictor was the presence of a material adjustment the previous year. Later, Kinney (1981) extended the initial study and expanded the available information to include ratios from other firms, an approach which resulted in better predictions.

Collins (1980) was concerned with identifying the appropriate form of regression model to use in ARPs, especially when stepwise regression was used to select the most appropriate set of predictor variables in the model. Collins found difficulties with the stepwise approach, in that the model often included variables that were inappropriate and excluded variables that should have been considered.

Kinney and Salamon (1979) evaluated the effects of using annual versus monthly data to obtain "best" estimates of the presence of material error in the account balances. Simulated account balances seeded with material accounting errors were assessed using the STAR model of DH&S, which relies on monthly data, and the regression model developed by Kinney and Salamon, which relies on annual data. STAR's monthly data were more effective than Kinney and Salamon's annual data in minimizing the standard error of prediction and in keeping model results within acceptable risk levels.

Kaplan (1978) used the regression modelling approach to build a financial model of a firm in order to determine which accounts were the "best" predictors for other account balances. This study yielded a series of regression equations that might be useful in predicting unaudited book values in ARPs.

In summary, the research on regression modelling approaches in ARPs has focused on the structural form of the regression equation, methods for selecting variables in the regression equation, the number of data intervals used to build the regression model, and the development of models of an entire firm through a series of regression equations to determine the "best" set of predictors for estimating unaudited account balances.

Time series models

While regression models use account balances, ratios, or other variables to predict the unaudited book value of an account, time series models use time as one of the predictor variables. The simplest statistical forecasting methods use a univariate model referred to as an Autoregressive-Integrated-Moving-Average (ARIMA) Box-Jenkins model. This procedure allows the auditor to consider numerous models in identifying the most appropriate model for a particular set of data.

Kinney (1978) and Albrecht and McKeown (1977) used the Box-Jenkins ARIMA models to compare with regression models in ARPs. Both found that the more sophisticated ARIMA time series models provide better prediction results, but not substantially better than regression analysis. Kinney (1978) suggests that regression will most likely be the preferred statistical model for use in ARPS, due to the added complexity and difficulty in training auditors to use the ARIMA time series models.

Dugan, Gentry and Shriver (1985) have suggested that the Census X-11 Model is superior to ARIMA models for time-series forecasting in that it provides a statistical decomposition of time series data. The components revealed by the X-11 model allow meaningful interpretations of underlying economic factors that increase the auditor's understanding of the time series under analysis. However, the authors provide no evidence of the application of the X-11 model in an analytical review setting.

Other

A variety of other statistical models have been reviewed for use in ARPs. Altman and McGough (1974) demonstrated the use of linear discriminate analysis to provide early warnings of client failure, by considering relationships among accounting variables. In this procedure, a discriminant function is used to predict possible financial difficulties. Kinney (1981) reports that both Touche Ross and Arthur Andersen have utilized this approach.

Lev (1980) has evaluated the use of index models in ARPs. In addition to the typical predictor variables found in regression, index models include indices of exogenous factors, such as changes in the inflation rate, technology, and consumer taste. Lev suggests that these models may be better predictors of unaudited book value than traditional time series or regression models, but that future extensions to research should be undertaken.

An implicit theme in the recent research was explicitly stated by Lev (1980, p. 543):

> The major benefits from using statistical techniques, such as index models, in analytical reviews are the increased objectivity of the auditor's tests and the closer, quantifiable relationship that can be achieved between analytical reviews and statistical sampling. Specifically, the use of statistical techniques in analytical reviews allows the auditor objectively to assess the likelihood of his actions, namely, the probability of accepting as correct a reported balance which, in fact, is materially misspecified, and the probability of rejecting as misstated a balance which is not materially in error.

Lev (1980), Wallace (1983), and others have suggested that simple, linear devices such as regression models can improve the judgment of experienced auditors, because of the objectivity of the models and their linkages to statistical sampling techniques. Lev (1980, p. 545) also cites psychological literature [e.g., Dawes and Corrigan (1974); Slovic, Fleissner, and Bauman (1974)] suggests that such models outperform expert judges, and that the consistent application of linear models leads to decisions that are better than those of the individuals who are being modelled. Hogarth and Makridakis (1981) cite similar references in the forecasting literature, and reach similar conclusions.

There would appear to be several limitations and weaknesses in the use of statistical models in ARPs:

(1) It may be difficult to satisfy the underlying assumptions of the model in audit practice. For example, Lev (1980, p. 527) assumes in his index model that the firm-industry-economy relationship is stationary over time, and that economic and industry factors can be reliably predicted. If this and other assumptions underlying these models are not met, the results of the modelling procedure cannot be relied upon;

(2) Auditors who use statistical models must specify the variables they include in the model. This implies the need for auditor judgment, and links the success of such variable selection to the experience of the auditor with the models and the client; (Some evidence of this is found in Chapter 7 of this monograph.)

(3) The reasonableness of the expectation obtained by a statistical model must be evaluated relative to the auditor materiality limits. This requires auditor judgment and experience, with both the models and the client;

(4) Most statistical models require a relatively large number of data points in order to reliably estimate the parameters of the model. If the historical data used to develop the model contain unusual fluctuations (due to economic conditions and/or operating characteristics of the firm), the model may not reflect current conditions and may bias the prediction results;

(5) For predictive purposes, the model must satisfy such underlying statistical assumptions as homoscedasticity of the error terms, uncorrelated error terms over time, independence of predictor variables, and linearity. If these assumptions are not met, the model results may be in error, or some judgment on the part of the auditor or analysts may be required to modify the model to satisfy the assumptions;

(6) Statistical model results are limited to the variables selected, and the data values from which the model was developed. These models may not be "rich" enough to capture other relevant information that may be useful to the auditor in forming his or her expectation;

(7) Available data may not be sufficient to develop a model;

(8) If sufficient data are available, they may not be reliable; and

(9) Special training, and therefore additional resources, are required to develop auditors with the necessary skills to work effectively with even simple statistical models.

Since the statistical models require considerable auditor judgment, Lev's (1980) suggestion that simple models often outperform experts may not be appropriate in ARP-related tasks. Statistical models may serve as decision aids to help the auditor assess the nature of unaudited account balances. But they should not be seen as a replacement for the auditor in analytical review.

Even if the statistical models were to be viewed as a potential substitute for auditor judgment, the research cited by Lev (1980) may be inappropriate for extrapolation to ARPs. Lev cites evidence that linear models of the decision maker's judgment process will outperform the decision maker. But this evidence is based on tasks that are very simple compared to the analytical review task facing a practicing auditor. This suggests the need for caution in applying the results of psychological research involving relatively simple tasks to the auditing environment, especially a diverse and complex process like analytical review. Even if prediction is based on statistical procedures, Einhorn and Hogarth (1982, p. 23-24) suggest that judgment is still required to determine the appropriate action.

This review of the statistical modelling literature clearly reveals the need for insight into the judgment process underlying ARPs.

2.5 JUDGMENT RESEARCH IN ANALYTICAL REVIEW PROCEDURES

Auditor judgment has been the focus of several recent research projects. One series of studies investigated whether auditors should use unaudited client data to develop an expected value for an account during analytical review. Some have argued that the practice increases audit risk and violates audit independence requirements [e.g., Kinney and Uecker (1982); Biggs and Wild (1985)]. Others have suggested that such a use of unaudited data may be appropriate under some circumstances [e.g., Shields, Solomon and Waller (1986); Heintz and White (1986a,b)]. Several studies have shown that the availability of unaudited client data influences auditors' estimates of account values.

An initial study addressing this issue, conducted by Kinney and Uecker (1982), involved analytical review of the gross profit percentage of a hypothetical manufacturing firm, where the experimental case contained two years' past audited information about the components of gross profit. By providing one group of auditors with a high unaudited gross profit and another group with a low unaudited gross profit, Kinney and Uecker confirmed their hypothesis that the non-investigation regions specified by each group would be "biased" by the unaudited value they received. Auditors' estimates of the client's gross profit percentage were generally proportioned to the unaudited gross profit percentage.

Biggs and Wild (1985) found similar results when they replicated Kinney and Uecker's (1982) experimental condition of giving auditors two years' audited information. However, Biggs and Wild also gave auditors five years' audited information while holding all other aspects constant. While the additional information reduced the effect of unaudited data on the auditors' non-investigation regions, there was still evidence that the unaudited values affected the auditors' analytical review estimates.

Several unpublished studies have also investigated this issue. Heintz and White (1986a) used nine-month data for the unaudited value, to emphasize the unaudited nature of the gross profit components, but found that auditors' estimates were still affected. In another study, Heintz and White (1986b) found that, regardless of whether the client had a material adjustment in the prior year, or experienced a system change in the current year, auditors' analytical review estimates were influenced by the unaudited data. Finally, Shields, Solomon and Waller (1986) found that auditors relied on unaudited data in making estimates, regardless of whether material misstatements were present.

This line of research points to some potential judgmental biases in analytical review. Wild and Biggs (1986) developed an analytical framework and provided simulation results showing that auditors will increase audit risk or costs when analytical review estimates are influenced by unaudited data, except when the client's financial statements contain no material errors. But for auditors to make that presumption would go counter to the essence of audit practice. Since unaudited values are readily available during an audit and since there are important risks associated with the use of such data in estimating account values, this line of research merits considerable attention by practicing auditors.

Libby (1985) asked experienced auditors to detect financial statement errors through a preliminary analytical review. Although the experiment was highly abstracted from the types of complexities found in auditing practice, he found the frequency and recency of auditor's experience with particular errors influenced their ability to generate or detect these errors. The results were attributed to the auditors' recent memory of errors. While his results require confirmation, Libby suggests the use of decision aids that take advantage of typical memory structures in order to enhance auditors' ability to detect errors during analytical review.

In a second experiment, Biggs and Wild (1985) had their subjects make intuitive extrapolations for a revenue account based on six deterministic time series patterns. Compared to mathematical extrapolations, auditors significantly underestimated the expected values for exponentially increasing and decreasing patterns. However, for linear and logarithmic patterns auditor estimates were considerably closer to the mathematical extrapolations. Since linear and logarithmic patterns were considered by Biggs and Wild to be more commonly encountered by practicing auditors, these results reflect favourably on auditors' ability to recognize time series patterns and form expected values.

Blocher, Esposito and Willingham (1983) investigated the effects of different situational and individual variables on auditors' judgments in planning and using ARPs. They detected considerable differences among auditor judgments in planning ARPs, but none of the situational variables could explain these differences. Auditor judgments for using ARPs showed much less variability, although the limited availability of data on actual usage may have influenced this finding. The viability of judgments found in this study are consistent with the lack of consensus found in studies of internal control judgments [Mock and Turner (1981); Biggs and Mock (1983)] and audit program planning [Joyce (1976)].

2.6 SUMMARY

The application of ARPs allows for the use of statistical measures, judgmental approaches, or both. While statistical approaches require continued research and development, special research attention should be focused on auditor judgment in ARPs. Judgmental research is important, because it plays a fundamental role in ARPs whether statistical techniques are used or not. In addition, some of the ARP judgment studies have shown the presence of judgment errors that could affect audit risk and costs. Thus, much more research is needed to understand the ARP judgment process. The next chapter presents a framework to guide judgment research in analytical review.

Chapter 3

FRAMEWORK FOR JUDGMENT RESEARCH IN ANALYTICAL REVIEW

The previous chapter established the need for a better understanding of the judgmental processes involved in analytical review. The purpose of this chapter is to provide a framework for judgment and decision research in ARPs. The framework is based on the cognitive science literature, a fairly new field devoted primarily to psychological and artificial intelligence research. The framework identifies issues and topics for research that may, at some time in the future, lead to theories that will help understand and improve auditor judgment in ARPs. It is not a complete theory of auditor judgment, but a first step in that direction. The framework also provides some perspective for the research described in later chapters.

3.1 PHILOSOPHICAL BACKGROUND

The theory presented in this chapter is concerned with understanding, at a cognitive level, how auditors make analytical review judgments. Such a theory should focus on experts because analytical review, like many auditing tasks, is complex and requires the knowledge and experience of experts for high level performance. Moreover, since knowledge and experience are the hallmark of expertise [Johnson (1986)] and are represented in the memory of experts, a theory that seeks to explain expert judgment must be concerned with cognitive processes.

The initial findings presented in this monograph fit into an overall research plan that is consistent with the development of cognitive science theory. From this cognitive perspective, an important long-term goal of our research is to obtain enough evidence to develop a computer program that models the observed behaviour of auditors conducting analytical review [Pylyshyn (1984); Johnson (1986)]. Of course, one research project cannot provide sufficient evidence to develop such a model. Johnson (1986) notes that such a model is developed in three phases:

(1) Systematic observation of expert behaviour to identify the "operative knowledge necessary for accomplishing a task or class of tasks";
(2) Theory development and testing, either through further empirical testing of the knowledge obtained in the first phase, or through the development of a computer model; and
(3) Theory manipulation, where the theory is tested under new, sometimes extreme conditions to determine and extend its boundaries.

The research reported in this monograph involves the first phase. Many might question a research project based on data from a few auditors performing analytical review, or the lack of specific, *a priori*, testable hypotheses. There are four fundamental reasons for this approach:

(1) **Need to conduct research in realistic task settings** — After approximately a decade of research to test hypotheses on relatively simple tasks, we are not much closer to a practical theory of auditor decision-making. Most of the research to date has been designed to settle small, specific issues [e.g. Joyce and Biddle (1981)]. It is not at all clear whether such experiments can be combined to provide a theoretical understanding of auditor judgment. The testing of experimental hypotheses will be most appropriate when it is based on factual evidence on auditor decision-making, as opposed to hypotheses borrowed from other fields;
(2) **Lack of theory for realistic task settings** — A review of the literature revealed that there is no theory specific enough to predict auditor behaviour in a realistic task setting, such as the one used in this study. The general theories of judgment and problem-solving developed by Einhorn and Hogarth (1981) and Newell and Simon (1972), which provided the initial basis for our research, are too general to support the *a priori* development of testable hypotheses. Given this lack of accounting theory, one can either follow the traditional approach of borrowing hypotheses from other disciplines and testing them in fairly simple task settings, or begin by gathering data about how auditors make analytical review judgments in realistic settings and attempt to build a new theory from the results.

While either of these approaches would be a reasonable way to proceed in developing scientific knowledge, the former would seem to be better accepted by accountants. Yet if accounting is in a pre-paradigm [Kuhn (1970)] or pre-theoretical [Lachman *et al.* (1979)] stage of scientific development, then the generation of hypotheses should be an important research priority. Moreover, there is little reason to question the value of theory induced from data. In fact, Ericsson and Simon (1984, p. 280) use a Bayesian framework to refute the traditional view that theory and hypotheses must be stated before data is gathered. While they recognize that prior statement of hypotheses has merit, they argue that theories and hypotheses which are generated out of data have considerable scientific value:

> The common view that hypotheses must be formulated before experiments are run in order for the data to have value as evidence is simply false.

(3) **Experienced auditors generally make good decisions** — The overall success of auditors [Willingham (1985)] suggests that good decisions predominate in auditing. This does not mean there is no room for improvement, or that judgmental biases are non-existent, but it does suggest that reasonable theories can be based on systematic knowledge of the way in which experienced auditors make decisions in complex task settings. In fact, the development of theory from observation of experts is providing some of the most dramatic advances in artificial intelligence [see Hayes-Roth *et al.* (1983); Feigenbaum and McCorduck (1983)]. The study of experts is likely to be particularly productive where decisions are made with minimal support from professional guidelines, so that the decision maker must rely on experience; and

(4) **New research tools allow modelling of complex behaviour** — The recent development of verbal protocol analysis and artificial intelligence techniques has advanced the ability to conduct research in complex task settings. Verbal protocol analysis allows systematic observation and analysis of the details of human decision-making, while new artificial intelligence techniques enable the researcher to develop computer models that incorporate highly complex and detailed behaviour [Pylyshyn (1984)]. Even though the development of computer models for complex behaviour is very time consuming (Davis (1982) estimates five person-years), the systematic observation and description of auditor behaviour in complex and realistic task settings should be encouraged. Research in psychology and medical decision-making has demonstrated the richness and comprehensiveness of human judgments in complex decision-making activities [Chi, Feltovich and Glaser (1981); Elstein, Shulman and Sprafka (1978)]; similar approaches may improve our understanding of the judgments underlying analytical review.

These factors suggest that observation of the auditor judgment in analytical review can be important. Analytical review is an accepted [SAS 23] means of providing "reasonable assurance" that the risk of material misstatement in a client's financial accounts is minimized. Analytical review may also improve audit efficiency, by serving as a substitute for tests of details. Since the environment in which analytical reviews are undertaken is complex, and is linked with other aspects of the audit such as planning, compliance testing, and review, research to determine how experienced auditors make trade-offs and judgments in complex environments can provide important insights into auditor decision-making.

FIGURE 1
Process Model of Analytical Review

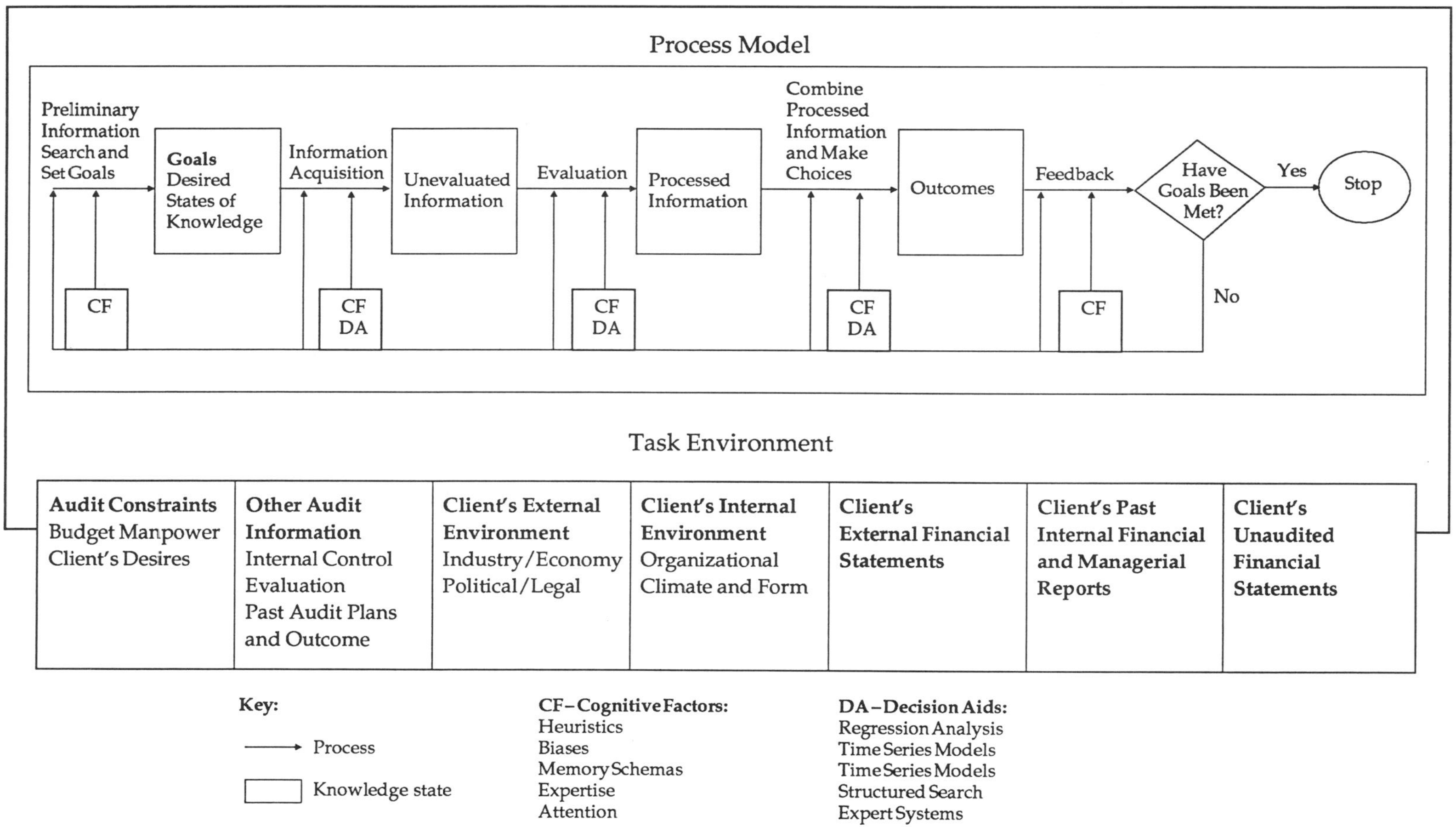

3.2 A JUDGMENTAL FRAMEWORK FOR ANALYTICAL REVIEW PROCEDURES

It is clear from Chapter 2 that analytical review is a highly complex task, involving judgment and the possible use of sophisticated statistical techniques. A research framework that reflects this complexity is presented in Figures 1 and 2. Figure 1 provides a model of the analytical review process, while Figure 2 presents the cognitive components that are implied by the process model.

The centre of Figure 1 depicts a process model of the auditor's decision making in conducting an analytical review. The task environment is shown as a box surrounding the process model. The process begins with a preliminary examination of the task environment to develop goals and a possible sequence of operations to accomplish the goals. Perception and evaluation of the task environment depend on cognitive factors relating the auditor's memory schemas and expertise, and the level of attention the auditor brings to the task. This preliminary analysis would lead to the development of a problem space [Newell and Simon (1972)] for the analytical review, involving goals, subgoals, knowledge states and a sequence of operations represented in the auditor's memory.

Figure 1 shows some possible aspects of the task environment for an analytical review. Although the individual aspects of the task environment are not discussed here, it is from these components of the environment that the auditor will acquire information, so that the auditor's decision behaviour may depend on which items are attended to. Unfortunately, the literature provides little insight into the effects of particular aspects of the task environment on auditor behaviour in analytical review or on the impact of variations in the quantity or quality of information available.

The flow of processes and states of knowledge in the centre of Figure 1 is consistent with Einhorn and Hogarth (1981), and includes: information acquisition, information evaluation, choice, and feedback. In addition, there is a "set-goal" operation which takes place after a preliminary information search, and provides direction for the remaining operations executed by the auditor.

It must be emphasized that the process described in Figure 1 is dynamic and interactive. At any step in the process, the auditor may decide to go back and acquire additional information or set different goals, so that each phase may influence behaviour in any other phase. There are also behavioural/cognitive factors that may influence the auditor's information processing at any phase. These factors include heuristics, memory schema, attention, biases, values, and personality. Finally, while Figure 1 indicates that decision aids might replace or complement the auditor at various phases in the process, the usefulness of these aids depends on many factors related to cost and benefit. Decision aids may range from checklists and formalized procedures, to statistical and other quantitative techniques, to expert systems.

While there is little literature on the processes involved in establishing goals, goals are an important component of current models in cognitive science, since they provide the primary rationale for the behaviour that follows [Newell and Simon (1972); Pylyshyn (1984)]. In addition, the professional literature does suggest some general aspects of analytical review related to goals, which suggest some of the cognitive processes that are involved in conducting ARPs. For example, Arens and Loebbecke (1980) suggest the following four goals for ARPs:

(1) Obtain a general understanding of the client's:

   (a) financial performance and position;
   (b) industry and competitive environment; and
   (c) internal managerial environment;

(2) Develop a set of expected boundaries for the values reported in the client's unaudited financial statements;
(3) Evaluate the fit between the expected values for the unaudited financial statements and the actual unaudited values; and
(4) Determine the extent to which other aspects of the audit (substantive testing, internal control evaluation, and so on) can be altered based on the results of analytical review.

These four goals are closely related to the planning or attention-directing phase of ARPs discussed in the professional literature [CICA *Handbook*; SAS 23; Smith (1983)]. As a decision-making activity, planning requires the existence or development of values and goals, the generation of alternatives, and the evaluation of the alternatives selected. Forecasts are also needed in the generation and assessment of alternatives, and in the prediction of future states of the environment. Monitoring and control are also integral elements of planning [Hogarth and Makridakis (1981)].

For complex problems like analytical review, planning involves a variety of inputs and skills. Goals and values can be difficult to communicate, and must often be sensed by the auditors rather than obtained directly from firm policies. The generation of alternatives requires imagination and creative thinking, topics that have been virtually ignored in the accounting literature [see Hogarth (1980, 1984)] for a review of the literature, and some interesting experiments in this area). On the other hand, the assessment of alternatives may call for a high degree of analytical competence, and facility with statistical and quantitative models. Thus, the planning process and the establishment of goals requires a variety of complex cognitive and judgmental processes.

Once goals have been established, as represented by the "set goals" operation in Figure 1, the remaining judgment operations in the problem space become essential elements of the analytical review. These operations include: search of the accounting and/or other information system, acquisition of information, evaluation of the acquired information, and selection of a decision rule leading to actions or decisions. These choices or actions involve the development of an analytical review program, and the decision to adjust other substantive tests based on evaluation of analytical review evidence. The choice/action stage results in an outcome. Feedback from this outcome makes it possible to assess effectiveness in meeting the goals of the analytical review, and to decide whether further sequencing through the operations is required.

In an extensive review of the psychological literature, Hogarth and Makridakis (1981) show that bias can affect the various components of human decision processes shown in Figure 1. While biases are not the focus of this monograph, it should be noted that auditor judgment could be subject to some of these biases. In fact, studies of internal control [Mock and Turner (1981)] and other components of the audit have been shown to be subject to bias [Joyce and Biddle (1981); Swieringa *et al.* (1976)].

Hogarth and Makridakis (1981) suggest that the most serious biases in a judgmental task such as analytical review are likely to be the illusion of control, the accumulation of redundant information, a failure to seek possible disconfirming evidence, and overconfidence in judgment. The illusion of control is related to the human need to control a task environment, and is most prevalent in planning and attention-directing activities. The acquisition of redundant information increases confidence in judgments, even though it does not increase judgment accuracy [Hogarth (1980)]. The failure to seek disconfirming evidence has been found to have adverse affects on doctors' diagnoses of diseases [Elstein, Shulman and Sprafka (1978)].

While auditors certainly may be subject to judgmental bias, caution should be exercised in generalizing the findings of the psychological studies reviewed by Hogarth and Makridakis (1981) to auditing practice [Shanteau (1987)]. Since most of the psychological studies have involved relatively simple tasks carried out by inexperienced subjects, they may not have any bearing on judgments made by expert auditors in more complex task settings such as analytical review. In fact, many of the models in the artificial intelligence literature, which has focused a great deal of research on expert judgment, include a component that recognizes when judgment is likely to be biased [see Davis (1982); Johnson *et al.* (1979)].

The analytical review process model presented in Figure 1 implies a variety of cognitive processes. But to discuss auditor judgment from a cognitive point of view, a different figure is required. Figure 2 presents a cognitive model of a human decision-maker. The model reflects aspects of models or discussion from Newell and Simon (1972), Johnson *et al.* (1979) and Pylyshyn (1984). While Figures 1 and 2 are consistent with each other, Figure 2 contains additional descriptive detail on the cognitive components involved in judgment and decision-making.

FIGURE 2
A Cognitive Model of Auditor Judgment

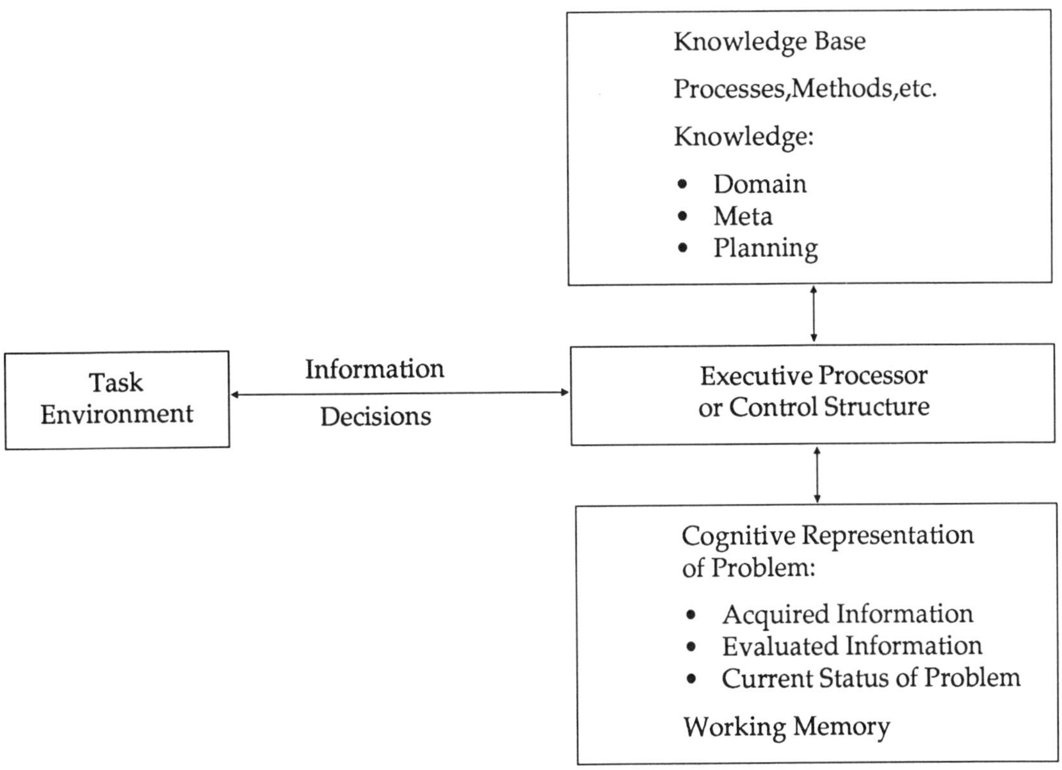

Figure 2 incorporates the task environment and three main cognitive components:

(1) **Task environment**—The problems facing the auditor in analytical review are described in Figure 1. Essentially, there is an audit to be conducted and the auditor must determine the role that analytical review can play. Various aspects of the task environment are shown at the bottom of Figure 1;

(2) **Executive processor or control structure** — This is a goal-directed process that controls the individual's decision-making. Following the flow in Figure 1, the Executive would first acquire some information from the task environment, to obtain an initial formulation of the problem. Based on this initial formulation, the Executive would seek relevant knowledge and decision-making methods from the Knowledge Base, which would be used to evaluate new information from the environment. The Executive would also transfer knowledge to and from the cognitive representation in working memory; and

(3) **Knowledge base** — This is the decision-maker's long-term memory, containing processes (decision methods) and stored knowledge. Based on experience, the decision-maker develops methods for performing tasks. These methods are collections of procedures that evaluate information and make decisions. These methods include heuristics, and rules used in decision-making. Three categories of knowledge are represented [see Johnson *et al.* (1979)]:

Domain knowledge, including:

(a) prototype knowledge, represented as idealized instances of task problems and solutions based on experience;
(b) system knowledge, represented as laws and principles that explain task prototypes; and
(c) feature knowledge, represented as categories of information, such as ratio or regression analysis, that allow recognition of the problem.

Meta knowledge, including the individual's awareness of the characteristics of his or her own knowledge, the nature of the way in which he or she uses that knowledge, and the nature and extent of his or her own limitations.

Planning knowledge, including goal structures and action sequences that can be used to perform tasks.

Cognitive representation of the problem

This is the decision-maker's conscious sensing of the problem to be solved, and identification of problem characteristics which may be useful for problem-solving. This sensing involves perception, based on cues derived from the problem characteristics. Perception is an interactive process in which the cues are compared to rules, concepts, experience, and other schema in the memory of the decision-maker. This perceptual process results in a representation of the problem that is held in working (short-term) memory. The representation contains the current formulation of the problem, facts and methods from the knowledge base, and any potential solutions.

A significant cognitive feature that can be derived from the model in Figure 2 is the concept of a schema, an organized set of knowledge and decision methods related to a particular task domain [Alba and Hasher (1983)]. Schemas and similar devices [e.g., scripts, Schank and Abelson (1977); frames, Minsky (1975); and templates, Nisbett and Ross (1980), Gibbins (1984)] provide the primary cognitive processes for decision-making and judgment. In the model in Figure 2, the Executive acquires information that activates a schema in the knowledge base. The schema becomes a part of the Executive's working memory, where it is used to evaluate new information and ultimately solve the problem.

The completeness, accuracy and effectiveness of schemas, and the ability to access the appropriate schema, is based primarily upon an individual's experience [Alba and Hasher (1983); Chi, Feltovich and Glaser (1981)]. There has been a great deal of research to investigate differences between experts and novices in such factors as the ability to properly formulate problems, and problem-solving accuracy and efficiency [Larkin *et al.* (1980); Chi, Feltovich and Glaser (1981); Johnson *et al.* (1981); Chi, Glaser and Rees (1982); Alba and Hasher (1983)]. This research has confirmed significant differences in the depth and completeness of schema.

Another aspect of cognitive research involves methods of measuring cognitive components, including response time, protocol analysis, and multi-dimensional scaling. While response time or reaction time has been used in a laboratory setting in a great number of psychological studies, in which responses to a variety of tasks such as phoneme recognition have been recorded, this approach is not particularly useful with real tasks and realistic cases. Protocol analysis, in which subjects verbalize their thought processes and the researchers attempt to understand the decision and reasoning process by evaluating the recorded protocols, was used in this study (see Chapters 4, 5 and 6). Multi-dimensional scaling, a means of measuring the perceptions of decision-makers to deduce the underlying cognitive structure from which the scaling model has been derived, was also used in this study, and is described in Chapters 4 and 7.

3.3 SUMMARY AND GENERAL RESEARCH CONCLUSIONS

This chapter has presented a process model of analytical review (Figure 1), and a cognitive model of individual decision-making (Figure 2). The process model reveals the complexity of the analytical review task and depicts a sequence of information processes an auditor would undertake in performing ARPs. This sequence forms a general model of auditor ARP processes based on Newell and Simon (1972) and Einhorn and Hogarth (1981). This model has guided the development of the verbal protocol coding scheme for operators used in the case phase of the study. The protocols were examined for auditor decision operations related to the major processes in Figure 1, including goal setting, information acquisition, information evaluation, and decisions. These processes are explained more fully in Chapters 4 (Research Design and Methods), 5 (Overall Decision and Information Acquisition Behaviour) and 6 (Information Evaluation and Decision).

Literature reviewed in this chapter and Chapter 2 revealed a lack of theoretical and empirical evidence related to complex auditor judgments in ARPs. This lack of guidance suggested the need for fundamental descriptive evidence of auditor judgment processes. The first part of this chapter provided the substantive rationale for such a descriptive study. The following general research questions are based on this need, and on the process model of analytical review (Figure 1):

> 3-A What is the nature of auditors' information acquisition behaviour during analytical review? What types of information are acquired, in what order, and with what emphasis?

> 3-B What is the nature of auditors' evaluation and decision processes during analytical review? What types of evaluation are used, what problems are identified, and what kind of decisions are made?

3-C What are the differences and similarities in the decision processes of experienced and inexperienced auditors? What are the information acquisition, evaluation and decision processes involved?

Decision-makers' information acquisition behaviour is important for several reasons. Information acquisition is an important component of the decision process model, because decision-makers must often select from a large volume of available information. The processes underlying the selective acquisition of information are therefore crucial to decision-making, especially in light of evidence that information acquisition may affect decision quality [Abdel Khalik and El Sheshai (1980)].

The auditor's evaluation and decision behaviour is equally important. Descriptive research concerning rationale and decision rules suggests that building lists of relevant variables, tentative behavioural rules, and other components may lead to useful theories of analytical review. An analysis of auditor evaluations and decisions may also identify decision biases discussed by Hogarth and Makridakis (1981), such as confirmation bias. Such knowledge may also play an important role in the development of expert systems for analytical review decisions.

Comparing the information acquisition behaviour and evaluation and decision processes of experienced and inexperienced auditors can provide important insights into expert judgment in ARPs. This is particularly important in task domains like analytical review, where there is a lack of theory to guide the evaluation of decision processes.

Figure 2 provides a detailed model of the cognitive components of the judgment process. Of particular importance to this research was the concept of schemas. One of the main reasons for investigating differences between experienced and inexperienced auditors is that schema development and access appear to be based primarily on experience. In addition, there are important issues related to the measurement of cognitive representations, specifically multidimensional scaling. This discussion has led to the following general research questions:

3-D What is the nature of auditors' reasoning processes? How do auditors make inferences and the nature of their evaluations?

3-E What are the schema-related differences in the reasoning processes of experienced and inexperienced auditors?

3-F What cognitive dimensions describe auditors' analytical decisions?

Chapter 4

RESEARCH DESIGN AND METHODS

The research methods involved six separate but related design and validation approaches to address the questions raised in Chapter 3. These approaches included:

(1) Development of a case study (Pacific Electronics) for use in the analytical review study;
(2) Statistical analysis of a case developed to test auditors' analytical review assessments (performed by the researchers);
(3) Ratio analysis of the case, to establish norms to evaluate auditor performance;
(4) Concurrent verbal protocol analysis of experienced and inexperienced auditors performing analytical review on the case;
(5) Multi-dimensional scaling analysis of the auditors' assessment of data supplied by the researchers in support of the ratio analysis; and
(6) Retrospective verbal protocol analysis of an experienced and inexperienced auditor, both of whom had performed statistical and judgmental analytical review procedures on an actual audit client.

This chapter describes the statistical and ratio analyses performed on the Pacific Electronics case by the researchers, and the concurrent verbal protocol, multi-dimensional scaling, and retrospective protocol methods that were used to assess auditor performance.

4.1 STATISTICAL AND RATIO ANALYSIS: TASK DESIGN AND CASE VALIDATION (PACIFIC ELECTRONICS)

Several factors were considered in the design of the task for this aspect of the study. It was important to make the case as realistic as possible to ensure that the case had some identifiable audit problems that could be detected through analytical review, and to develop a comprehensive case that would allow observation of the way in which auditors link analytical review judgments to audit program planning decisions. Given these design factors, it was felt that the use of a single, comprehensive case would yield the most relevant descriptive data.

The case study of Pacific Electronics, a large retailer of electrical appliances, was based on an actual client of a medium-sized audit firm. The original audit had resulted in an adjustment in the valuation of the client's accounts receivable. The case included the pre-adjusted, or unaudited financial statements for the year in which the adjustment was made. In addition, a "standard" audit program from an international accounting firm was adapted for use as the basis for audit program planning decisions.

For validation, the case was reviewed by several experienced auditors from two international accounting firms. The reviewers were asked to check the case for realism, completeness, and any features that would represent a firm bias. The final case contained over 100 pages of material, covering economy, industry and company background; audit planning material; internal control evaluation information; five years of financial statements including footnotes; analyses of sales, aging of accounts receivable and operating expenses, and quarterly financial statements; and standard audit programs for four major accounting cycles (Non-Trade Notes, Revenue, Inventory, and Accounts Payable). The audit objectives for the revenue cycle are summarized in Appendix C; the actual case may be obtained by contacting any of the authors.

Statistical and ratio analyses were conducted to determine whether analytical review of the case data would yield reasonable and potentially useful results, and to provide a reference point for comparison to the judgmental phase of the study.

Statistical analysis

Several statistical techniques were used to predict the 1980 unaudited account balances for Pacific Electronics. These included regression analysis, and time-series modelling such as exponential smoothing, Box-Jenkins, and related procedures. In order to specify equations for use in the regression analysis, the authors computed correlations between all account balances to determine which pairs of accounts had the highest correlations and to help identify the pairs of variables that had the most meaningful relationships. Pairs of correlations were considered, since the underlying interdependence of various accounts would have made it more difficult to develop meaningful prediction equations. Each of the regression equations derived from the more significant and reasonable correlations involved two variables with high correlations, where one served as a dependent variable and the other as an independent variable. The resulting equations are shown in Table 1.

After all aspects of the case had been examined through a variety of statistical procedures, the most appropriate procedures were applied to the accounts most relevant to the audit program.

TABLE 1
Regression Equations for Statistical Analytical Review of Pacific Electronics

SALES	=	a + b(CGS)
CGS	=	a + b(OE)
OE	=	a + b(SALES)
DEPR	=	a + b(CPLTD)
PPLE	=	a + b(CPLTD)
DEP	=	a + b(OCA) + c(AP)
INT	=	a + b(CPLTD)
AR	=	a + b(SALES)
INV	=	a + b(AP)
INV	=	a + b(CGS)
NR	=	a + b(PPE)
PPE	=	a + b(OCA)
OCA	=	a + b(PPE)

Note:

AP	=	Accounts Payable
AR	=	Accounts Receivable
CGS	=	Cost of Goods Sold
CPLTD	=	Current Portion of Long-Term Debt
DEP	=	Deposits
DEPR	=	Depreciation
INT	=	Interest
INV	=	Inventory
NR	=	Notes Receivable
OCA	=	Other Current Assets
OE	=	Operating Expenses
PPE	=	Prepaid Expenses
PPLE	=	Property, Plant and Equipment

4.2 STATISTICAL ANALYSIS OF ACCOUNTS WITHIN THE SCOPE OF PACIFIC ELECTRONICS AUDIT PROGRAM

The purpose of using statistical models in analytical review is to predict the true book balances of various accounts. The relationship between the predicted balance and the unaudited balance is then assessed by the auditor in light of audit materiality and investigation intervals, and the audit program is adjusted as necessary.

Several statistical models were used in this analysis, with the following results:

Regression analysis based on quarterly data for the years 1976 through 1979

This analysis utilized the data for the 16 quarters preceding the 1980 unaudited book values of the Sales, Accounts Receivable (AR), Cost of Goods Sold (CGS), Accounts Payable (AP) and Inventory (INV) accounts. Table 2 shows the resulting predictive equations, the point estimates of the "true" book value, the difference between book value and predicted value (residuals), and the residuals expressed as a percentage of book value.

The magnitude of the difference between book value and predicted value, and the direction of difference, are of particular interest.

TABLE 2
Pacific Electronics Regression
Analysis of Selected Accounts Based on Quarterly Data

(in $000's)

	Selected Accounts		Time as Independent Variable		
Model	**AR[(a)]**	**INV[(b)]**	**AR[(c)]**	**SALES[(d)]**	**CGS[(e)]**
Unaudited Book Value	$1,505	$2,003	$1,505	$15,601	$10,187
Predicted Value	1,369	1,839	1,350	15,596	10,540
Residual Value*	135	-839	155	3	-352
Residual as % of Book Value	10	-29	10	0	-3

(a) AR	=	-385 +	0.417	SALES	R^2 = 0.91
(b) INV	=	412 +	0.63	AP	R^2 = 0.98
(c) AR	=	78 +	63	TIME	R^2 = 0.91
(d) SALES	=	1,144 +	148	TIME	R^2 = 0.96
(e) CGS	=	760 +	101	TIME	R^2 = 0.94

* Residual value is the difference between the unaudited book value and the predicted value

The purpose of this and the other statistical analyses is to attempt to accurately predict the "true" value of the account balance, which may or may not be the same as the unaudited book balance. Criteria for reasonableness of the magnitude (materiality) of any difference would be set by auditors' or audit firms' policies, and would form investigation intervals around the point estimate for the account balance.

The results in Table 2 show that the predicted value of accounts receivable on sales is 10% less than the book value. Given that accounts receivable were actually overstated in this case, the regression result does predict in the correct direction. The regression of accounts payable on inventory shows an even higher percentage difference between the book value and the predicted value. Since the results of the actual audit on Pacific Electronics did not result in major adjustments to any account balances other than accounts receivable, the book values may be regarded as the "true" values, *a posteriori*, in this case. Therefore, the regression result on the inventory account would appear to be overstated based on most reasonable materiality standards, since the relative difference between the book and predicted values is -29%.

Regression analysis using time as the independent variable — trend analysis, quarterly data

In this regression model, quarterly data were used as the dependent variable, but time was the independent variable. Trend analysis was used on the assumption that historical trends may be representative of future trends. The results of this analysis are shown on the right side of Table 2.

The results of time regressions show relatively close correspondence to book value. Table 2 shows percentage differences between book and predicted values between -3% and 10%. As in the previous analysis, the book value of sales and the cost of goods sold can be regarded as being materially accurate. Thus, the time series models, with relatively small residuals between unaudited book and predicted values, can be regarded as satisfactory models. Like the previous regression on accounts receivable, the analysis shows the correct direction of difference for predicted accounts receivable relative to book balance: it implies that the book value is overstated. Once again, auditor investigation intervals would be based on the materiality of any differences between book and predicted values.

Time series analysis — triple exponential smoothing

An exponential smoothing model was applied to quarterly data for sales, cost of goods sold, accounts receivable, inventory and accounts payable. Table 3 shows that the differences between book and predicted values are moderately large. Since this particular model shows accounts receivable to be understated (a negative residual), the auditor runs the risk of making an incorrect inference.

TABLE 3
Pacific Electronics Exponential Smoothing
Analysis of Selected Accounts Based on Quarterly Data

(in $000's)

	SALES	CGS	AR	INV	AP
Unaudited Book Value	$15,601	$10,197	$1,505	$2,003	$3,547
Predicted Value	13,327	8,978	1,597	2,431	3,209
Residual Value*	2,274	1,209	-92	-428	338
Residual as % of Book Value	15	12	-6	-21	10

* Residual value is the difference between the unaudited book value and the predicted value

Box-Jenkins time series methods — moving average, autoregressive, and constant factor models

Several Box-Jenkins time series models, including moving average, autoregressive, and constant factor, were applied to the quarterly data. Table 4 shows the actual and percentage differences between predicted and book value from the various time series models. All three time series models have relatively small differences for the income statement items: sales and cost of goods sold. The moving average and the autoregressive transfer function models also show small differences for the inventory account.

TABLE 4
Pacific Electronics Box-Jenkins Time Series Analysis of Selected Accounts Based on Quarterly Data

(in $000's)

Account	SALES	CGS	AR	INV
Unaudited Book Value	$15,601	$10,187	$1,505	$2,003
(1) Moving Average				
Predicted Value	16,190	10,854	1,046	1,968
Residual Value*	-589	-667	459	35
Residual as % of Book Value	-4	-7	30	2
(2) Autoregressive				
Predicted Value	16,089	10,770	1,047	2,012
Residual Value*	-488	-583	458	9
Residual as % of Book Value	-3	-6	30	0
(3) Constant Factor				
Predicted Value	16,040	10,952	922	1,095
Residual Value*	-439	-765	583	908
Residual as % of Book Value	-3	-8	39	45

* Residual value is the difference between the unaudited book value and the predicted value

The predicted accounts receivable account shows relatively large differences from book value (30, 30 and 39 percent) using all three time series models. The direction of the differences is correct, given that the account was, in fact, overstated. The inventory account also shows a relatively large difference for the constant function time series model. In general, the Box-Jenkins analysis predicted the unaudited book values of the various accounts reasonably well. The direction of the differences was correct for the accounts receivable account, although the magnitude was much greater than in simple and time series regression. In some cases, the Box-Jenkins analysis yielded the most accurate predictions of all the models utilized.

4.3 OVERALL COMPARISON OF STATISTICAL MODELS

The analysis shows that the various statistical models predict the unaudited book values of selected accounts with mixed success. Simple regression and the Box-Jenkins time series provided very accurate predictions, in the correct direction. For some accounts, the magnitude of the Box-Jenkins prediction was much greater than with other methods. Although the Box-Jenkins models are more elegant and complex, and are theoretically more accurate, the simple regression model based on trend performs reasonably well. This is in line with previous research [Kinney (1978)], suggesting that simple regression models may perform very well for the cost. With more cyclicality and/or seasonality in account balances, trend analysis may not perform as well as it has in the case analysis, unless these factors are included in the model. And without materiality guidelines, these models cannot be used to raise questions concerning the potential need for audit program adjustments. However, the analysis does show that several statistical models could be successfully used to estimate account balances for Pacific Electronics, and that the data are reasonably well-behaved for statistical analysis.

Ratio analysis

In order to understand auditors' evaluations and decisions during analytical review, it is helpful to get a picture of Pacific Electronics' financial condition. Tables 5 through 8 show selected financial ratios, many of which were included in the auditors' analytical review. A review of the ratios would be expected to yield evaluations relevant to the four audit cycles covered by the research. Some of the expected evaluations would be as follows:

Analysis of short-term asset and liabilities

Measures of short-term liquidity (Table 5) reveal a relatively consistent deterioration. The current ratio shows a steady decline over five years.

Table 5 also raises serious questions about the quality of accounts receivable, which declined each year from a high of 25.88 in 1976 to 15.18 in 1979, and an unaudited turnover of only 10.37 in 1980. The pattern is similar for the combined turnover of accounts receivable and notes receivable.

TABLE 5
Short-Term Liquidity Ratios

Unit	Ratio	1980*	1979	1978	1977	1976
Times	Current Ratio	1.23	1.40	1.26	1.32	2.34
Times	Quick Ratio	0.40	0.38	0.24	0.23	0.50
Times	Accounts Receivable Turnover	10.37	15.18	10.80	11.81	25.88
Days	Days in Accounts Receivable	69.70	55.80	33.80	30.90	14.10
%	Allowance to Accounts Receivable	5.70	7.49	8.60	2.26	0.00
	Aging of Accounts Receivable:					
%	0- 30 days	34.60	36.10			
%	30- 60 days	26.10	28.50			
%	60- 90 days	17.80	18.50			
%	90-180 days	9.80	7.80			
%	180-360 days	10.80	8.30			
%	Over 360 days	0.90	0.80			
Times	All Accounts Receivable Turnover**	4.84	6.00	9.59	10.09	17.31
Days	Days in all Accounts Receivable**	75.40	60.80	38.10	36.20	21.10
%	Allowance to all Accounts Receivable**	5.91	6.92	7.88	2.73	0.00
Times	Inventory Turnover	4.07	5.11	6.56	7.42	6.59
Times	Accounts Payable Turnover	3.03	3.56	2.38	2.79	19.62

* Unaudited
** Includes accounts receivable, and current and non-current notes receivable.

TABLE 6
Capital Structure and Long-Term Solvency

Unit	Ratio	1980*	1979	1978	1977	1976
%	Current Liability to Total Assets	52.1	47.9	65.5	58.9	30.6
%	Long-Term Liability to Total Assets	27.2	25.5	11.8	17.5	25.1
%	Total Liability to Total Assets	79.6	73.7	78.2	76.6	56.2
%	Property Plan & Equity to Total Assets	30.8	26.5	10.9	15.9	16.0
Times	Times Interest Earned	4.6	5.0	7.3	6.6	6.6

* Unaudited

TABLE 7
Return on Investment

Unit	Ratio	1980*	1979	1978	1977	1976
%	Return on Assets	4.3	6.0	3.8	4.5	11.4
%	Return on Equity	16.3	17.2	12.2	15.6	22.1

* Unaudited

TABLE 8
Operating Performance Relative to Net Sales

Unit	Ratio	1980*	1979	1978	1977	1976
%	Net Sales	100.0	100.0	100.0	100.0	100.0
%	COGS	65.3	69.2	67.0	67.3	67.9
%	Gross Profit	34.7	30.8	33.0	32.7	32.1
%	Operating Expense	30.0	25.2	24.5	26.2	24.3
%	Operating Profit	4.7	5.6	8.5	6.5	7.8
%	Interest Expense	1.1	1.4	1.3	1.2	1.4
%	Income Taxes	2.0	2.8	3.6	3.0	3.9
%	Net Income	2.1	2.2	1.6	2.5	3.5
	Operating Expenses:					
%	Salary & Wages	13.2	11.3			
%	Insurance	6.6	6.1			
%	Supplies	3.1	2.2			
%	Rent	1.6	0.9			
%	Bad Debt	3.1	3.0			
%	Amortization	0.2	0.2			
%	Pension	1.0	0.9			

* Unaudited

In addition, the aging schedule shows a greater percentage of accounts contained in the older categories in 1980 than in 1979. In 1979, 16.9 percent of accounts receivable were 90 days or older; in 1980, 21.5 percent were past 90 days. Yet the allowance for doubtful accounts as a percentage of gross accounts receivable has declined from 7.4 percent in 1979 to 5.7 percent in 1980. Bad debt expense as a percentage of sales has remained constant, at about 3.0 percent for both 1979 and 1980 (see Table 8). Thus, analytical review would suggest serious potential problems in collecting accounts receivable. Auditors would be expected to identify this problem, and make appropriate adjustments to the audit program for the revenue cycle.

The inventory turnover ratio also shows a decline over a four-year period. Turnover reached a high of 7.42 in 1977, before declining steadily to an unaudited 1980 turnover of 4.07. Since inventory in this case is composed of electronic stereos, televisions, stoves, refrigerators, and washing machines, obsolescence could be causing the decline in turnover. Auditors would be expected to take this possibility into account during their analytical review and evaluation of the audit program for inventory.

The accounts payable turnover ratio has been relatively steady since 1977, and actually improved from 2.79 in 1977 to 3.03 in 1980, suggesting that few audit problems are present in accounts payable.

Other analyses of financial condition

In general, the financial condition of Pacific Electronics has declined over the five-year period. Capital and return on investment measures (Table 7) have been erratic, and have generally declined. Capital structure is increasingly based on debt financing, with the ratio of total liabilities to total assets growing from 56.2 percent in 1976 to nearly 80 percent in 1980 (see Table 6). Moreover, Table 9 indicates that long-term debt is one of the fastest-growing items on the balance sheet. The company would appear to be using the increased debt to finance an expansion of its fixed assets, since net property, plant and equipment have also increased substantially. But the higher debt increases the risk in the capital structure, since the debt must be serviced. This burden is reflected in the decline in interest coverage. Table 6 shows the Times Interest Earned ratio at a five-year low of 4.64 in 1980, suggesting that Pacific Electronics is not doing a good job managing its balance sheet. In terms of operating performance, the company appears to have some problems in managing its expenses. Table 8 shows operating expenses increasing as a percentage of sales. In fact, all but one component of operating expenses increased as a percentage of sales from 1979 to 1980. Table 9 confirms that Pacific Electronics has been unable to translate sales growth into an equivalent growth in operating income. While the company does not face any immediate threats to its survival, its high level of debt and deteriorating performance add uncertainty to its future. It was expected that auditors would recognize these potential risks.

4.4 CONCURRENT PROTOCOL STUDY OF THE PACIFIC ELECTRONICS CASE

To gain insight into the decision processes underlying the analysis of Pacific Electronics, concurrent verbal protocols were obtained from auditors. Verbal protocol analysis requires subjects to verbalize their thoughts as they perform a task. This verbalization is recorded for subsequent analysis. The verbal protocols trace the subjects' information acquisition and evaluation processes, the judgments and decisions made, and the reasoning and rationale for the judgments and decisions. Concurrent verbal protocols are obtained as subjects perform the task, in order to capture the reasoning and judgment process as it occurs.

TABLE 9
Indexed Trends for Selected Accounts

	1980*	1979	1978	1977	1976
Sales	152.7	131.1	100.0	69.7	58.7
Cost of Sales	141.4	128.6	100.0	71.2	60.5
Gross Profit	179.7	137.1	100.0	66.0	54.4
Operating Expenses	170.5	125.3	100.0	75.7	59.1
Operating Income	71.6	73.3	100.0	51.8	64.0
Interest Expense	129.2	136.0	100.0	63.7	63.3
Income Before Taxes	74.8	87.6	100.0	56.8	56.0
Net Income	192.3	171.1	100.0	112.5	134.4
Accounts Receivable	314.8	216.5	100.0	63.7	24.5
All Receivables	302.5	209.7	100.0	66.2	32.5
Inventory	95.8	69.5	100.0	82.8	25.4
Current Assets	119.1	81.6	100.0	77.1	32.2
Net Property Plant & Equipment	432.4	244.0	100.0	119.3	54.6
Other Assets	114.3	94.5	100.0	77.5	67.0
Total Assets	152.9	100.2	100.0	81.7	37.1
Current Liabilities	121.4	73.2	100.0	73.4	17.3
Long-Term Debt	351.9	216.2	100.0	121.4	78.9
Capital Stock	100.0	100.0	100.0	100.0	100.0
Retained Earnings	151.9	125.1	100.0	85.3	68.9
Stockholders' Equity	143.2	120.8	100.0	87.8	74.1
Working Capital Provided by Operations	168.5	110.1	100.0	74.0	84.6

* Unaudited

Subjects

Since protocol analysis is a time-consuming research method for subjects as well as researchers, protocol studies tend to have small numbers of subjects who supply relatively large quantities of data [Payne, Braunstein, and Carroll (1978)]. Reflecting this constraint, the concurrent protocol study involved four subjects. Criteria for subject selection included audit experience (preferably with small to medium-sized clients), multiple firm representation, proximity to researchers, and subject availability. The four subjects were all considered, by their respective partners, to be among the most competent in their offices at their level of experience to perform the analytical review task.

An important research objective was to compare the decision behaviour of auditors with different levels of experience. Two experienced managers, each with seven years of audit experience, were assigned to the project by international accounting firms in Los Angeles. Two senior auditors, each with less than three years of audit experience, were appointed from the Milwaukee offices of the same participating firms. For the purposes of the paper, these auditors have been assigned the codes M1 and M2 for the two managers, and S1 and S2 for the two seniors.

Data collection and compilation

To analyze the Pacific Electronics case, subjects were required to participate in two different sessions with the researchers, in which they were required to verbalize their thoughts as they performed the tasks.

In the first session (Phase I), subjects were asked to review the case and prepare a program of analytical review procedures for the Pacific Electronics audit. This included the generation of a list of information items which might facilitate the analytical review, and which would be supplied by the researchers at a later date. For the second session (Phase II), subjects were supplied the information they had requested in the previous session and were asked to evaluate the planned audit program for Pacific Electronics. On the basis of the subjects' analytical review, each step of the planned substantive audit program was to be evaluated with respect to nature, timing, and extent. Any adjustments to the program were to be noted on the audit program.

The audio tapes were transcribed by breaking the verbalizations into short phrases consistent with procedures outlined by Newell and Simon (1972) and Payne, Braunstein and Carroll (1978). The instructions, which simply asked the subjects to verbalize all their thoughts as they performed the task, were consistent with procedures outlined by Ericsson and Simon (1984, 1980), for generating valid information about the cognitive processes of subjects performing the task. The transcripts were analyzed and coded using the operators in Appendix A.

Newell and Simon (1972) describe human decision-making as an information processing dynamic, in which decisions are composed of elementary operations applied to information acquired from memory and the external task environment. This theory provides the basis for assuming that information processing operations (called "operators", and described in Appendix A) are the primary type of behaviour to look for in the data. While Newell and Simon's theory of human information processing is very basic, it is also sufficiently general to apply to most decision situations. It also suggests that the most significant factors to explain decision behaviour are those relating to information processing (i.e. task environment, knowledge possessed by the subject, and the operations employed). Alternative theories might suggest factors such as personality or other individual differences as the first place to look to explain decision behaviour.

Einhorn and Hogarth (1981) suggest four interacting phases of operation that underlie decision-making processes:

(a) information acquisition;
(b) information evaluation;
(c) action/choice; and
(d) feedback.

Simon (1977) provides a similar framework, but Einhorn and Hogarth (1981) use component labels that seem to describe auditor decision-making better. The "feedback" component was not specifically addressed, since the research involved a single decision. Our research examined auditors' decision behaviour for operators that were consistent with Figure 1.

Multi-dimensional scaling analysis

Multi-dimensional scaling techniques (MDS) were utilized to analyze similarity judgments made by the subject auditors on the data supplied by the researchers. MDS helps identify the structure underlying a set of similarity judgments, with the hope of gaining insights into the way in which auditors organize certain concepts or constructs in memory. Thus MDS was viewed as a complementary procedure to the concurrent verbal protocol analysis. MDS purports to measure perceptual constructs of memory that have been conditioned on prior experiences, or expectations formulated from knowledge or rules in memory.

In the analytical review of Pacific Electronics, auditors requested various kinds of information to help them make audit program judgments. After this information was supplied, each auditor was asked to perform a number of similarity judgments which were then analyzed according to MDS procedures. Details on the nature and type of judgments, as well as the results, are presented in Chapter 7.

4.5 RETROSPECTIVE PROTOCOL ANALYSIS OF ACTUAL AUDIT CLIENT

The concurrent verbal protocol study utilized real auditors with a case adapted from a real electronics firm. Some constraints were placed on the subjects, in that they were working with a case, had no prior experience with the client, and had limited financial and other information. To make the case more realistic, and to evaluate other analytical review approaches such as those involving statistical methods, the study included a phase in which real auditors' performance of analytical review on a real client could be evaluated. Johnson (1986) recommends this approach as a key element in understanding expert judgment. Although some internal validity is sacrificed in this approach, in that the researchers had no control over the subjects or the task, a great deal of realism and insight can be gained.

Subjects

Two auditors assigned by an international accounting firm were in the midst of an audit of a large conglomerate company headquartered in Los Angeles. These auditors included a high-level senior (experienced) and a junior (inexperienced). The senior had approximately seven years' experience, while the junior auditor had less than one year of experience.

Task

For the protocol study, three divisions of the firm were considered: drug manufacturing, medical/surgical supplies, and a new, unnamed division which had been purchased at the end of the previous fiscal year. The drug and medical/surgical divisions had been audited by the same firm in prior years, while the new division had no audit history with the current audit firm. The senior auditor had several years' audit experience with this client, and thus was very familiar with its past history. The junior auditor had no prior experience with the audit client. The auditors used the normal analytical review procedures employed by their firm. Both a statistical analytical review approach and a judgmental approach were utilized as a means of reducing substantive testing. As a matter of accounting firm policy, these analytical review procedures were applied only to income statement accounts; the firm utilized other approaches for balance sheet accounts. Since the audit client was large and three divisions were under audit, the scope of the protocol analysis was limited to three selected income statement accounts: net sales, cost of sales, and expenses.

4.6 RETROSPECTIVE PROTOCOL METHOD

The protocols for these auditors differed from those in the Pacific Electronics case. The auditors evaluating the actual audit client provided *retrospective* verbal protocols, whereas the auditors evaluating Pacific Electronics provided *concurrent* protocols. Retrospective protocols are obtained after the analysis has been performed, not in the course of the analysis. The auditors were asked to come to the researcher's office and provide a description of the process they went through as they performed analytical review. All audit work papers pertaining to analytical review were available during the protocol session. The verbalizations were tape recorded and then transcribed in a manner similar to the concurrent protocols.

There are important limitations to the use of retrospective verbal protocols. Since they are collected after the task has been performed, the subject must verbalize factors about the task from memory. As a result, the subject may not remember the task performance accurately, or may respond in ways that he/she thinks he/she should respond, rather than describing the way in which the task was actually performed. Nevertheless, there is value in obtaining systematic observational data about judgments related to an actual audit.

Chapter 5

OVERALL DECISION AND INFORMATION ACQUISITION BEHAVIOUR

This chapter presents the overall coding results and descriptive evidence of auditors' information acquisition behaviour in completing the Pacific Electronics case. The overall coding of the auditors' decision processes is presented as a perspective on their information acquisition behaviour, and on the evaluation and decision behaviour presented in Chapter 6. As well, specific research questions are derived based on research questions 3-A and 3-C from Chapter 3.

5.1 OVERALL CODING RESULTS

The overall coding results give a general indication of the type of process each subject completed, especially in terms of the specific activities performed. Given that the research design allows for comparison between managers and seniors, each of the research questions listed below could also be stated as a comparison between these two groups.

> 5-A What specific behaviours, in terms of operators used, were evident in the protocol?

> 5-B What relative proportion of behaviour categories (e.g. information acquisition, evaluation and choice) was evident?

> 5-C What overall process did the auditors utilize?

Table 10 presents data about the subjects' task performance, and the results of operators employed by each subject and by manager versus senior. The mean values for the categories are also reported. The table indicates that subjects spent approximately 4.5 hours completing the two phases of the task, and each generated about 19,000 words of protocol. Table 10 also shows the percentage of operators generated by each subject. This table provides the basis for answering research questions 5-A and 5-B.

As discussed earlier, operators were coded using the definitions found in Appendix A, which were derived from general theories of human decision-making [Newell and Simon (1972); Einhorn and Hogarth (1981)] and tailored based on codes used by Newell and Simon (1972), Biggs (1978), and Biggs and Mock (1983). The categories of operators follow the components of Figure 1, and of Einhorn and Hogarth's decision process model: information acquisition, information evaluation, and action/choice. Klersey and Mock (1986) present a comparison of codes used in previous protocol studies.

The operators reported in Table 10 reflect various types of cognitive processes employed by subjects as they performed the task. At a macro level, there are some rather significant differences in the use of operators by each auditor. For example, while 21 percent of subject M1's activity and 49 percent of M2's activity involved "information acquisition", only 11 percent of S1's comments were coded as information acquisition activities. In addition, subject M2 generated almost twice as many operators than any of the other auditors which, in conjunction with the relatively large percentage of his efforts directed at acquiring information, implies an exceedingly information-intensive decision process.

There were also differences between managers and seniors. For instance, the seniors spent relatively more effort on analytical and information evaluation. This difference appears to be related primarily to the more complete information acquisition conducted by the two managers, which will be discussed in more detail later.

TABLE 10
Tabulation of Subjects' Performance of Task

Data Collected	Managers		Seniors	
	M1	M2	S1	S2
Audit experience (years)	7	7	2.5	3
Approximate time (hours)	4.75	5	4	4.5
Words in protocol (estimated)	17,900	24,544	15,838	18,902
Operators generated, Phase I	510	1,439	236	587
Operators generated, Phase II	329	689	495	607

Percentage of Operator Use for Each Phase

Operator Type	M1 Phase		M2 Phase		S1 Phase		S2 Phase	
	I	II	I	II	I	II	I	II
Task structuring:								
Set goal	2%	1%	0%	0%	2%	1%	1%	1%
Information acquisition:								
Information search	9	12	22	6	11	5	12	3
Direct reading	8	19	1	24	0	12	9	16
Algebraic calculation	1	0	9	0	0	0	2	0
Information retrieval	2	3	7	6	0	3	4	3
Sub-total	21%	33%	49%	36%	11%	19%	26%	23%
Information evaluation:								
Assumption	3	3	1	0	1	0	4	4
Conditional judgment	13	5	5	4	4	7	17	14
Comparison	5	4	10	5	8	1	4	1
Evaluation	36	29	24	21	40	35	28	33
Decision support	1	0	1	5	0	0	0	0
Generate query	6	4	4	1	7	1	12	2
Sub-total	64%	46%	44%	36%	60%	45%	65%	53%
Action/Choice:								
Generate alternative	1	2	1	1	6	5	1	3
Audit decision	8	14	5	26	22	29	5	19
Other decisions	0	0	1	0	0	0	2	1
Decision rule	3	3	0	0	0	1	0	0
Sub-total	12%	19%	7%	27%	28%	35%	8%	23%
Total	100%	100%	100%	100%	100%	100%	100%	100%
Total operators generated	510	329	1,439	689	236	495	587	607

5.2 OVERALL DECISION PROCESS: EPISODE ABSTRACTS

In responding to research question 5-C, which focused on modelling each of the four auditors' overall decision process, two types of models were developed. The more detailed involved the preparation of episode abstracts for each auditor. The second was based on highly summarized decision flowcharts, called macro flowcharts.

Episode abstracts

An episode abstract describes a subject's significant decision activities in terms of the sequence of goals accomplished [see Newell and Simon (1972)]. In essence, an episode abstract provides a detailed summary of the sequence of decision processes identified in the protocols. Because of their length (original text was approximately 40 pages), the episode abstracts are included in Appendix B.

For example, the episode abstract for M1 in Appendix B shows five major goals or episodes for Phase I: (1.0) familiarization with the Pacific Electronics case and with the task requirements; (2.0) evaluation of 1980 financial statements; (3.0) review of task requirements and an initial attempt to specify an analytical review program; (4.0) overview of audit program; and (5.0) completion of the analytical review program. The sub-episodes show the sequence of significant information acquisitions (e.g. 2.1), evaluations (e.g. 2.1.1) and decisions (e.g. 5.4.6) that the subjects chose to accomplish in completing the case.

Macro flowcharts

The second step in modelling subjects' overall decision processes involved the development of macro flowcharts, which summarize the vast amount of decision behaviour described in the episode abstracts. Macro flowcharts of each auditor's decision process are presented in Figures 3 through 6. In Phase I, the flowcharts generally provide a sequential review of case planning memoranda leading to decisions concerning requested analytical review information, and indicate that each auditor performed a significant amount of analytical review of the client's financial history, and internal control data, and of the planned audit approach. A number of audit decisions and alternatives were typically generated during this phase, although auditors differed in their emphasis on certain information, and in the decisions and alternatives they generated.

For example, managers generally identified a broad range of issues throughout the case, reflecting a more detailed managerial review. The large range of issues and problems identified during Phase I of Subject M1's episode abstract (Appendix B) reveals a rich base of knowledge about finance, taxation, and a variety of industry and economic factors.

The macro flowcharts also show a sequential approach toward the Phase II task, which required the subjects to review the analytical review procedure results and modify the planned audit program accordingly. The nature of the process was similar to Phase I in terms of information acquisition, evaluation, and choice behaviour. A large number (241) of audit decisions concerning the planned audit program were made. The Phase II macro flowcharts for M1, M2 and S2 were essentially the same, emphasizing a sequential search and review of the planned audit program. S1 differed somewhat by beginning with the revenue cycle, which was the most important cycle affecting audit risk.

FIGURE 3
Macro Flowchart of Analytical Review for Subject M1

Phase I

Sequential Search and Evaluation of Case:
- Case Study Overview
- Planning Work Paper
- Summary of Compliance Tests

↓

Evaluation of Financial Statements through Comparative Analysis of 1980 with prior years, primarily 1979

Identification of Critical Audit Areas

Directed/Contingent Analysis of
- Audited Financial Statements for 1976-1979
- Supplemental Schedules

↓

Specify Analytical Review Program

Phase II

Review Information from Analytical Review Program

↓

Sequential Search and Evaluation of the following cycles:
- Non-trade Notes and Other Receivables
- Revenue, Sales, Shipping,Trade Receivables
- Cash Receipts
- Production Costs and Inventories
- Purchasing Cycle

Evaluation of Specific Audit Problems Identified in the Analytical Review:
- Salary and Wage Expense
- Contingent Liability

FIGURE 4
Macro Flowchart of Analytical Review for Subject M2

Phase I

Sequential Search and Evaluation of Planning Memo:
- Case Study Overview
- Planning Work Paper
- Summary of Compliance Tests

↓

Sequential, Detailed & Complete Evaluation of Financial Information to Identify Critical Areas:
- Evaluate 1980 Financial Statements
- Comparative Analysis of 1979/80 Financial Statements
- Comparative Analysis of 1977/78 Financial Statements
- Comparative Analysis 1976/77 Financial Statements
- Evaluate Supplemental Schedules
- Evaluate Quarterly Balance Sheets
- Evaluate Quarterly Income Statements

↓

Specify Analytical Review Program

Phase II

Review Analytical Review Program Information

↓

Sequential Search, Evaluate, & Change Audit Program:
- Non-trade Notes and Other Receivables
- Revenue, Sales, Shipping, Trade Receivables, Cash Receipts
- Production Costs and Inventories
- Purchasing Cycle: Receiving, Accounts Payable and Cash Disbursements

FIGURE 5
Macro Flowchart of Analytical Review for Subject S1

Phase I

Sequential Search and Evaluation of Planning Memo:
- Case Study Overview
- Planning Work Paper
- Summary of Compliance Tests

Comparative Analysis of Unaudited (1980) and Audited (1979) Financial Statements

Directed Evaluation of Audit Approach as Presented in Planning Memo

Initial Evaluation of Time Requirements

Evaluation of Supplemental Schedules:
- Sales Analysis & AR Aging
- Schedule of Operating Expenses
- Summary Quarterly Financials (1976-79)

Final Review of Phase I Decisions

Phase II

Review Analytical Review Results Requested During Phase I

Directed Search through the audit program (Based on Materiality):
- Revenue Cycle
- Non-trade Notes and Other Receivables
- Purchasing
- Inventory

Modification and Adjustments to the Planned Substantive Audit Program as Necessary

FIGURE 6
Macro Flowchart of Analytical Review for Subject S2

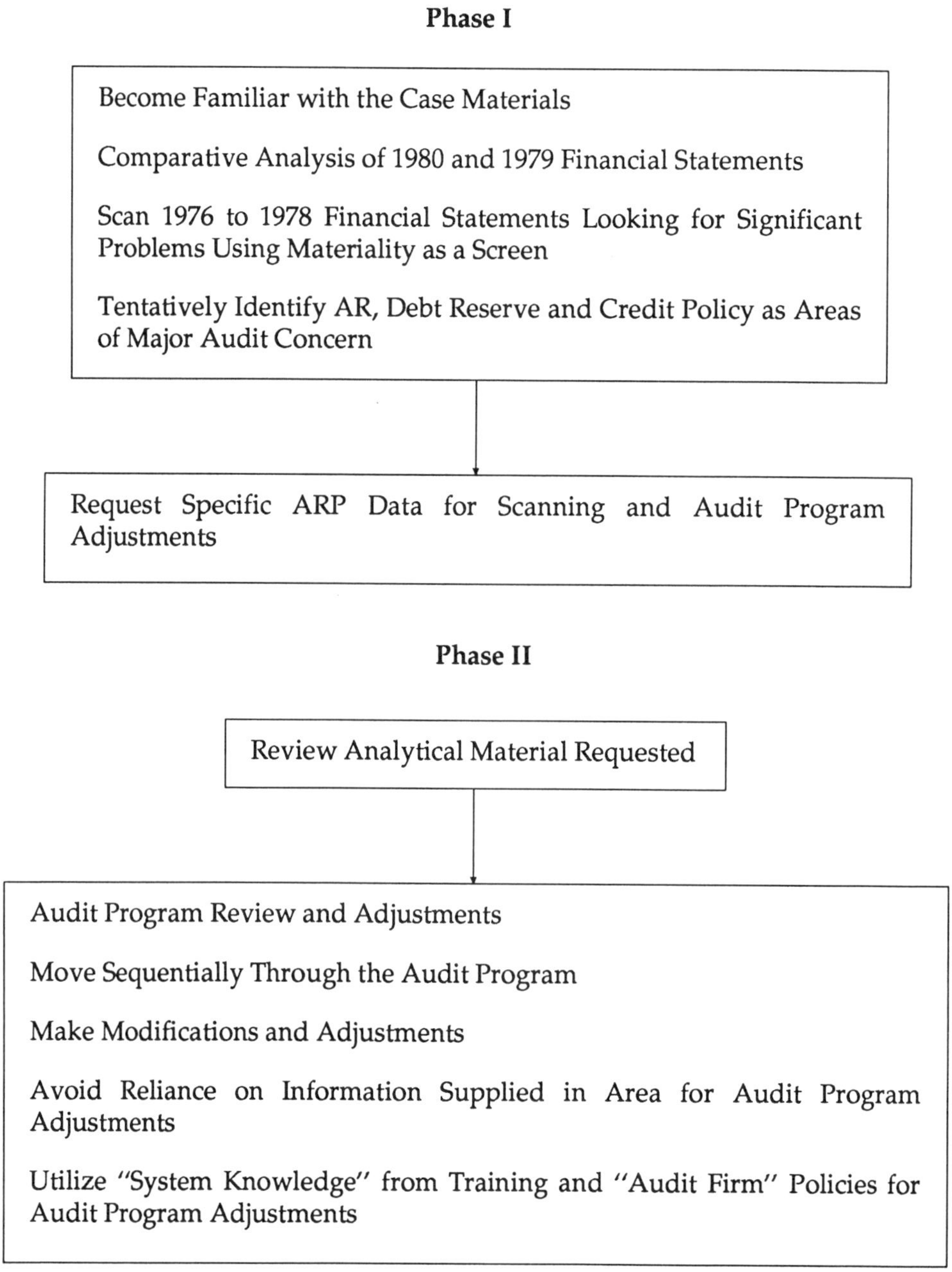

There is sufficient similarity among the four macro flowcharts to suggest that the auditors tended to use the following four-step approach:

(1) Read through all or portions of the case, conducting a preliminary analytical review to identify audit problems (areas of potential concern) or "opportunities" (areas of little concern);
(2) Request analytical review information (usually financial ratios) to further clarify problems and opportunities found in the first step;
(3) Evaluate requested information to confirm problems and opportunities; and
(4) Adjust the audit program based on analytical review information from the previous steps.

This process is similar to the diagnostic reasoning found in medical studies, where doctors generate and test hypotheses in identifying diseases in patients [Elstein, Shulman and Sprafka (1978); Johnson *et al.* (1982)]. These medical studies provide a basis to evaluate the decision processes of auditors. The results of this examination are shown in Chapter 6.

5.3 DESCRIPTION OF INFORMATION ACQUISITION BEHAVIOUR

The operator category entitled "information acquisition" includes information search, direct reading, algebraic calculation, and information retrieval functions. The coding of these operators provided the basic evidence of the auditors' information acquisition activities (see Appendix A for definitions of the information acquisition operators). This section addresses the following research questions:

5-D In what order did the auditors acquire information?

5-E How comprehensive was the auditors' search of the audit work papers?

5-F What components of the audit work papers did the auditors emphasize in the information acquisition?

In order to measure information acquisition behaviour, the available "cues" or bits of information must be divided in some manner. In this study, the work papers were organized according to the major categories traditionally used in auditing. The primary categories are:

Category Code	**Content of Category**
1.0	Case Overview
2.0	Planning Work Paper
3.0	Internal Control Summary
4.0	Unaudited (1980) Financial Report
5.0, 6.0 & 7.0	Historical Financial Reports
8.0	Supplementary Financial Schedules
9.0	Phase II Instructions
10.0	ARP Results from Phase I
11.0-14.0	Planned (standard) Audit Program

In some cases, as in Table 11, the general categories were coded in more detail. While it is recognized that any such partitioning of case information is likely to be somewhat arbitrary, the categories represent a normal partitioning of audit work papers, and give a satisfactory indication of the types of information that were or could be attended to.

TABLE 11
Frequency of Information Search

		M1		M2		S1		S2	
Case	**Category**	**Phase**		**Phase**		**Phase**		**Phase**	
Sequence	**Name**	**I**	**II**	**I**	**II**	**I**	**II**	**I**	**II**
PHASE I									
1.0	Case Overview:	2	0	8	1	9	2	1	0
2.0	Planning Workpaper:								
2.1	General Information	12	2	9	8	12	1	9	1
2.2	Audit Completion	3	7	1	1	2	0	2	0
2.3	Personnel & Critical Areas	4	0	3	0	1	0	1	0
2.4	Internal Audit Involvement	1	0	1	0	1	0	1	0
2.5	Audit Schedule	4	0	4	4	8	0	9	0
3.0	Internal Control Summary:	5	3	12	2	14	4	13	0
4.0	1980 Financial Reports:	2	6	0	0	1	0	0	0
4.1	1980 Balance Sheet	36	6	38	12	27	4	20	7
4.2	1980 Earnings Statement	10	1	22	2	8	1	6	0
4.3	1980 Retained Earnings	0	0	1	0	0	0	1	0
4.4	1980 Changes in Fin. Position		3	0	22	0	0	0	4
4.5	1980 Fin. Statement Notes	33	5	51	11	3	2	28	3
5.0	1979 Financial Reports:	0	2	0	0	0	0	0	0
5.1	1979 Auditor's Report	1	0	0	0	0	0	1	0
5.2	1979 Financial Statements	25	5	59	10	13	1	8	0
5.3	1979 Fin. Statement Notes	0	1	27	1	0	0	1	0
6.0	1978/77 Financial Reports:	7	0	112	1	0	0	4	0
7.0	1977/76 Financial Reports:	4	0	64	0	0	0	12	0
8.0	Supplemental Schedules:	1	0	0	0	1	0	0	0
8.1	Sales Analysis & Aging	11	0	17	4	9	1	5	2
8.2	Operating Expenses	6	0	9	0	2	0	7	1
8.3	Quart. Fin. Reports (1976-79)	6	0	57	0	5	0	17	3

TABLE 11 (Continued)
Frequency of Information Search

Case Sequence	Category Name	M1 Phase I	M1 Phase II	M2 Phase I	M2 Phase II	S1 Phase I	S1 Phase II	S2 Phase I	S2 Phase II
PHASE II									
9.0	Phase II Instructions:	NA	9	NA	0	NA	0	NA	0
10.0	ARP Results from Phase I:	NA	27	NA	24	NA	15	NA	17
11.0	Nontrade Notes: Intro	NA	5	NA	4	NA	1	NA	3
11.1	Existence & Propriety	NA	7	NA	19	NA	5	NA	9
11.2	Collectibility & Valuation	NA	8	NA	7	NA	6	NA	10
11.3	C/NC Classification	NA	3	NA	3	NA	1	NA	3
11.4	Int. Income Recognition	NA	3	NA	3	NA	1	NA	3
12.0	Revenue Cycle: Intro	NA	5	NA	10	NA	2	NA	4
12.1	Existence & Recording	NA	1	NA	23	NA	11	NA	10
12.2	Collectibility & Valuation	NA	2	NA	19	NA	10	NA	11
12.3	Rev. Recog. & Consistency	NA	1	NA	8	NA	4	NA	4
12.4	Sales Properly Recorded	NA	1	NA	17	NA	1	NA	9
12.5	Proper Sales Cutoff	NA	3	NA	4	NA	4	NA	4
12.6	Cash Receipts Recording	NA	1	NA	4	NA	2	NA	3
12.7	Cash Receipts Cutoff	NA	3	NA	4	NA	4	NA	3
13.0	Inventory Cycle: Intro	NA	5	NA	5	NA	3	NA	5
13.1	Existence & Ownership	NA	2	NA	33	NA	7	NA	19
13.2	Cost Inclusion	NA	4	NA	10	NA	2	NA	6
13.3	Recording Cost of Sales	NA	2	NA	7	NA	7	NA	7
13.4	Inventory Valuation	NA	4	NA	9	NA	5	NA	5
13.5	Purchases & Sales Cutoff	NA	1	NA	7	NA	7	NA	4
14.0	Purchasing Cycle: Intro	NA	1	NA	6	NA	3	NA	1
14.1	A/P Valid & Classification	NA	2	NA	15	NA	7	NA	8
14.2	Recording of Liabilities	NA	6	NA	5	NA	5	NA	8
14.3	Proper Purchases Accounting	NA	4	NA	7	NA	2	NA	5
14.4	Recording of Cash Disburs.	NA	1	NA	5	NA	0	NA	6

Note: NA indicates information not available during Phase I.

Research question 5-D concerns the order of information acquisition, a factor which has been related to expertise in solving physics problems. For example, physics experts tend to use a "working forward" model of information acquisition and problem-solving, while novices tend to use a "working backward" model [Chi, Glaser and Rees (1982); Larkin, *et al.* (1980)]. Essentially, working forward involves a sequence of information search and problem-solving in which known values are used to solve unknowns. In working backward, the decision-maker begins with various potential solutions and acquires the information needed to support each solution.

Biggs and Mock (1983) found that auditors had similar approaches to solving auditing problems. Their "systemic" and "directed" decision strategies were analogous to the working forward and working backward models, respectively, and were similarly associated with audit experience.

In this study, a table was prepared for each subject that recorded the protocol line number in which each information cue was the object of an information acquisition operator (information search, direct reading, algebraic calculation and information retrieval). A sequential information acquisition pattern would result in a general increase in protocol line numbers as one scans down such a table. This was the pattern observed in the tables for all the subjects except S1, one of the less experienced auditors.

While S1's information acquisition pattern was to a large extent sequential, a substantial amount of information acquisition was not. In six out of 25 information search operators during Phase I, S1 referred back to the planning materials in the introduction to the case, to seek guidance from what had been previously planned. During Phase II, S1 again made numerous references to planning materials, and relied upon his firm's guidelines for making many decisions.

In addition, S1 was the only auditor to evaluate and revise the planned audit program in an order that was not sequential. He began with the revenue cycle, then worked on the non-trade notes receivable, followed by the purchasing cycle and finally the inventory cycle. As might be expected of a less experienced auditor, S1's behaviour was similar to physics novices' use of a working backward strategy, in that previous decisions in the case materials provided the primary guidance for his decision process.

The results on the order of information acquisition may support several theories about auditor judgment that have recently been reported in the auditing literature. Gibbins (1984), for example, suggests that "judgment is a conditional process. The judgment process is conditional on information which arrives (is perceived) as the process unfolds."

A sequential search of information would support the essential elements of this proposition. Similarly, in a task that involved internal control evaluation, Biggs and Mock (1983) categorized several auditors as "systemic", noting that they completed their information search before finalizing their response (selecting an appropriate sample size).

These propositions would be quite difficult to verify without testing the same subject in a second case, where information arrives in a different sequence. However, they do underscore the importance of auditor information search. If judgments are conditional on the information that is acquired and perceived, the study of information search will be necessary to understand auditor judgments.

Research question 5-E concerns the comprehensiveness of information acquisition. Table 11 shows the frequency of each auditor's information acquisition operations directed at each category of information in the case. Zeros indicate a category of information for which there is no evidence of acquisition by a particular auditor. The NA entries reflect the fact that the planned audit program was not made available during Phase I.

During Phase II, there was one instance of an auditor failing to examine a part of the audit program. There is no protocol evidence of subject S1 examining recording cash disbursements in the purchasing cycle. The other three auditors carried out complete searches of the entire audit program. But while information acquisition appears to have been very comprehensive during Phase II, there were considerable differences in the comprehensiveness of information acquisition during preliminary analytical review (Phase I).

Table 11 shows that M2 searched all the Phase I materials, virtually reading every word. The only item of information he missed was the 1979 auditor's report, which he looked for but was unable to find in the case materials. He conducted a very thorough search, raising numerous questions and making notations for management letter comments throughout. Subjects M1 and S2 were also very thorough, although they did skip a few items in some of the early financial statements.

S1 basically concentrated his information search on the 1980 unaudited information, making a cursory pass through the 1979 financial statements and ignoring the earlier financial statements.

Research question 5-F concerns the relative emphasis of information acquisition. Table 12 reveals an important difference in emphasis between seniors and managers. The two seniors concentrated, on average, over 32 percent (S1 40.6 percent and S2 24.1 percent) of their information acquisition activities on the "introductory" case materials (sequence numbers 1-3). S1, in particular, referred frequently to case instructions and audit procedures.

By contrast, the two managers spent an average of only 12.5 percent (M1 17.6 percent and M2 7.3 percent) of their information acquisition effort on this introductory material. This behaviour is consistent with previous research on experts and novices. Chi, Feltovich and Glaser (1981) found that physics experts have internal schemata (problem representations in memory) that make it easier for them to categorize and solve the problem. Novices, on the other hand, do not seem to have well-developed internal schemata to help them solve problems and must therefore create problem discriminations based on the features of the problem they are dealing with. The lack of such internal schemata would explain why seniors spent much of their information acquisition activity referring back to instructions and procedures presented in the introductory part of the case. The managers, after reading the introductory material once, were apparently able to draw on a wider base of experience that provided the principles on which they could proceed to the rest of the case.

TABLE 12
Emphasis of Information Search

Case Sequence	**Category Name**	**M1**	**M2**	**S1**	**S2**
PHASE I					
1.0	Case Overview:	1.1%	1.5%	7.8%	0.7%
2.0	Planning Workpaper:				
2.1	General Information	6.8	1.7	10.3	6.0
2.2	Audit Completion	1.7	0.2	1.7	1.3
2.3	Personnel & Critical Areas	2.3	0.6	0.9	0.7
2.4	Internal Audit Involvement	0.6	0.2	0.9	0.7
2.5	Audit Schedule	2.3	0.8	6.9	6.0
3.0	Internal Control Summary:	2.8	2.3	12.1	8.7
4.0	1980 Financial Reports:				
4.1	1980 Balance Sheet	20.5	7.4	23.3	13.3
4.2	1980 Earnings Statement	5.7	4.3	6.9	4.0
4.3	1980 Retained Earnings	0.0	0.2	0.0	0.7
4.4	1980 Changes in Fin. Position	1.7	4.3	0.0	2.7
4.5	1980 Fin. Statement Notes:				0.0
4.5.1	Sig. Accounting Policies	3.4	1.5	0.0	5.3
4.5.2	Inventory	0.6	0.6	1.7	1.3
4.5.3	Notes Receivable	1.7	0.6	0.0	0.7
4.5.4	Plant, Property & Equipment	0.6	0.2	0.0	1.3
4.5.5	Intangible Assets	0.6	0.4	0.0	0.7
4.5.6	Long Term Debt	4.0	3.1	0.9	2.0
4.5.7	Commitments	1.7	2.1	0.0	4.0
4.5.8	Contingent Liabilities	1.7	0.4	0.0	0.7
4.5.9	Income Taxes	0.6	0.2	0.0	0.7
4.5.10	Pension & Profit Sharing	0.6	0.4	0.0	0.7
4.5.11	Discontinued Operations	1.7	0.2	0.0	1.3

TABLE 12 (Continued)
Emphasis of Information Search

Case Sequence	Category Name	M1	M2	S1	S2
PHASE I (cont.)					
5.0	1979 Financial Reports:				
5.1	1979 Auditor's Report	0.6%	0.0%	0.0%	0.7%
5.2	1979 Financial Statements	14.2	11.4	11.2	5.3
5.3	1979 Fin. Statement Notes	0.0	5.2	0.0	0.7
6.0	1978/77 Financial Reports:	4.0	21.7	0.0	2.7
7.0	1977/76 Financial Reports:	2.3	12.4	0.0	8.0
8.0	Supplemental Schedules:				
8.1	Sales Analysis & Aging	6.3	3.3	7.8	3.3
8.2	Operating Expenses	3.4	1.7	1.7	4.7
8.3	Quart.Fin. Reports (1976-79)	3.4	11.0	4.3	11.3
	Total	100.0%*	100.0%*	100.0%*	100.0%*
PHASE II					
1.0	Case Overview:	0.0	0.3	1.5	0.0
2.0	Planning Workpaper:	3.2	0.0	0.0	0.0
2.1	General Information	1.3	2.5	0.8	0.5
2.2	Audit Completion	4.5	0.3	0.0	0.0
2.3	Personnel & Critical Areas	0.0	0.0	0.0	0.0
2.4	Internal Audit Involvement	0.0	0.0	0.0	0.0
2.5	Audit Schedule	0.0	1.3	0.0	0.0
3.0	Internal Control Summary:	1.9	0.6	3.1	0.0
4.0	1980 Financial Reports:	3.9	0.0	0.0	0.0
4.1	1980 Balance Sheet	3.9	3.8	3.1	3.8
4.2	1980 Earnings Statement	0.6	0.6	0.8	0.0
4.3	1980 Retained Earnings	0.0	0.0	0.0	0.0
4.4	1980 Changes in Fin. Position	0.0	0.0	0.0	0.0
4.5	1980 Fin. Statement Notes:	3.2	3.4	1.6	1.6
5.0	1979 Financial Reports:	1.3	0.0	0.0	0.0
5.1	1979 Auditor's Report	0.0	0.0	0.0	0.0
5.2	1979 Financial Statements	3.2	3.2	0.8	0.0
5.3	1979 Fin. Statement Notes	0.6	0.3	0.0	0.0
6.0	1978/77 Financial Reports:	0.0	0.3	0.0	0.0
7.0	1977/76 Financial Reports:	0.0	0.0	0.0	0.0
8.0	Supplemental Schedules:				
8.1	Sales Analysis & Aging	0.0	1.3	0.8	1.1
8.2	Operating Expenses	0.0	0.0	0.0	0.5
8.3	Quart. Fin. Reports (1976-79)	0.0	0.0	0.0	1.6
9.0	Phase II Instructions:	5.8	0.0	0.0	0.0
10.0	ARP Results from Phase I:	17.5	7.6	11.5	9.2

TABLE 12 (Continued)
Emphasis of Information Search

Case Sequence	Category Name	M1	M2	S1	S2
PHASE II (cont.)					
11.0	Nontrade Notes : Intro	3.2%	1.3%	0.8%	1.6%
11.1	Existence & Propriety	4.5	6.0	3.8	4.9
11.2	Collectibility & Valuation	5.2	2.2	4.6	5.4
11.3	C/NC Classification	1.9	1.0	0.8	1.6
11.4	Int. Income Recognition	1.9	1.0	0.8	1.6
12.0	Revenue Cycle: Intro	3.2	3.2	1.5	2.2
12.1	Existence & Recording	0.6	7.3	8.4	5.4
12.2	Collectibility & Valuation	1.3	6.0	7.6	6.0
12.3	Rev. Recog. & Consistency	0.6	2.5	3.1	2.2
12.4	Sales Properly Recorded	0.6	5.4	0.8	4.9
12.5	Proper Sales Cutoff	1.9	1.3	3.1	2.2
12.6	Cash Receipts Recording	0.6	1.3	1.5	1.6
12.7	Cash Receipts Cutoff	1.9	1.3	3.1	1.6
13.0	Inventory Cycle: Intro	3.2	1.6	2.3	2.7
13.1	Existence & Ownership	1.3	10.5	5.3	10.3
13.2	Cost Inclusion	2.6	3.2	1.5	3.3
13.3	Recording Cost of Sales	1.3	2.2	5.3	3.8
13.4	Inventory Valuation	2.6	2.9	3.8	2.7
13.5	Purchases & Sales Cutoff	0.6	2.2	5.3	2.2
14.0	Purchasing Cycle: Intro	0.6	1.9	2.3	0.5
14.1	A/P Valid & Classification	1.3	4.8	5.3	4.3
14.2	Recording of Liabilities	3.9	1.6	3.8	4.3
14.3	Proper Purchases Accounting	2.6	2.2	1.5	2.7
14.4	Recording of Cash Disb.	0.6	1.6	0.0	3.3
	TOTAL	100.0%*	100.0%*	100.0%*	100.0%*

* Rounding error

This evidence is consistent with Gibbins' (1984) proposition that "judgment begins with a search for a template. When an environmental demand is made on an experienced public accountant, the immediate mental response is to search long-term memory for an existing judgment template."

The term "template" is very similar to the schema concept. Again, although the results are preliminary and must be verified by further research, the evidence is consistent with this class of theory about the cognitive processes of decision-makers.

Table 12 also indicates differences in auditor emphasis and approach. Subjects M1 and S1 are more oriented toward the balance sheet (20.5 percent and 23.3 percent of their information acquisitions) and both place relatively more weight on the client's recent financial history. In contrast, subject M2 places more emphasis on accounting issues (1980 footnotes), and on historical trends as represented in pre-1979 financial statements and quarterly summaries. While all subjects emphasized historical financial information, indicating a significant amount of preliminary, informal analytical review, there is some evidence that the auditors used unaudited 1980 data in forming their prior expectations for 1980 balances. This approach, as noted by Kinney and Uecker (1982) and Biggs and Wild (1985), is controversial and may lead to biased judgments.

Finally, there was an important difference in the goals of managers and seniors during the information acquisition phase. While the seniors' activity was oriented strictly toward understanding the client well enough to revise the audit program, the managers tended to acquire information for other purposes as well. Much of the managers' information acquisition activity during Phase I was directed at understanding the client, the nature of its business, and any business problems it faced. The many management letter comments made by the two managers during Phase I reflect information acquisition oriented toward this latter goal. For example, both noted the tax savings the client could achieve by switching from FIFO to the LIFO inventory cost flow assumption. These differences probably reflect the difference between managers, who are used to taking a global approach, and seniors who simply carry out orders.

5.4 SUMMARY

Chapter 3 presented some general research questions related to auditors' overall decision processes and information acquisition behaviour. These questions were more specifically addressed in this chapter. The auditors' overall decision processes were modelled in the form of episode abstracts and macro flowcharts. In general, the auditors' decision process was similar to diagnostic reasoning models that have been found in the medical literature.

The protocol analysis of the auditors' information acquisition behaviour focused on questions of order, completeness and emphasis. The auditors tended to search the case materials completely (although S1 was an exception), in sequence, but some important differences in search emphasis were detected. In particular, the inexperienced auditors spent a greater proportion of their search activities referring back to case materials than their more experienced colleagues, a finding that was attributed to differences in memory schemas. The experienced auditors apparently had a richer, more complete problem schema that allowed them to perform the case with minimum return to case instructions and introductory materials.

Chapter 6

INFORMATION EVALUATION AND DECISION

The decision process model presented in Figure 1 included information evaluation and action/choice, as well as information acquisition, among its components. The previous chapter described the auditors' information acquisition processes in performing the Pacific Electronics case. This chapter describes how the auditors evaluated the information, and made decisions on analytical review procedures to perform and audit program changes to undertake. The more specific research questions presented below are derived from general research questions 3-B through 3-F in Chapter 3.

6-A What was the nature of the auditors' evaluations and decisions during the analytical review phase of the task?

6-B What decisions did auditors make while adjusting the planned audit program, and on what basis?

6-C What decision errors were made, if any, and what were their apparent causes?

6-D What was the nature of the auditors' reasoning process?

6.1 OVERALL DECISION PROCESS

The main purpose of this chapter is to describe the auditor's specific evaluations and decisions. However, to better understand these specific decision processes, it is helpful to review the four subjects' overall decision frameworks. In Chapter 5, there was sufficient similarity among the four auditors to suggest that they used the following four-step approach:

(1) Read through all or portions of the case, conducting a preliminary analytical review to identify audit problems (areas of potential concern) or "opportunities" (areas of little concern);
(2) Request analytical review information (usually financial ratios) to further clarify problems and opportunities found in the first step;
(3) Evaluate requested information to confirm problems and opportunities; and
(4) Adjust the audit program based on analytical review information from the previous steps.

It has already been noted that this process is similar to the diagnostic reasoning found in medical studies, where doctors generate and test hypotheses to identify diseases in patients [Elstein, Shulman and Sprafka (1978); Johnson *et al.* (1982)]. This research linked poor diagnostic performance to confirmation bias, demonstrating that doctors who made incorrect diagnoses tended to search for additional information that confirmed their initial hypotheses rather than search for information that might disconfirm it. With this in mind, the protocols were examined to determine what problems were initially identified, and to seek evidence of confirmation bias in the subsequent evaluation of information. This chapter explores the subjects' specific evaluations and decisions during the analytical review (Phase I) and audit program adjustment (Phase II) components of their task.

6.2 AUDITORS' EVALUATIONS AND DECISIONS DURING ANALYTICAL REVIEW (PHASE I)

Information acquired by auditors must be evaluated for relevance and importance before it can be incorporated into decisions. Thus, an understanding of auditors' decision processes must be based on knowledge of the way in which the acquired information is evaluated, as well as the process by which actual decisions are made. The distinction between an evaluation and a decision is somewhat arbitrary, and the two components should not be seen as independent aspects of the decision process. But to understand how decisions are made, it is helpful to look at the two components separately.

For the purposes of this study, an evaluation was defined as a conclusion drawn about some aspect of the case, while a decision was defined as an audit action. For example, if an auditor indicated that the current ratio should be included in the analytical review program or made a change in the audit program, the action was considered a decision. If the auditor reviewed the current ratio and concluded that the company had a liquidity problem, his conclusion was deemed an evaluation. If the evaluation of liquidity led to increased audit attention to current assets or current liabilities, the increase was considered a decision.

Expected evaluations

In order to understand the evaluations and decisions made by auditors during the analytical review portion of the case, it is helpful to review the ratio analysis of Pacific Electronics' financial condition presented in Chapter 4. Tables 5 through 8 presented selected financial ratios, many of which were included in the auditors' analytical review. Based on the analysis presented in Chapter 4, an analytical review of Pacific Electronics was expected to yield evaluations relevant to the four audit cycles included in the audit program for the research. The anticipated results of the auditors' analytical review of Pacific Electronics were as follows:

Analysis of liquidity

Measures of Pacific Electronics' short-term liquidity revealed a relatively consistent deterioration. The current ratio showed a steady decline over the five years.

Collectibility of accounts receivable

The analysis in Chapter 4 raised serious questions about the quality of Pacific Electronics' accounts receivables. Accounts receivable turnover declined in each year, from a high of 25.88 in 1976 to 15.18 in 1979, and an unaudited turnover of only 10.37 in 1980. The aging schedule placed a greater percentage of accounts receivable in the older categories in 1980 than in 1979. In 1979, 16.9 percent of accounts receivable were 90 days or older; in 1980, 21.5 percent were past 90 days. Pacific Electronics' allowance for doubtful accounts as a percentage of gross accounts receivable declined from 7.4 percent in 1979 to 5.7 percent in 1980. Bad debt expense as a percentage of sales remained constant, at about 3.0 percent, in 1979 and 1980.

This analysis suggested serious concerns about the collectibility of Pacific Electronics' accounts receivable. It was expected that the auditors would identify this problem, and make appropriate adjustments to the audit program for the revenue cycle.

Potential inventory obsolescence

Pacific Electronics' inventory turnover ratio declined over the four-year period. Turnover declined steadily, from a high of 7.42 in 1977 to an unaudited 1980 turnover of 4.07. Since Pacific Electronics' inventory was composed of electronic stereos, televisions, stoves, refrigerators and washing machines, it was considered possible that the declining turnover was caused by obsolescence. It was expected that auditors would take this possibility into account during their analytical review and evaluation of the audit program for inventory.

Analysis of accounts payable

The analysis of accounts payable revealed an apparent opportunity for the auditor to rely on analytical review to reduce further substantive testing of the account. Since the accounts payable turnover ratio had been relatively steady, and had actually improved from 2.79 in 1977 to 3.03 in 1980, the auditors could consider accounts payable less risky and possibly reduce the relevant tests of detail in the audit program phase of the task.

Decisions made by auditors during analytical review

Research question 6-A is aimed at describing the evaluations and decisions made by the auditors during the analytical review phase of the task. In analyzing their performance, the prior ratio analysis of Pacific Electronics is used as a point of comparison.

Problems and opportunities identified during analytical review

The auditors' decision processes reflected the use of analytical review as a diagnostic tool to help direct the audit function. Since their evaluations effectively identified potential problems and opportunities in the client's financial statements, the protocols were analyzed to identify all the analysis that took place during Phase I analytical review.

The analysis of the problems and opportunities identified in the initial analytical review was concerned with two issues. The first issue was whether the auditors would identify the problems associated with Pacific Electronics' financial statements that were discussed in the previous section, bearing in mind that the case was based on a real company that actually had an adjustment to its allowance for doubtful accounts. The second issue was whether auditors used analytical review to identify "problem" areas that should be subjected to increased audit effort, and opportunities to reduce the level of effort. The role of analytical review in problem identification is described by Smith (1983) as follows:

> Analytical review procedures applied early in the audit examination tend to isolate errors and omissions . . . . The auditor would want to investigate items of this nature further and discuss them with the client at the earliest possible date . . . .

As for identifying opportunities, Smith notes:

> It is important to consider the cost effectiveness of performing more or less analytical review procedures as opposed to decreased or increased tests of detail to arrive at the same level of audit assurance.

Table 13 presents the auditors' identification of problems (no opportunities were identified). It is evident that all four subjects identified an extensive set of problems during initial analytical review, although managers identified substantially more than seniors. All four auditors noted that accounts receivable were potentially overstated, pointing out that accounts receivable grew more rapidly than the allowance for doubtful accounts, or the overdue accounts shown in the accounts receivable aging schedule. An example of the reasoning appears in sections 2.4, 2.5, and 2.24 of subject M1's episode abstract (see Appendix B).

As well, all four auditors noted the potential obsolescence of Pacific Electronics' inventory, based on increases in inventory and declines in the inventory turnover ratio over the preceding four years: an example can be found in section 2.10 of the episode abstract for subject M1 (Appendix B). At least one auditor identified all the significant problems in the Pacific Electronics case. Overall, in identifying critical problems in the case, the auditors' performance was quite impressive.

TABLE 13
Problems Identified by Auditors During Phase I

Problem Identified	**M1**	**M2**	**S1**	**S2**
Pacific Electronics not on Lifo	X	X		X
Possible Inventory obsolescence	X	X	X	X
Accounts Receivable overstated	X	X	X	X
Accounts Payable increasing faster than inventory, possible liquidity problem	X	X	X	
Installations in Process overstated	X	X		X
Notes Receivable overstated	X			
Long-Term Debt too high	X			X
Interest Expense too high	X	X		
Salary and Wages not controlled	X			X
Bad Debt Expense understated		X		
Insurance Expense understated		X		
Acquisitions unclear		X		
Depreciation understated			X	
Sales Returns	X			
Potential Going-Concern problem	X			

With respect to the identification of both problems and opportunities, the evaluations are subject to some criticism.

There is no evidence of any auditor using analytical review during Phase I to identify areas where audit effort could be reduced (see Table 13), even though some areas, like accounts payable, showed no unusual fluctuations and might have lent themselves to a reduction in tests of details. This issue will be discussed further in the section on decisions made during Phase II.

Decisions made by auditors during analytical review

Research question 6-A is also concerned with identifying the analytical review information the auditors requested at the conclusion of Phase I. These requests constituted audit decisions about an analytical review program, and therefore provide descriptive evidence of auditors' approach to analytical review. Auditors' requests for additional ARP information also provide insight into the existence of confirmation bias and indicate whether the subjects tended to request information that simply confirmed the problems and opportunities they had already identified.

Table 14 lists the ARPs that were requested in Phase I. As might be expected, the auditors were interested in liquidity, profitability and other traditional financial indicators. There is also considerable correspondence between the problems identified in Table 13 and the information requested shown in Table 14, a finding which lends credence to the possibility of confirmation bias.

However, it is important to be cautious in drawing conclusions about bias. It appears that auditors did request additional information to confirm problems that had been identified earlier. There is obviously nothing wrong with such an approach, as long as the information search is not so restricted that it prevents previous hypotheses from being disproved. From this standpoint, the auditors appeared to request a very comprehensive set of additional information, which was used in at least one instance to disprove a previous hypothesis.

TABLE 14
Analytical Review Information Items Requested in Phase II of the Pacific Electronics Case

Information Requested	Subject Selection of Information Item			
	M1	M2	S1	S2
Inventory Turnover Ratio	–	X	X	X
Acid Test Ratio	X	X	–	X
Debt to Equity Ratio	–	X	–	–
Current Ratio	X	X	X	–
Gross Profit Percentage	–	X	X	X
Operating Income to Sales	–	X	–	–
Effective Tax Rate	–	X	–	–
Earnings from Continuing Operations as a Percentage of Sales	–	X	–	–
Days Outstanding Accounts Receivable	X	X	–	–
Accounts Payable Turnover	X	X	–	–
Accounts Receivable Turnover	–	X	–	X
Aging of Accounts Receivable	–	X	X	X
Collection Period	–	–	–	X
Total Liabilities to Total Assets	–	–	–	X
Dollar Days Sales	X	–	X	–
Operating Expense Analysis	X	–	–	–
Quarterly Gross Profit Percentage	–	–	X	X
Industry Ratios	–	–	–	X
Dollar and Percent Changes of Income Statement Items:				
Sales	–	–	X	–
Cost of Goods Sold	–	–	X	–
Gross Profit	–	–	X	–
Operating Expense	–	–	X	–
Interest	–	–	X	–
Operating Income	–	–	X	–
Other Income	–	–	X	–
Earnings Before Taxes	–	–	X	–
Earnings from Continuing Operations	–	–	X	–
Loss from Discontinued Operations	–	–	X	–
Net Income	–	–	X	–

In Phase I, subject M1 identified accounts payable as a problem area that could lead to liquidity deficiency for the company. He requested two related ratios: accounts payable turnover, and inventory turnover. Based on his analysis of these ratios, he concluded that there was no evidence to support his earlier concern, noting that, while receivables and inventory may represent liquidity problems, the company had kept its accounts payable in order.

Thus, M1 used the information he had requested to disconfirm an earlier hypothesis of a serious liquidity deficiency.

6.3 DECISIONS MADE DURING AUDIT PROGRAM ADJUSTMENT (PHASE II)

Research question 6-B is concerned with describing the decisions made during Phase II to adjust the planned audit program. The discussion of results explains the protocol coding methods used to identify the auditors' decisions and associated rationale, describes the decisions, with emphasis on increases and decreases in nature, timing and extent, and presents a detailed analysis of decisions in the revenue cycle.

Coding methods for describing decisions

A set of action/choice operators was used to code Phase II protocols for each subject. Four coding operators were developed:

Audit Decision (AD)	Assigned when an auditor reaches a definite decision concerning a specific audit task (either to specify an analytical review procedure during Phase I or adjust the audit program during Phase II).
Generate Alternative (GA)	Assigned when an auditor generates a potential decision that requires further evaluation.
Other Decision (OD)	Assigned when an auditor reaches a definite decision that could not be coded as an AD operator. OD operators typically involved an auditor making a management letter comment.
Decision Rules (DR)	Assigned when an auditor specifies a method of making a decision.

The protocols were further analyzed to determine which audit procedure or procedures, if any, were affected by the decision, the type of change being considered, and the reasoning or rationale that could be linked to each action. More specifically, each audit program decision was coded using the following classifications:

Type of change

Nature (N)	Changes in type of procedures performed in the audit step.
Timing (T)	Changes in the stage at which the audit step is performed.
Extent (E)	Changes in the amount of work performed in the audit step.
Editorial (O)	Minor changes in the wording of the audit step.
Miscellaneous (O)	A number of other decision categories, including deletion of an audit step and management letter comments.

Type of Rationale	
Analytical Review (A/R)	Changes based explicitly on analytical review considerations.
Internal Control (IC)	Changes based explicitly on internal control considerations.
Materiality/Risk (M) (R)	Changes based on or involving audit risk and materiality.
Efficiency/Effectiveness (EF)	Changes in the interest of efficiency or effectiveness.
Statistical (ST)	Changes based upon statistical criteria (e.g. statistical sampling).
Tailoring (TL)	Changes made to fit the program to the characteristics of the client.
Technical (DP)	Changes made to accommodate technological factors, such as computerized audit techniques.
Firm-Specific Standards (O)	Changes based on firm audit policies and procedures.

Overview of decisions made by auditors

The analysis of the decisions and their associated rationales resulted in a "decision coding table" for each auditor and phase, which is presented in Table 15. From this summary table alone, one can see the significant scope of review and analysis that each auditor went through. Table 15 summarizes some 532 actions; although 80 of these actions were "editorial" in nature (most of them involving auditors from the firm least familiar with the standardized audit program), 422 involved explicit changes in nature, extent or timing. In 29 instances, steps deemed irrelevant to a retail-wholesale enterprise were eliminated by the subjects.

Increases and decreases in planned audit program

Of the 422 changes to nature, timing and extent on the audit program, only 19 simplified or reduced the nature of work, while 403 represented increases or meant no change in overall audit effort. This is consistent with the earlier finding that the auditors identified problems but no opportunities during Phase I. At least in this study, the auditors did not use analytical review to reduce tests of details, which is one of the primary purposes of the procedure as outlined in SAS 23 [AICPA (1978, Section 318.03)]:

> A basic premise underlying the application of analytical review procedures is that relationships among data may reasonably be expected by the auditor to exist and continue in the absence of known conditions to the contrary. The presence of those relationships provides the auditor with evidential matter required by the third standard of field work. The application of analytical review procedures may indicate the need for additional procedures or may indicate that the extent of other auditing procedures may be reduced.

TABLE 15
Summary of Subject Decisions

	M1 Phase		M2 Phase		S1 Phase		S2 Phase		Total Phase	
Decisions	I	II	I	II	I	II	I	II	I	II
Audit Decision	40	30	45	85	17	76	30	75	132	266
Gen. Alternative	13	25	0	1	15	36	1	11	29	73
Other Decision	2	0	7	0	1	1	10	4	20	5
Decision Rule	4	0	0	0	0	1	1	1	5	2
Change Type										
Change Nature	40	21	46	7	15	49	40	23	141	100
Change Timing	7	7	0	3	9	23	1	6	17	39
Change Extent	1	10	0	0	6	56	0	8	7	83
Combination	0	4	0	18	0	13	0	0	0	35
No Change	0	4	0	4	2	0	0	0	2	8
Delete Procedure	0	8	0	8	0	0	0	13	0	29
Editorial Change	3	0	0	37	0	1	0	39	3	77
Management Letter	1	0	3	0	1	1	1	0	6	1
Disclosure	0	0	2	0	0	0	0	0	2	0
Other Changes	7	1	1	0	4	0	0	2	12	3
Change Rationale										
Analytical Review	43	16	19	18	7	11	40	16	109	61
Internal Control	0	0	0	2	4	4	0	5	4	11
Materiality/Risk	2	12	0	2	1	9	0	4	3	27
Efficiency	6	11	1	12	6	11	0	29	13	63
Technical	0	0	0	0	3	5	0	5	3	10
Statistical	0	0	0	0	2	9	0	1	2	10
Tailoring Program	0	0	0	1	0	2	0	27	0	90
Firm Standards	1	0	0	1	0	2	0	0	1	3
Unspecified	1	12	32	15	10	40	2	4	45	71
N/A	1	3	0	0	4	5	0	0	5	8

While there is little evidence of auditors reducing the nature, timing or extent of planned audit procedures on the basis of analytical review, it is difficult to identify the cause. Is this purely a case specific finding, or do auditors simply not get enough comfort from the procedure to reduce more traditional audit tests? Either way, this study found that the primary role of analytical review was to provide "red flags" to identify areas of audit risk. This is an appropriate but limited role that fails to reflect the full benefit of the procedure.

Rationale for decisions

Table 15 shows the underlying rationale for the decisions made during Phase II. The 116 actions with "unspecified" rationale primarily reflect the large number of decisions to make minor adjustments (e.g. editorial), whose rationales were often not explicitly stated. It is important to note that "analytical review" was the most frequently cited reason for decisions, followed by tailoring of the general audit program to the specifics of the case (90) and efficiency considerations (76). Analytical review was clearly an important factor in the decisions reached in this task.

Table 16 summarizes the significant analytical review conclusions and their effect on the audit program for all cycles except revenue, which is the focus of a detailed analysis that follows. Table 16 shows that analytical review provided the basis for increases in the program for inventory, and for the materiality judgment with respect to notes receivable. New analytical review procedures were added to the audit program, areas of audit risk were identified as a result of ARP information, and the nature, extent, and timing of other substantive audit procedures were adjusted. For example, on the basis of analytical review, both M1 and M2 added new audit steps to the planned program. M1 added steps related to salary and wages, supplies expense, rent expense and potential "off balance sheet" notes receivables, based on problems identified during analytical review. M2 added a step on insurance expense after identifying a substantial increase in this account during analytical review.

6.4 AUDIT PROGRAM CHANGES IN THE REVENUE CYCLE

Since the Pacific Electronics case was based on an actual client whose problems with the revenue cycle were discovered through analytical review, a more complete analysis of auditor decisions in this cycle follows. (See Appendix C for a summary of the revenue cycle audit program.) The analysis shows the explicit reasoning leading to revenue cycle audit decisions, with special emphasis on decisions based on analytical review rationale, and psychological theories that may underlie the auditors' reasoning processes.

TABLE 16

Specific Effects of Analytical Review on Audit Program Other than Revenue Cycle

	Analytical Review Conclusion	**Effect on Audit Program**
Notes Receivable Cycle		
M1	Immaterial	No Change
M2	Immaterial	Editorial Changes
S1	Immaterial	No Change
S2	Immaterial	No Change
Inventory Cycle		
M1	Possible Obsolescence	No Change
M2	Possible Obsolescence	Increase Scope
S1	Possible Obsolescence	Increase Scope
S2	Inventory Increase	Increase Scope
Accounts Payable Cycle		
M1	Accounts Payable Turnover, Possible liquidity Problem	No Change
M2	None	Editorial Changes
S1	None	Some Increase
S2	None	No Change

TABLE 16 (Continued)
Specific Effects of Analytical Review on Audit Program Other than Revenue Cycle

	Analytical Review Conclusion	Effect on Audit Program
Other Procedures Added		
M1	Lack of Control Over Operating Expenses	Adds Procedures for: Salary Expense, Rent Expense, Supplies Expense, and Contingent Liabilities
M2	Lack of Control Over Operating Expenses	Adds Procedure for: Insurance Expense

Revenue cycle decisions

Table 17 presents a detailed analysis of all Phase II decisions that affected the revenue cycle audit program.

This table indicates that the majority of the revenue cycle decisions were not explicitly based on analytical review rationale. The most common decision involved "tailoring" a standard audit program to reflect the specifics of the client, or to enhance the efficiency or effectiveness of the program. Analytical review was evident in the protocols for 21 of the choices, which are examined in more detail below.

Revenue cycle decisions with analytical review rationale

Table 18 focuses on those audit decisions that were explicitly based on ARP evidence or rationale. What is immediately evident from this table is that most of the audit changes or alternatives involved increasing the extent of the program, or moving the timing of a particular step forward. This result was expected, given that the case involved a client whose revenue cycle accounts were overstated. But it is clear that the ARPs served as an effective "red flag" to identify an audit risk area.

Decision strategies for revenue cycle

Tables 17 and 18 also provide insight into the character of the auditors' decision strategies for this part of the task. Subject M1 decided to react to the risk he identified by changing the timing of some audit steps, largely through the use of general instructions that established broad audit goals and objectives. He expected subordinates to meet these objectives by making more detailed decisions in the field, contingent upon conditions existing during the audit. In his protocols for Phase II, M1 made explicit statements to this effect:

> My theory on that is really that if the people are really aware of the objectives
>
> I would rather make sure they understand the objectives and what we're doing
>
> and maybe tailor or mention a few specifics unusual to their industry

TABLE 17

Detailed Summary of Program Change Decisions for the Revenue Cycle

	M1					M2					S1					S2				
Audit Objective	**N**	**E**	**T**	**O**	**Rationale**	**N**	**E**	**T**	**O**	**Rationale**	**N**	**E**	**T**	**O**	**Rationale**	**N**	**E**	**T**	**O**	**Rationale**
A: Existence & Recording	NC	NC	+	O	A/R,R						*				IC,C					
A1 Arithmetric Accuracy			+		A/R,R				*	EF,TL			*		UN				*	A/R,EF
A2 Obtain Confirmations							*			EF			+		EF		+		*	A/R,EF
												+			IC,ST					
A3 Investigate Exceptions									*	EF									*	EF
A4 Send Second Requests						NC				UN	*				EF				*	EF
A5 Check Undelivered Requests						NC				UN	*				EF				*	EF
A6 Followup for Positives							–			EF	*	+			TL				*	EF
A7 Summarize Results						NC				UN						*	+	*	*	A/R,EF
A8 Ascertain Amount Non-Current						NC				UN	*				EF	*				A/R
A9 Investigate Material Balances									*	EF	*				TL	NC				UN
B: Collectibility & Valuation			+		UN						*		+		TL					
B1 Arith. Accuracy of Allowance						NC				UN			+			*				DP,A/R
B2 Examine Material Chargeoffs						*				TL			+			*	+			DP,A/R
B3 Test Aging									*	TL	*	+	+		A/R,O				*	EF
B4 Compare to Preceding Year						NC				UN			+						*	EF
B5 Computer No. of Days Sales						NC				UN	*		+		AR,EF				*	UN
B6 Check Subsequent Receipts							+		*	EF,A/R			+		A/R	*	+		*	A/R,EF
B7 Invest. Material Chargeoffs						NC				N/A	*		+		TL			*		EF
B8 Determine Allowance Adequacy						NC				UN									*	A/R,EF
C: Recognition & Consistency	NC	NC	NC		UN						*		*		UN					
C1 Check Accuracy of Sales & Cos						*				EF	*		*		TL				*	EF
C2 Review Recognition Methods						*			*	EF	*		+		A/R				*	UN
C3 Investigate Large Contracts						NC				UN			+						*	EF

TABLE 17 (Continued)

Detailed Summary of Program Change Decisions for the Revenue Cycle

	M1					M2					S1					S2				
Audit Objective	**N**	**E**	**T**	**O**	**Rationale**	**N**	**E**	**T**	**O**	**Rationale**	**N**	**E**	**T**	**O**	**Rationale**	**N**	**E**	**T**	**O**	**Rationale**
D: Sales Properly Recorded																				
D1 Review Sales Postings							–			EF						NC				UN
D2 Foot & Trace Sales to G/L									*	EF							–			EF
D3 Check Numerical Sequence						NC				UN						NC				UN
D4 Examine Supporting Documents						D	D	D		EF						*				EF
D5 Trace Postings to Sales Register						NC				UN						*		*		UN
D6 Examine Shipping Records						NC				UN						D	D	D		UN
D7 Check Credit Memos						*				EF							*		*	EF
E: Proper Sales Cut-off																				
E1 Review Shipping Records			–		EF	NC				UN		*	*		TL	*				EF
E2 Review Subsequent Credits										UN		+			A/R				*	M
E3 Review Returns/Warranties	*	*	*		EF	NC				UN		+			A/R	NC				UN
F: Cash Receipts Recording											*	+	*		TL,IC					
F1 Check Significant Cash Postings						NC				UN						*			*	A/R,EF
F2 Foot & Trace to G/L									*	EF						*			*	A/R,EF
F3 Reconcile with Bank						NC				UN						*			*	A/R,EF
G: Cash Receipts Cut-off											*	*			TL					
G1 Review Cash re Cut-off	D	D	D		EF	*				EF,A/R						D	D	D		EF
G2 Review Subsequent Receipts	D	D	D		EF				*	EF						D	D	D		EF

Change Type

N = Nature
E = Extent
T = Timing
O = Other

Nature of Change

D = Delete Step
– = Decrease Extent/Timing
+ = Increase Extent/Timing
* = Unspecified Change
NC = No Change
O = Other

Change Rationale

A/R = Analytical Review
EF = Efficiency/Effectiveness
TL = Tailoring
IC = Internal Control
C = Cost Considerations
ST = Statistical
R = Risk Considerations
M = Materiality
DP = Computer Considerations
UN = Unspecified Rationale
NA = Not Applicable
O = Other

TABLE 18

Revenue Cycle Change Decisions Based on Analytical Review Evidence or Rationale

	Subject M1				Subject M2				Subject S1				Subject S2			
Audit Objective	**N**	**E**	**T**	**O**	**N**	**E**	**T**	**O**	**N**	**E**	**T**	**O**	**N**	**E**	**T**	**O**
A: Existence & Recording	NC	NC	+						*							
A1 Arithmetric Accuracy			+					*			*					*
A2 Obtain Confirmations						*				+	+			+		*
A7 Summarize Results					NC								*	+	*	*
A8 Ascertain Amount Non-Current					NC				*		+		*			
B: Collectibility & Valuation			+								+		*			
B1 Arith. Accuracy of Allowance					NC						+		*	+		
B2 Examine Chargeoffs					*				*	+	+					*
B3 Test Aging								*	*		+					*
B5 Compute No. of Days Sales					NC						+		*	+		*
B6 Check Subsequent Receipts						+		*								*
B8 Determine Allowance Adequacy					NC				*		*					
C: Recognition & Consistency	NC	NC	NC						*		+					*
C2 Review Recognition Methods					*			*								
E: Proper Sales Cut-off										+						*
E2 Review Subsequent Credits										+			NC			
E3 Review Returns/Warranties	*	*	*		NC				*	+	*					
F: Cash Receipts Recording													*			*
F1 Check Significant Cash Postings					NC								*			*
F2 Foot & Trace to G/L								*					*			*
F3 Reconcile with Bank					NC				*	*						
G: Cash Receipts Cut-off													D	D	D	
G1 Review Cash re Cut-off	D	D	D		*											

Change Type

N = Nature
E = Extent
T = Timing
O = Other

Nature of Change

D = Delete Step
– = Decrease Extent/Timing
+ = Increase Extent/Timing
* = Unspecified Change
NC = No Change
O = Other

I like to think my people are thinking on their feet and not just following steps.

Usually that's the way most of ours do it.

They have to be willing to change the approach as we get new wrinkles.

Subject S1, who was from the same firm as M1, decided to move timing back and increase audit scope. Four of his audit decisions are explicitly tied to ARP evidence. For Step 3, Objective B, which entails "test aging of receivables balance", he decides to increase extent and change timing. For Step 5, which involves number of days' sales computations, timing is also changed. For Objective E, involving proper sales cut-off, the extent of Step 2 (credit memo review) and Step 3 (warranty and product return review) are both increased.

Subject M2 made only one decision in the revenue cycle that could be related to analytical review. However, S2, his colleague from another office, made several decisions based on ARP evidence, four of which involved increases in audit scope. Specifically, he recommended increasing confirmations (Objective A, Steps 2 and 7), examining additional supporting documents for material charge-offs (Objective B, Step 2), and checking additional subsequent receipts of receivables (Objective B, Step 6).

6.5 DECISION ERRORS

Research question 6-C addresses the issue of decision errors made by auditors during Phase II. In a case as complex as the one used here, errors cannot be identified with precision. But it is still important to address the issue, even if it involves some speculation. There are two primary bases on which decision errors can be assessed. First, the case was based on an actual client, where an audit adjustment was made to the accounts receivable: while this is not a perfect criterion, in that the real world auditors may have been mistaken, it is a measure that has "passed" a market test. Second, it is possible to compare managers and seniors. While this, too, is an imperfect criterion, the combination of protocol evidence of the reasoning behind decisions, knowledge of the auditing literature, and *prima facie* evidence that managers are more expert than seniors justifies some comment on decision errors.

In at least one area, there is very clear evidence. All auditors identified accounts receivable as a primary concern, and there was considerable agreement regarding the evidence that supported their conclusion. Analytical review revealed that accounts receivable were increasing faster than the associated allowance account, and found evidence of deterioration in the aging schedule. All auditors explicitly cited both sources of evidence.

However, while the auditors performed very well in identifying the problem with accounts receivable, their decisions based on the identification of a problem suggest important differences in the reasoning processes and memory structures of managers and seniors. In the discussion of information acquisition behaviour, it was suggested that managers appeared to have internal memory schemata that were more developed than seniors, and that this was consistent with evidence presented by Chi, Feltovich and Glaser (1981). Further support for this conclusion emerges from the decisions made about the revenue cycle, where managers seem to apply a more complex and deeper understanding of the auditing task. All four auditors identified the potential overstatement of accounts receivable during their analytical review. But while the seniors used this evidence to make numerous increases in nearly all the steps of the audit program for this cycle, the managers were much more selective in increasing the audit effort.

A particularly revealing decision involves Objective A, Step 2, Confirmation. Both seniors increased the number of confirmations (extent), while neither manager increased this step. In the following protocols, subject M2 clearly states why he made no change:

The confirmation scope, I think, would be the same.

Confirmation scope doesn't have anything to do with collection.

Just has to do with propriety

and existence.

In Objective B, however, Subject M2 indicates a different decision based on analytical review evidence:

As far as scope changes there

Since we do have a deterioration (in aging of accounts receivable), we want to look closer

I would say that in Step 6

Where we're discussing collectibility

Our scope . . . it's difficult to say what our scope should be

Our balance is twice the size that it was in the prior year.

This reasoning suggests that M2 used a deeper and more complex schema related to the problem of linking analytical review evidence with audit program changes. In contrast to S1 and S2, M2 recognized that confirmations would provide little insight about the collectibility of accounts receivable. Rather, confirmations, a fairly expensive procedure, should be increased when problems of existence and propriety are involved. The seniors, evidently having a more shallow understanding of the problem, increased audit work throughout the revenue cycle. The seniors' decisions are similar to those of physics novices in the Chi, Feltovich and Glaser (1981) study, whose reasoning reflected attention to the surface features of the problems but did not identify more complex and deeper relationships. In this study, the seniors' failure to adequately identify steps requiring increased audit effort could increase the cost of audits.

6.6 NATURE OF REASONING PROCESSES

Research question 6-D is concerned with describing the auditors' reasoning processes. The research focused on an analysis of the evaluation operators the auditors used during their task performance.

Types of evaluation operators

Operators in the "Evaluative" category in Table 10 reflect the auditors' information evaluation behaviour. General decision process models, such as Einhorn and Hogarth (1981), establish that information evaluation is likely to be a part of an auditor's decision process, but do not indicate what specific types of evaluative behaviour to expect. The protocols revealed a rich variety of evaluative operators. In fact, five operators were required to capture the various types of evaluations the auditors made in performing the case. These operators ranged from resolute evaluations (Evaluation Operator) to more tentative evaluations (Conditional Judgment Operator). The category also includes such behaviour as assumptions and queries, as well as rationales for decisions (Decision Support Operator).

In examining the evaluative operators in Table 10, two results stand out. The first is the substantial amount of evaluative behaviour that took place. In the two phases of the study, the percentage of operators involving evaluative behaviour ranged from 36 percent (M2 in Phase II) to 65 percent (S2 in Phase I), suggesting that evaluative behaviour took up most of the auditors' decision process activities. It can also be noted that the highest percentage of evaluative behaviour involved the Evaluation operator.

As well, the auditors in this study were much more resolute in their evaluation of the case information than the subjects in a study by Biggs, Messier and Hansen (1987), whose results revealed a much higher percentage of the more tentative evaluative operators (conjecture, assumption, and queries).

One plausible explanation for the difference is that the case in this study was much longer than the one used by Biggs, Messier and Hansen. A long case can be expected to include a large number of evaluations that are relatively minor in importance, and can thus be made with greater certainty. Another plausible explanation is the nature of the task. The Biggs, Messier and Hansen study involved evaluation of EDP controls, about which there may be less knowledge than the financial analysis inherent in analytical review. The large number of decisions made during Phase I supports both explanations, illustrating that the auditors made a great many decisions and recommendations about various management issues as they read through the case. The issues were often fairly straight-forward, such as recommending that Pacific Electronics consider switching from FIFO to LIFO.

The second important result concerns the auditors' use of tentative evaluative operators. While the more resolute "evaluation" operator was used most often, there were still a large number of tentative evaluations. These tentative operators tend to be used when the auditor has some uncertainty about the information being evaluated.

In general, auditors make evaluative judgments and decisions in an environment of uncertainty. That is, at the time they make a judgment or decision, they may have no way of knowing whether they are making a correct choice [Mock and Turner (1981); Biggs (1985)]. Uncertainty does not stop auditors from making decisions: they, like all decision makers, adapt their reasoning processes to fit uncertain circumstances [Norman and Bobrow (1975)]. In this study, the protocols show that the auditors adapted to uncertainty by making conditional judgments and assumptions during their evaluative reasoning processes. As an example, S2 gave the following protocols during Phase II:

> Throughout the program, I noted the first steps began: obtain and check accuracy of the schedules.
>
> I'm assuming, since P.E. has an IBM computer, that all of these schedules are computer-generated for the most part.
>
> Some may be manually maintained by accounting personnel.
>
> However, most of the larger ones I would think would be computerized.

In the above protocols, S2 is evaluating the audit program for notes receivable, specifically checking the accuracy of schedules. Although he is uncertain about whether the schedules are computer-generated, he makes an assumption (AS operator) that they are. He adds some detail to the assumption by making some tentative evaluations (conditional judgment operators were assigned to both of these comments). This process of reasoning under conditions of uncertainty was observed throughout the protocols of all four auditors, and is similar to results from two other studies where detailed protocols were taken from auditors [see Biggs and Mock (1983); Biggs, Messier and Hansen (1987)].

Since uncertainty is a common characteristic of their decision environment, information on auditors' reasoning under conditions of uncertainty is important to any understanding of their overall decision processes. Decision-making under uncertainty in other domains has also been studied at great length, so that there is a basis for comparison between fields of expertise. One reasoning process that is prevalent in the literature is probabilistic reasoning [Tversky and Kahnemann (1974)]. But in auditing, Gibbins (1984) has developed a system of propositions and corollaries relating to template selection that would predict behaviour that is not probabilistic:

Proposition 10.	Template selection depends on circumstantial fit.
Corollary 10(i).	The routine template selection process depends on matching present perception with past learning, so it is not a forward-looking, probabilistic, or expectation process.
Corollary 10(ii).	If a response template is not located immediately, processes of perception, search, and retrieval will continue until halted by an environmentally determined "stopping rule".

The lack of probabilistic behaviour that characterized the subjects in this study is somewhat consistent with Corollary 10(i).

Another approach has recently been proposed in the artificial intelligence literature. Rather than deriving from probabilistic quantities, the reasoning process is considered to be more qualitative in nature. Doyle (1983a and 1983b) proposes a model of reasoning by assumption, while Cohen (1984) suggests a model of reasoning by endorsements. Both suggest that individuals deal with uncertainty by considering the conditions under which a particular outcome would occur with certainty. That is, the reasoning process is more like "A will occur if conditions B, C, and D are present", rather than a probabilistic approach, "there is a probability of 0.5 that A will occur".

This study found no evidence that auditors were using probabilistic reasoning processes, but there is considerable support in the protocols for the alternative approaches. When faced with an uncertain situation, the auditors made assumptions and conditional judgments which allowed them to make decisions and evaluative judgments. It must be noted that no steps were taken to test the various theories of reasoning under uncertainty, so the implications of this evidence must not be overstated. Nevertheless, when simply asked to think aloud, the auditors showed no evidence of probabilistic reasoning. Future research will be required to determine how far this result can be generalized and to gauge its implications for auditor decision-making.

6.7 SUMMARY

The analysis of the auditors' evaluations and decisions revealed asymmetric use of analytical review, in that they only used analytical review to identify problems and increase other audit procedures. There was no evidence that analytical review was used to reduce other audit procedures, even though there were areas where such a reduction seemed plausible and the authoritative literature allows (even recommends) it. If this finding can be verified in future research, it will mean that analytical review is not achieving all of its possible benefits.

There were also significant differences between experienced and inexperienced auditors. Although auditors made few decision errors (except for the apparent asymmetric use of analytical review), the seniors increased confirmations of accounts receivable while the managers did not. This mistake on the part of inexperienced auditors was attributed to a more shallow understanding of the problem. The experienced auditors appeared to have richer memory schema that enabled them to make more cost-effective decisions.

When the protocols were examined for evidence of various types of judgmental biases, the problems identified and the subsequent requests for analytical review information revealed a potential for confirmation bias. However, the auditors' reasoning revealed little evidence of confirmation bias. In fact, in one instance, there is specific evidence of an auditor using information to disprove a previously hypothesized problem.

Finally, the auditors revealed no evidence of probabilistic reasoning. Their reasoning processes were more consistent with reasoning by assumption and reasoning by endorsements models which are proposed in the artificial intelligence literature.

Chapter 7

MULTI-DIMENSIONAL SCALING OF AUDITORS' ANALYTICAL REVIEW INFORMATION ASSESSMENT

7.1 INTRODUCTION

In Phase I of their task, the auditor subjects reviewed the Pacific Electronics case and prepared a suitable program of analytical review procedures. Program preparation included the generation of a list of requested information pertaining to the analytical review which would be provided by the researchers at a subsequent session. In Phase II, subjects were given the information they had requested, and were asked to evaluate the planned audit program.

Thus, by the beginning of Phase II, the subjects had three types of knowledge relating to the analytical review task:

(1) Prior knowledge of general audit principles, including the prototype, system and feature knowledge described in Chapter 3, acquired from previous auditing experience;
(2) Knowledge of the Pacific Electronics case based on preliminary analytical review; and
(3) Information supplied in response to each subject's request for additional information.

The cognitive representation of a problem is described more fully in Chapter 3. Briefly, for Pacific Electronics, the cognitive representation process includes the subject's conscious sensing of the issues and problems to be addressed through analytical review and the identification of characteristics which may lead to recommendations for audit program adjustments in Phase II of the audit task. The sensing of issues involves perception, based on information cues derived from the preliminary analysis of Pacific Electronics. Perception is an interactive process, in which information cues are compared to rules, concepts, experiences and other schema in the subject's memory. The results of this perceptual process is a representation of the Pacific Electronics case that is held in working (short-term) memory. Multi-dimensional scaling (MDS) measures perceptual constructs that have been conditioned on prior experiences or expectations, and can be applied to a problem or task such as Pacific Electronics. Multi-dimensional scaling was used to measure the underlying perceptual structure that each auditor utilized in performing the Pacific Electronics case. One result of the MDS study is a geometric representation of constructs derived from underlying psychological distance or perceptions, through the use of a variety of statistical and mathematical algorithms [see Reynolds, Schiffman and Young (1980); Carroll and Arabie (1980); Watkins (1984)].

This chapter describes the attempt to discover and measure the underlying cognitive representation of the Pacific Electronics case in each subject's memory at the beginning of Phase II of the task. The multi-dimensional scaling methodology was intended to complement the protocol analysis presented in the preceding chapters. MDS, when utilized with another method such as protocol analysis, can provide valuable insights into the way in which subjects organize and "frame" the particular decision task [Shepard (1974)].

7.2 THE MULTI-DIMENSIONAL SCALING TASK

As described above, the auditors began their task with a preliminary analytical review, based on financial statements and other materials in the case, then indicated what information they would require to recommend audit program changes in the third step. Since the adjustments could be conditioned in part by the additional information supplied, it was felt that this information should be an important factor in describing the auditors' cognitive representation of the problem. For this reason, the MDS study was used to identify similarities in the types of data requested by the subjects.

The information requested was summarized in Table 14. For convenience, the list is reproduced in modified form in Table 19. Each auditor was asked to rank the relative similarity of the information items supplied, by selecting one information item at random and then listing the remaining items in terms of similarity to the selected referent. Depending on the volume of information requested, auditors ranked from six to 15 information items.

TABLE 19

Information Items Requested in Phase II of the Pacific Electronics Case and Ranked for Multi-dimensional Scaling Analysis

Information Requested	Acronym for MDS Solution	Subject Selection of Information Items			
		M1	M2	S1	S2
Inventory Turnover Ratio	IT	–	X	X	X
Acid Test Ratio	ATR	X	X	–	X
Debt to Equity Ratio	DTE	–	X	–	–
Current Ratio	CR	X	X	X	–
Gross Profit Percentage	GP%	–	X	X	X
Operating Income to Sales	OI	–	X	–	–
Effective Tax Rate	ETR	–	X	–	–
Earnings from Continuing Operations as a Percentage of Sales	EFCO	–	X	–	–
Days Outstanding Accounts Receivable	DOAR	X	X	–	–
Accounts Payable Turnover	APT	X	X	–	–
Accounts Receivable Turnover	ART	–	X	–	X
Aging of Accounts Receivable	AAR	–	X	X	X
Collection Period	CP	–	–	–	X
Total Liabilities to Total Assets	TLTA	–	–	–	X
Dollar Days Sales	DS	X	–	X	–
Operating Expense Analysis	OEA	X	–	–	–
Quarterly Gross Profit Percent	QGP%	–	–	X	X
Industry Ratios	IR	–	–	–	X
Dollar and Percent Changes					
Income Statement Items:					
Sales	SL	–	–	X	–
Cost of Goods Sold	CS	–	–	X	–
Gross Profit	GP	–	–	X	–
Operating Expense	OE	–	–	X	–
Interest	IT	–	–	X	–
Operating Income	OI	–	–	X	–
Other Income	OTI	–	–	X	–
Earnings Before Taxes	EBT	–	–	X	–
Earnings from Continuing Operations	ECO	–	–	X	–
Loss from Discontinued Operations	LDO	–	–	X	–
Net Income	NI	–	–	X	–

7.3 MODEL SELECTION CRITERIA

Selection of an appropriate MDS model for the data depended on the empirical content of the data, the nature of the underlying error process, and the collection method. Empirical content refers to the kind of conceptual relationship portrayed. Since most MDS studies presuppose the use of similarity judgments or comparisons, and Tversky and Gati (1978) argue that similarity judgments are fundamental to human judgment and decision processes, a similarity model was deemed appropriate for this study. It was decided that a "representation model" of the data should be identified, to reflect the auditors' underlying model of similarity.

Observed data gathered in studies such as this can be highly sensitive to measurement error. Since the treatment of errors can have important effects on the MDS solution, reasonable assumptions must be made about the error process, and about the point at which randomness enters the data generation process.

There are different methods of gathering and analyzing similarity data ranging from paired comparisons to correlations. Takane (1981a, p.11) states that different types of judgments require different mental operations on the part of subjects. The scaling procedure should reflect reasonable assumptions about the psychological processes involved in a specific task situation which generates a specific type of data. These underlying mental processes of similarity can be represented in a response model.

To satisfy the model selection criteria, a specialized MDS algorithm, MAXSCAL4.1 [Takane and Carroll (1981b)], was used to analyze the auditors' similarity data. This algorithm is based on maximum likelihood estimation procedures, and the response model is especially suited for conditional and general rank order data. The assumption of a euclidian model can be generalized to other types of models, including those not based on distance concepts, such as Tversky's (1977) feature model and others.

The error model in MAXSCAL4.1 can be either additive or multiplicative. The additive model assumes that measurement error is normally distributed over replications of judgments, with constant variance within each subject. The multiplicative model, on the other hand, assumes that the log transform of the error follows the normal distribution with a constant variance. Rather than requiring an *a priori* choice of the most appropriate error model, MAXSCAL4.1 incorporates both models in the estimation procedure, so that the same set of data can be analyzed under both assumptions. The fit can then be compared, to determine which model best reflects a given situation.

MAXSCAL4.1 provides statistical guidance in terms of the appropriate number of dimensions (constructs) to represent the geometric solution, the best fitting model for the data, variance-covariance estimates of estimate model parameters (these estimates are useful for developing asymptotic confidence regions surrounding the estimated points in the MDS representation), standard errors of the estimated stimulus coordinates, and other measures.

7.4 RESULTS

Figures 7 through 10 show the derived stimulus configuration for each of the subjects. The stimulus configuration is a spatial representation of the data items requested by each subject, based on the most appropriate number of constructs or dimensions underlying the similarity data. Since this spatial representation is mathematically derived by the model from the data, it sometimes provides clusters or groupings in which some items may not coincide with the researcher's personal views. Each figure in this chapter contains a horizontal line (the X axis) and a vertical line (the Y axis), which intersect at the origin (zero point) of the figure. These two lines represent the two dimensions that can easily be plotted in a plane. A label at the top of each figure indicates which two dimensions are shown in the body of the figure. The figures may be interpreted by looking at the points and possible clusters of points on each side of the horizontal or vertical line, and attempting to give some meaning to the collection of points along a dimension. Appendix D contains summary information, including the coordinates of the stimulus configurations for each subject, and data showing various model statistics and standard errors for each of the stimulus coordinates.

Figure 7 shows the configuration for Subject M1. M1 was supplied with six information items on which he performed his similarity rankings. Largely due to the sparsity of items to rank, M1's optimal scaling solution provides only one dimension, with the information items distributed along the horizontal axis. The vertical axis separates the two extremes of the dimension. The resulting figure shows a separation of the current ratio (CR), days sales (DS) and operating expense analysis (OEA) from the acid test ratio (ATR), days outstanding accounts receivable (DOAR), and accounts payable turnover (APT); and ultimately, of sales and operating items (OEA, DS, CR) from liquidity (ATR, DOAR, APT) items. M1 is an experienced auditor, and this unidimensional representation is consistent with the notion of expertise expressed by Roshi (1986): "In the beginner's mind there are many possibilities. In the expert's, there are few."

M1's underlying bi-polar construct is consistent with the problems identified in Table 13. M1's cognitive representation of the Pacific Electronic's problem is based on his prior experience as an auditor, his preliminary analytical review and the specific data items requested and subjected to MDS. Thus, he cognitively represents the many aspects of the problem in a single continuum of liquidity versus sales and operating items which, of course, is consistent with the real underlying problems of Pacific Electronics.

S1's three-dimensional configuration is shown in Figure 8. Dimension one separates loss from discontinuing operations (LDO), net income (NI), operating expense (OE), interest (INT), earnings from continuing operations (ECO), and earnings before taxes (EBT) from gross profit (GP), cost of sales (CS), quarterly gross profit percentage (QGP%), sales (SL), operating income (OI), other income (OTI), inventory turnover (IT), current ratio (CR), and aging of accounts receivable (AAR). This dimension appears to separate items related to net earnings (LDO, NI, ECO, OE, EBT, INT) from gross earnings and cash flow (GP, QGP%, IT, CS, OI, OTI, SL, CR, AAR). Since operating income and other income fall right at the mid-point of the dimension, they are not particularly useful in interpreting the dimension.

Dimension two separates loss of discontinued operations (LDO), net income (NI), gross profit (GP), earnings from continuing operations (ECO), quarterly gross profit percentage (QGP%), cost of sales (CS), sales (SL), and inventory turnover (IT) from operating expense (OE), operating income (OI), interest (INT), current ratio (CR), aging accounts receivable (AAR), earnings before taxes (EBT), and other income (OTI). This dimension appears to separate normal operating determinants of income from financing and other determinants of income. Dimension three is plotted against dimensions one and two, and separates loss from discontinued operations (LDO), operating expense (OE), earnings before taxes (EBT), and operating income (OI) from the remaining information items on the bottom part of the dimension. This dimension appears to focus primarily on aspects of operating income.

FIGURE 7
Relative Plot of Derived Stimulus Configuration
M1's Information Structure

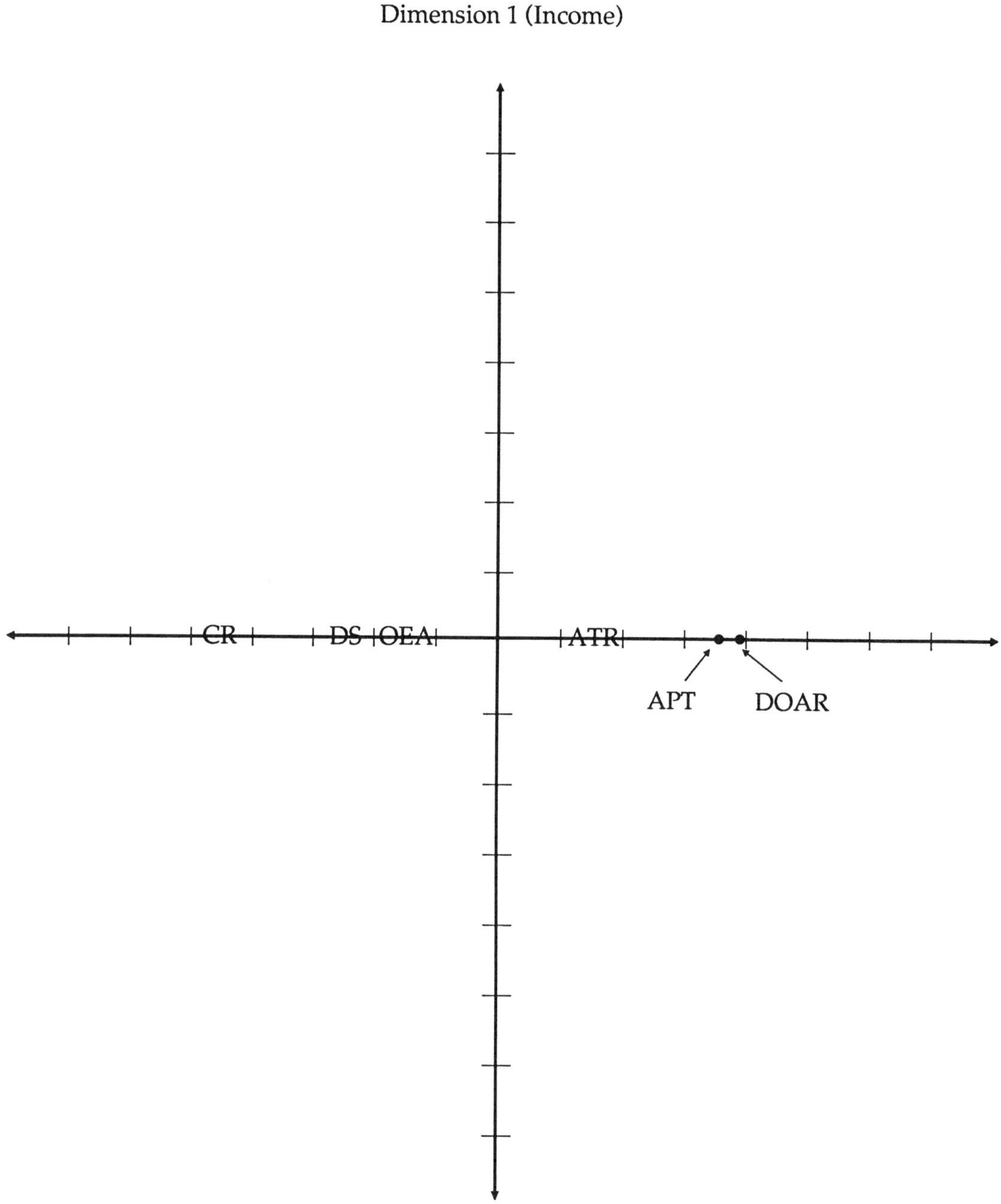

FIGURE 8
Relative Plot of Derived Stimulus Configuration
S1's Information Structure

Dimension 1 (Income-Financing) vs Dimension 2 (Operating)

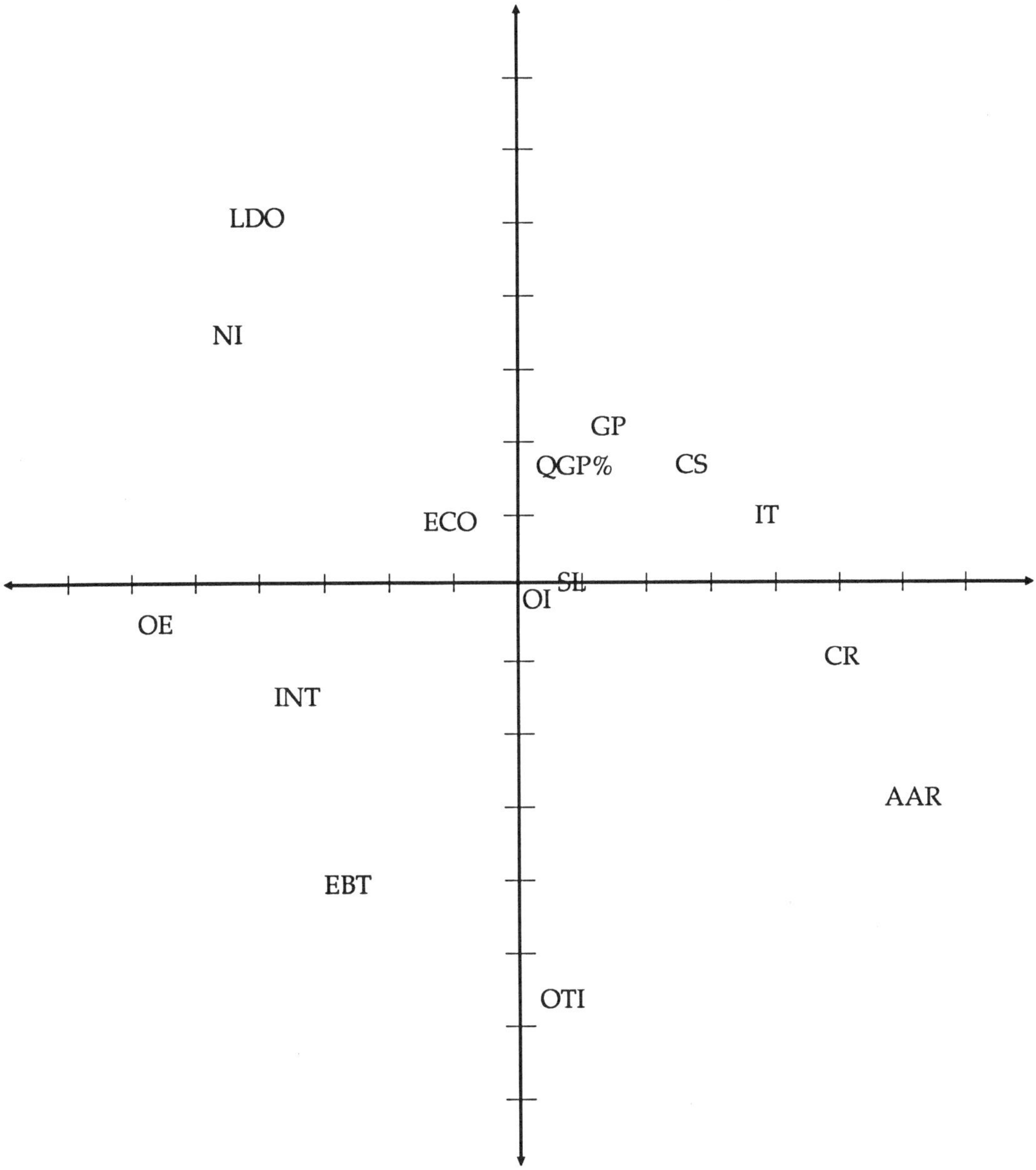

FIGURE 8 (Continued)
Relative Plot of Derived Stimulus Configuration
S1's Information Structure
Dimension 1 (Income-Financing) vs Dimension 3 (Net Earnings-Gross Earnings)

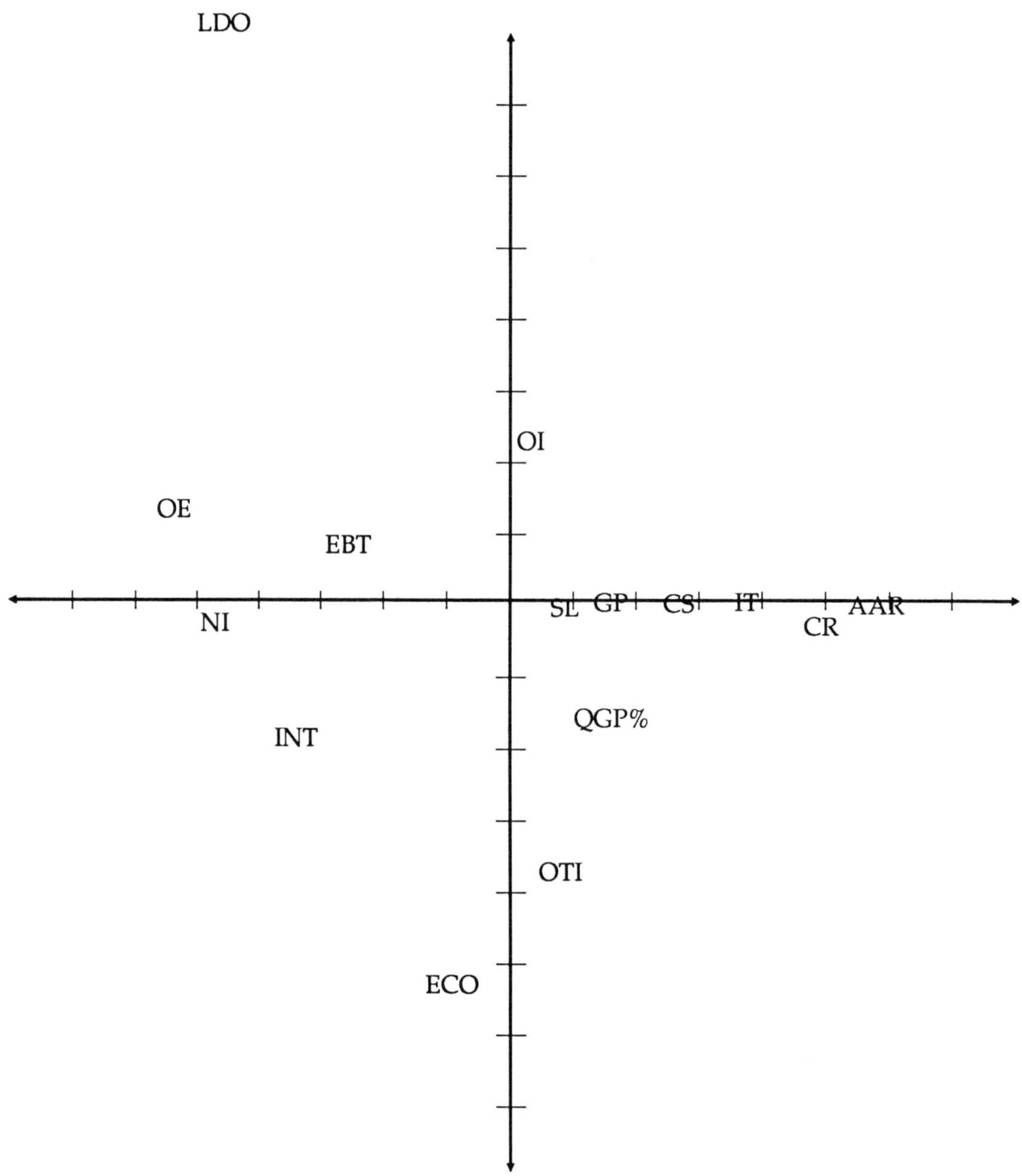

FIGURE 8 (Continued)
Relative Plot of Derived Stimulus Configuration
S1's Information Structure
Dimension 2 (Operating) vs Dimension 3 (Net Earnings-Gross Earnings)

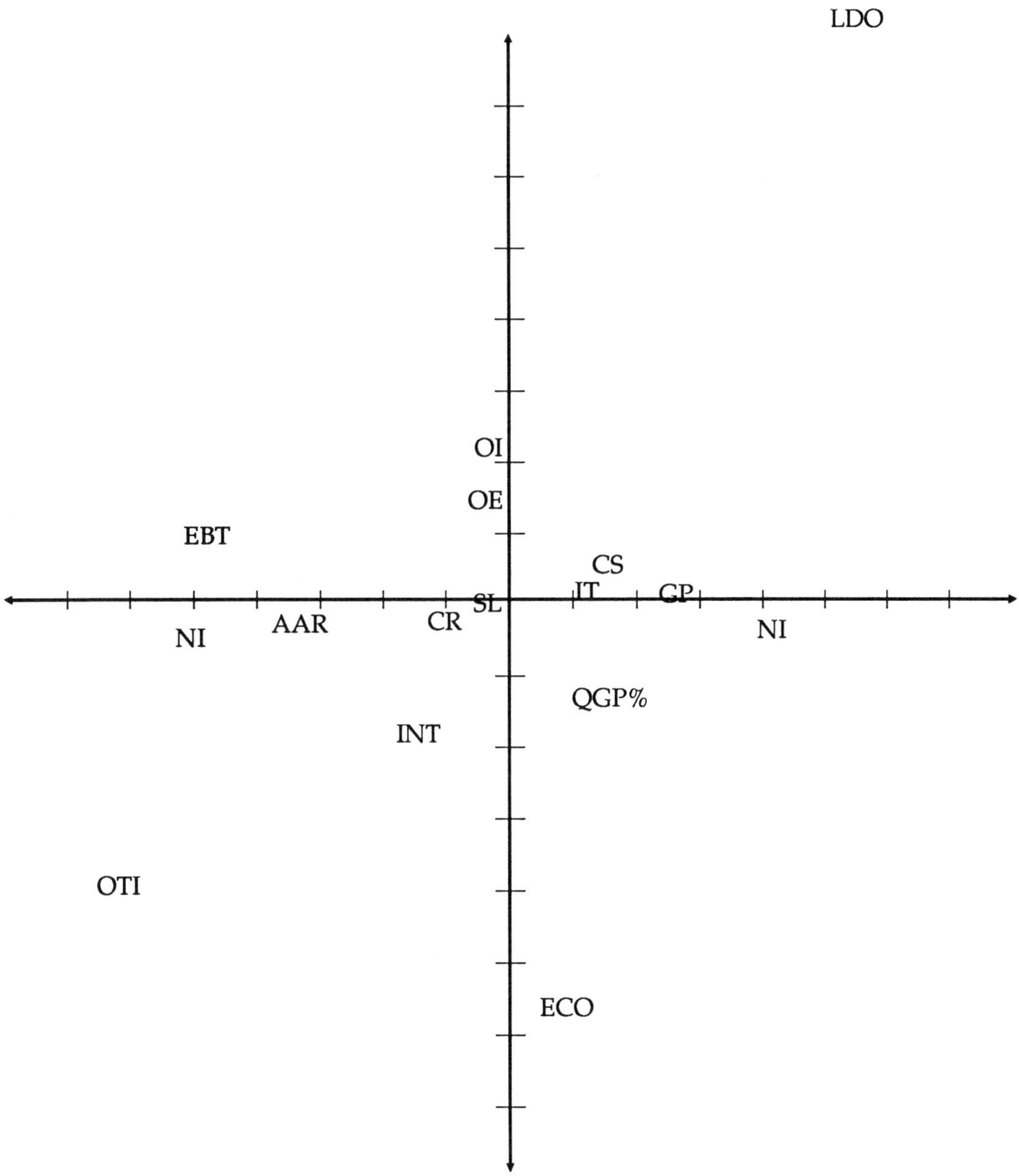

In Table 13, S1 did not identify as many problems and opportunities as the other three auditors. This may be attributed to his relative inexperience as an auditor, and is consistent with the above MDS solution. The MDS results show that S1's representation of the data was somewhat independent of any prior experience or domain knowledge, and of the preliminary analytical review (Phase I). His three dimensions reflect the almost textbook analysis one would apply to a set of financial statements in a context-free environment. S1 would appear to be unsure and unfocused as to real problems in the sample case.

M2's scaling solution (Figure 9) results in a two-dimensional representation. Dimension one separates effective tax rate (ETR), earnings from continuing operations as a percent of sales (EFCO), and gross profit percentage (GP%) from debt-to-equity ratio (DTE), current ratio (CR), acid test ratio (ATR), days outstanding-accounts receivable (DOAR) and aging of accounts receivable (AAR). This dimension appears to separate income items from balance sheet items, or income from cash flow.

Dimension two separates debt-to-equity (DTE), current ratio (CR), acid test ratio (ATR), inventory turnover (IT), and effective tax rate (ETR) from gross profit percentage (GP%), accounts payable turnover (APT), aging of accounts receivable (AAR) days outstanding accounts receivable (DOAR), earnings from continuing operations as a percentage of sales (EFCO), and accounts receivable turnover (ART). This appears to be a liquidity-collectability dimension.

M2, like M1, appears to have a focused representation of the problem in mind, based on prior experience (domain knowledge), the preliminary analytical review and current data. M2 and M1 had identified similar kinds of problems in Table 13. But rather than focusing directly and exclusively on liquidity and collectability, M2 also compares the balance sheet to the income statement, a concern that relates to PE's inventory turnover and accounts receivable problems. M2 appears to have a rich and focused understanding of the case, which enables him to efficiently and effectively make appropriate audit program adjustments.

S2's derived stimulus configuration is shown in three dimensions in Figure 10. Dimension one separates gross profit percentage (GP%), quarterly gross profit percentage (QGP%), accounts receivable turnover (ART), collection period (CP), and aging accounts receivable (AAR) from industry ratios (IR), inventory turnover (IT), acid test ratio (ATR), and total liabilities to total assets (TLTA). This dimension appears to track sales-income versus liquidity.

Dimension two separates industry ratio (IR), inventory turnover (IT), gross profit percentage (GP%), and quarterly gross profit percentage (QGP%) from accounts receivable turnover (ART), acid test ratio (ATR), collection period (CP), total liabilities to total assets (TLTA), and aging of accounts receivable (AAR). This dimension emphasizes sales versus collections and liquidity. Dimension three separates industry ratio (IR), collection period (CP), accounts receivable turnover (ART), and aging of accounts receivable (AAR) from gross profit percentage (GP%), quarterly gross profit percentage (QGP%), inventory turnover (IT), acid test ratio (ATR), and total liabilities to total assets (TLTA). This dimension seems to show collection items separated from all others.

S2's cognitive representation of the problem is somewhat closer to that of the more experienced auditors, since two of his underlying dimensions emphasize collectability and the other emphasizes liquidity. This is consistent with his problem identification in Table 13, where he identified more areas than S1 but fewer than the two more experienced auditors. While S2's need to adequately represent the problem in three dimensions is indicative of his relative inexperience, his analysis focuses much more on PE's real, underlying problems than S1's.

FIGURE 9
Realtive Plot of Derived Stimulus Configuration
M2's Information Structure
Dimension 1 (Income-Cash Flow) vs Dimension 2 (Liquidity)

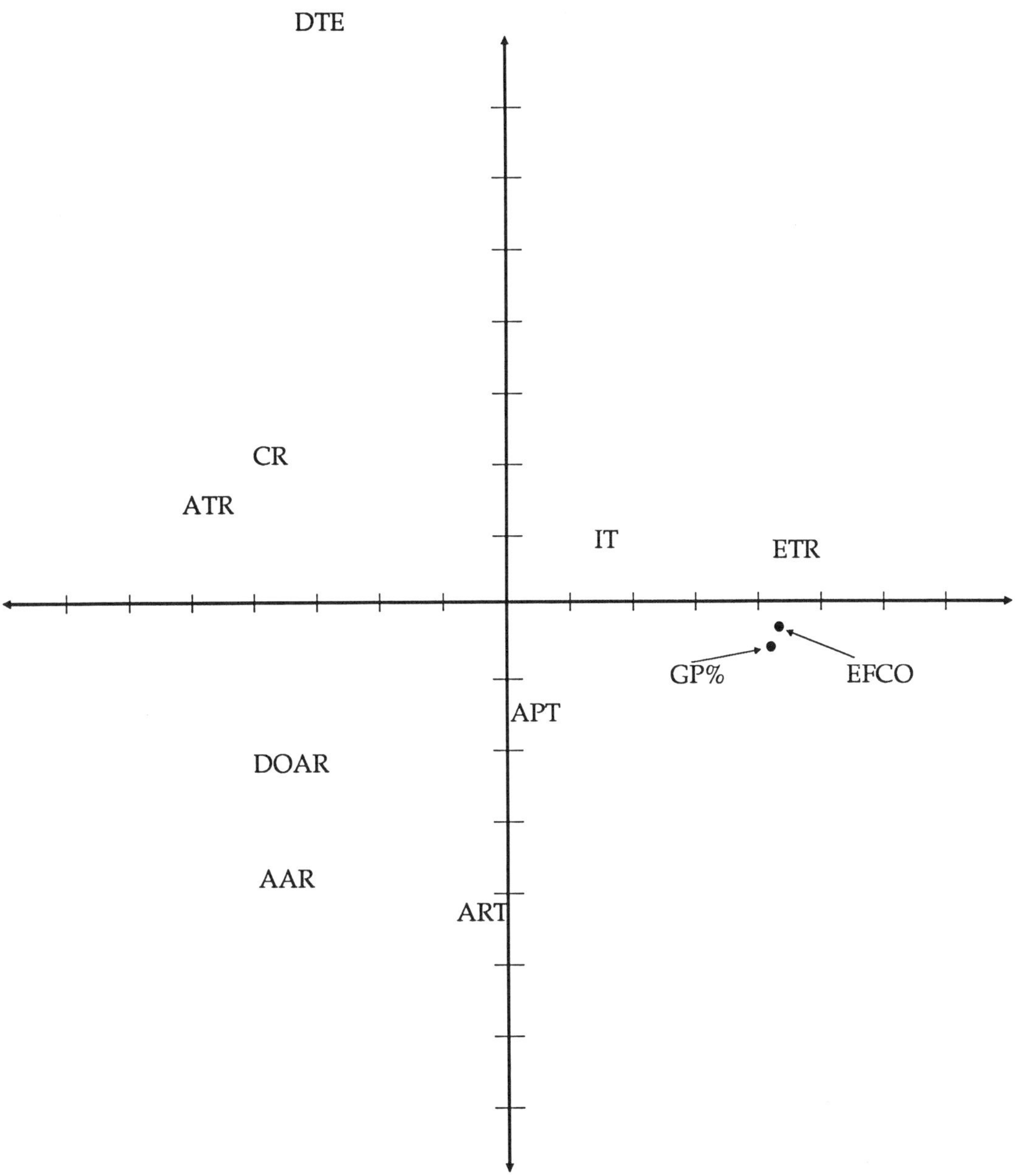

FIGURE 10
Reltive Plot of Derived Stimulus Configuration
S2's Information Structure
Dimension 1 (Liquidity-Income) vs Dimension 2 (Collections)

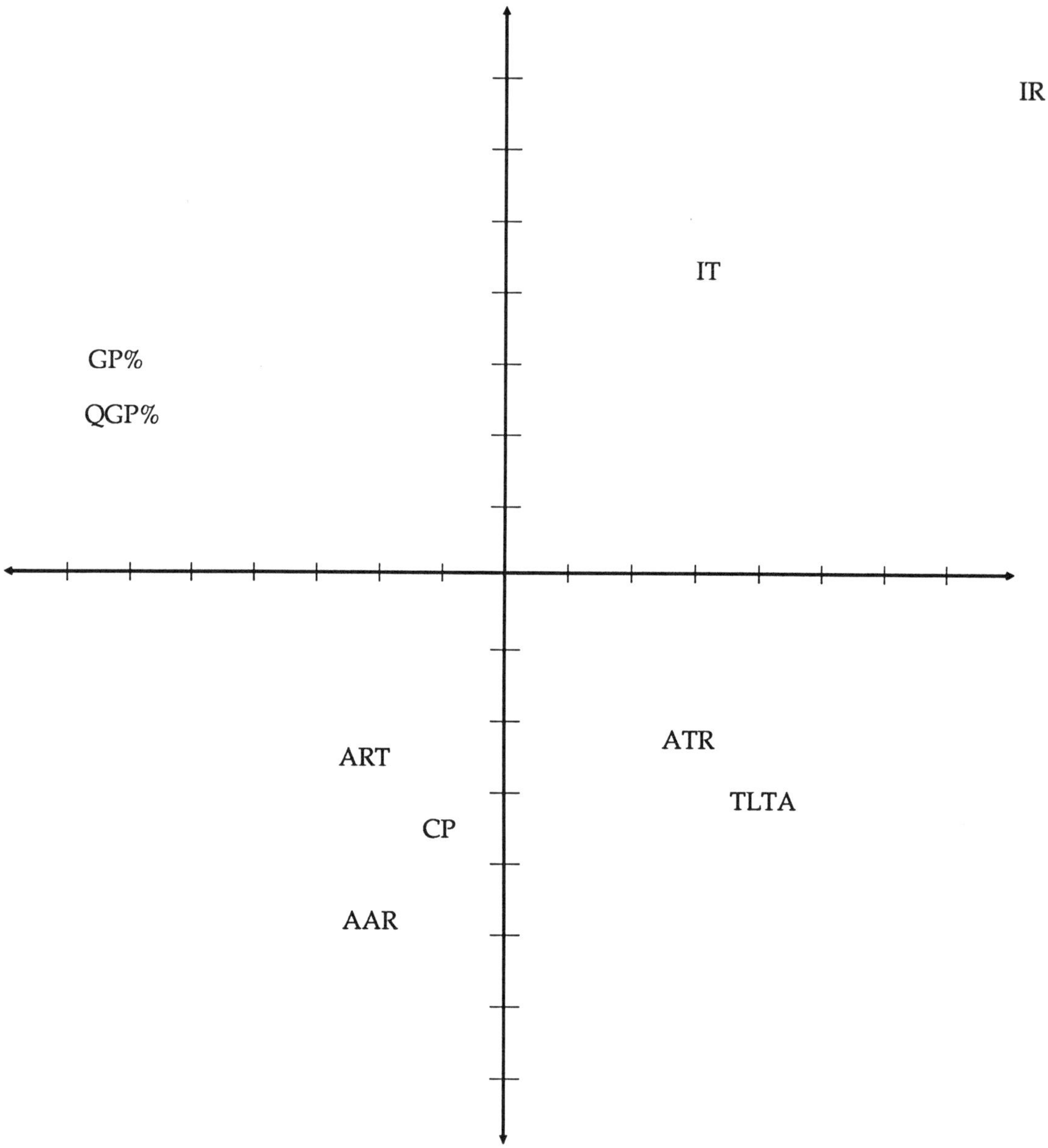

FIGURE 10 (Continued)
Relative Plot of Derived Stimulus Configuration
S2's Information Structure
Dimension 1 (Liquidity-Income) vs Dimension 3 (Sales-Collections)

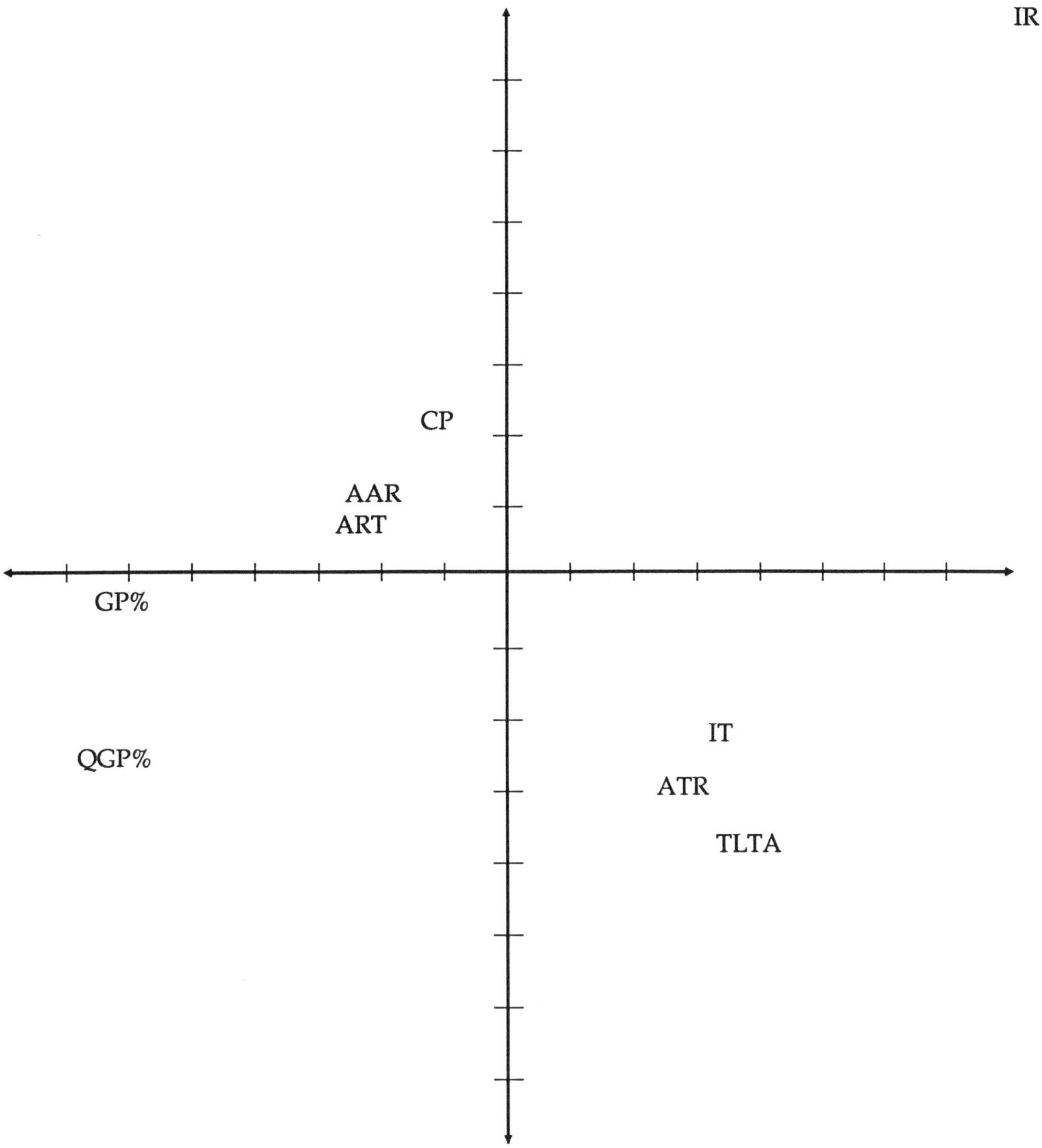

FIGURE 10 (Continued)
Relative Plot of Derived Stimulus Configuration
S2's Information Structure
Dimension 2 (Collections) vs Dimension 3 (Sales-Collections)

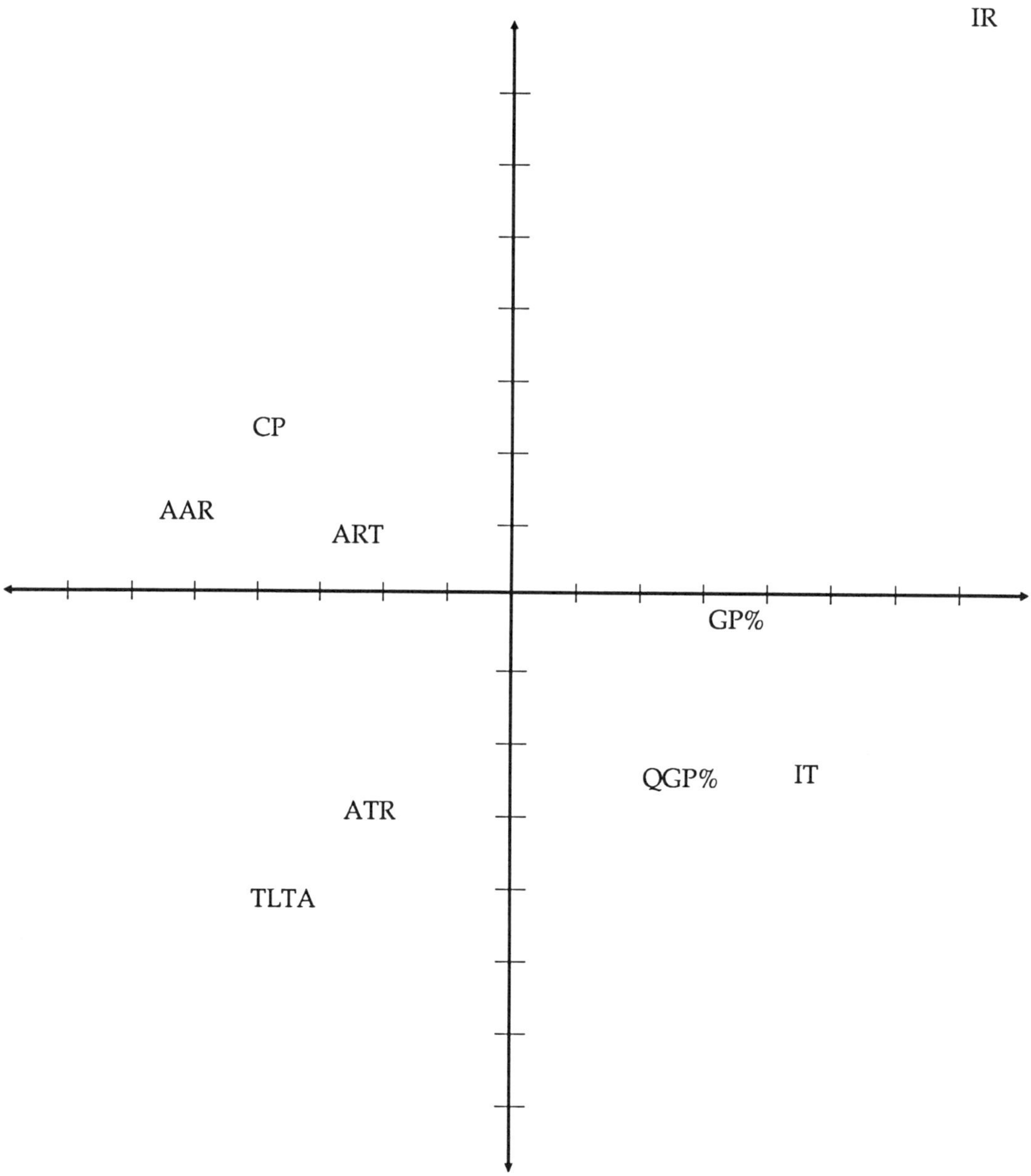

7.5 SUMMARY AND CONCLUSIONS

Overall, all the auditors' dimensions are consistent with the protocol study in Chapter 5 and 6. Table 20 summarizes the dimensions and tentative interpretations. The experienced auditors, M1 and M2, appear to have a clearer perception of the task, and thus require a more limited set of relevant information represented in one and two dimensions. Their focus on the liquidity-earnings aspects of the case suggests that their schema, based on prior experience and information related to the task, provide efficient analysis of the Pacific Electronics case.

TABLE 20
Summary of Dimensional Interpretations from Multi-dimensional Scaling Analysis

	M1	M2	S1	S2
Dimension				
1	Income	Income vs Cash Flow	Income vs Financing	Liquidity vs Income
2	N/A	Liquidity	Operating	Collections
3	N/A	N/A	Net Earnings vs Gross Earnings	Sales vs Collections

On the other hand, the inexperienced auditors have a more complex representation of the information environment. Both required three-dimensional representations, and their distinctions in the underlying structure of the information set are less clear. Table 20 shows a more fuzzy, less definite cognitive structure, which is more complex and detailed and less efficient in representing the problem. This is consistent with studies in other fields, such as cognitive science, which have shown that the complexity of knowledge representation and search paths is greater with novices than with expert judges [see Reiser (1986); Kolodner and Simpson (1986); Abelson and Black, (1986)].

In Table 20, the sequencing of dimensions is unimportant: what matters is that the concept underlying a given dimension is the same across several subjects. For example, dimension one for S1 and dimension two for M2 are both liquidity. The main point is that both subjects have a liquidity dimension; the dimension number is of no consequence.

The use of MDS in this study is limited by the size of the data set from which the similarity judgments were drawn, and the lack of complementary criteria or adjective descriptors to support the interpretation of the MDS results. The scaling was also based on a different set of data for each subject. While this is not a problem for the scaling algorithm, it does raise the question of whether subjects perceived the data sets in the same manner. However, since the subjects were all knowledgeable in general accounting principles and had experience as auditors, it seems likely that net income, current ratio, and the other information items were perceived in the same manner.

Chapter 8

ANALYSIS OF STATISTICAL AND JUDGMENTAL ANALYTICAL REVIEW FROM AN ACTUAL AUDIT

The concurrent verbal protocol study described in Chapters 5 and 6 utilized real auditors, and a case adapted from a real electronics firm. Some constraints were placed on the subjects, in that they were working with a case, with no prior experience with the client and limited financial or other information. To gain additional realism and evaluate other analytical review approaches, such as those involving statistical methods, it was decided to evaluate real auditors performing analytical review on a real client.

8.1 TASK

For this protocol study, three divisions of the firm were considered: drug manufacturing, medical/surgical supplies, and a new, unnamed division which had been purchased at the end of the prior fiscal year. The drug and medical/surgical divisions had been audited by the same firm in prior years, while the new division had no audit history with the current firm. The senior auditor had several years' audit experience with this client, and thus was very familiar with its past history. The junior auditor had no prior experience with the audit client. The auditors used the normal analytical review procedures employed by their firm, including a statistical and judgmental analytical review. Both ARP approaches were utilized with the objective of reducing substantive testing. As a matter of policy, these analytical review procedures were applied only to income statement accounts; the accounting firm used other approaches for balance sheet accounts. Since the audit client was large, and three divisions were under audit, the scope of the protocol analysis was limited to three selected income statement accounts: net sales, cost of sales, and expenses.

8.2 RETROSPECTIVE PROTOCOL METHOD

The protocols for this audit differed from those used in the Pacific Electronics case, in that the auditors provided *retrospective* verbal protocols rather than *concurrent protocols*. Retrospective protocols are obtained *post hoc*, that is, after the analysis has been performed rather than during the analysis. The auditors were asked to come to the researchers' office and to describe the process they went through in performing their analytical review. All audit workpapers pertaining to analytical review were available during the protocol session. The descriptions were tape recorded and transcribed, in a manner similar to the concurrent protocols in Chapters 5 and 6.

The auditors used the analytical review procedures normally employed by their accounting firm. They also agreed to perform judgmental analytical review, even though this was not a normal part of the audit for the particular client, to provide a basis for comparison to the statistical method.

The retrospective protocols contain rationales for search, reasoning and decisions, rather than a direct trace of the process as obtained with the concurrent protocols. Thus, the normal coding procedures, the generation of episode abstracts, the trace of search procedures and the other procedures used in the concurrent analysis were not utilized here. Rather, the rationale developed by the auditors was abstracted, summarized and organized in narrative fashion. The retrospective protocols do show the general approach to the task of analytical review, and provide insights into judgmental differences between the experienced and inexperienced auditors.

The remainder of this chapter summarizes the retrospective protocol analysis. First, the two auditors' statistical ARP results are summarized, and assessed for similarities and differences. Then, the judgmental ARP results are summarized and compared in a similar manner. The chapter concludes with a general summary and synthesis of the retrospective analysis.

Three of the research questions identified in Chapter 6 are appropriate for the retrospective study:

6-A What was the nature of the auditors' evaluations and decisions during the analytical review phase of the task?

6-B What decisions did auditors make while adjusting the planned audit program, and on what basis?

6-C What decision errors were made, if any, and what were their apparent causes?

8.3 STATISTICAL ANALYTICAL REVIEW

Both auditors performed a statistical analytical review on the real audit client. This is a matter of audit firm policy for many clients when there are at least 24 data points from which to develop and run a time series regression model.

Less experienced auditor

The less experienced auditor, hereinafter referred to as RJ, took a very pragmatic and somewhat naive approach to the statistical analytical review. He noted that statistical review had previously been performed on net sales, cost of sales, and total expenses, and concluded that these were reasonable accounts to test again this year. He also decided to break total expenses into compensation expenses and other, to check for "some correlation between the number of employees and the total compensation expense for the company". No rationale is provided for this breakout, other than an apparent interest in seeing whether any relationship would be present.

After deciding which accounts to look at, the first step in RJ's statistical ARP was to calculate the respective account balances. This is apparently a matter of firm policy, since he was able to articulate set formulae for accomplishing the task. RJ apparently relied exclusively on firm procedures, as there was no evidence of any other reasoning. The next step was to look for a base of at least 24 periods, with which to run the statistical model with the hope of identifying trends or any other "logical" relationships in the data. Again, the 24 base period is based on firm policy, and not auditor judgment.

The next step, also apparently a matter of firm policy, was to develop a materiality factor. RJ looked at the company's net income and shareholders' equity and arrived at a value of $1.8 million. Based on prior audit work, he assigned an internal control reliance factor of 1, indicating good internal control. To establish the reasonableness of the net sales account, it was decided to look at possible understatement of the account. This too is a matter of firm policy in most cases, since the tendency of the statistical tests is toward understatement on revenue items and overstatement on many expense items. Thus, the decisions reached were to test net sales for understatement, and cost of sales and compensation expense for overstatement.

Since the data had already been gathered and submitted for computer processing, RJ proceeded to analyze the results.

The first two steps were to look at the correlation between net sales (dependent variable) and cost of sales (independent variable), and identify any time series trend in the data for the base periods. As RJ examined the computer data, he noted a very high correlation of .9993 between net sales and cost of sales, suggesting a strong underlying relationship between sales and cost of sales. Next, RJ evaluated the residuals for any material deviations from the specified threshold. He noted that none of the residuals appeared excessive, and thus suggested that detailed testing for net sales be reduced. But then, he regressed cost of sales on net sales, just the reverse of the prior procedure. He concluded that the account appeared to be in order, since the correlation of .9993 between cost of sales and net sales was also high, and no significant deviations (residuals) were noted. RJ exhibited a surprising naiveté toward statistics in general, since the regression of two variables, with one serving as dependent and the other as independent, will by definition yield the same pattern of residuals and correlation coefficient as if the variables are reversed! Based on this analysis, RJ concluded that detailed testing of inventory relative to cost of goods sold could be reduced.

The next step in the analysis was to evaluate the total expenses account, by regressing total expenses on net sales. Based on a correlation coefficient of .9138 and no difficulties with residuals, RJ concluded that detailed testing of total expense could be reduced.

The analysis of compensation expense proceeded in a similar manner, with a regression of total compensation expense on total employee count. The results were acceptable, but since this was the first year for which the analysis was run, RJ repeated the process without a trend factor and found the correlation coefficient to be zero. Based on this analysis, RJ concluded that extensive, detailed testing would have to be undertaken on this account.

As a result of his analysis, RJ concluded that the budget for detailed testing of the accounts examined in this study should be 24 hours. Overall, he followed a very structured approach to the statistical audit, relied almost exclusively on firm guidelines and exhibited very little reasoning or judgment. When he did use his own judgment, as in the case of reversing the regression of sales and cost of sales, he erred in the selection of the analysis. While the error was unimportant in this case, it suggests that RJ was indeed a novice and inexperienced in the use of regression analysis. Given his error in variable selection, one might also question his understanding of fundamental statistical concepts, and his ability to apply other statistical methods such as sampling.

In contrast to the auditors evaluating Pacific Electronics, RJ used the ARP to recommend reductions in tests of detail for two of the three accounts. This difference is important, since failure to reduce tests of detail based on analytical review is contrary to the expectations described in the professional and academic literature discussed in Chapter 2.

Experienced auditor

The experienced auditor, hereinafter referred to as RS, gave a more comprehensive description of the statistical analysis than RJ. He analyzed the same basic accounts of cost of sales, total expenses and net sales, but omitted compensation expense. One notable difference between RS's and RJ's analysis was that RS also looked at corollary tests to help validate his tests on each account. For example, cost of sales and total expenses were tested for understatement, in accordance with testing of inventory for overstatement. Net sales were tested for overstatement, by testing accounts receivable for overstatement. Thus, RS used a richer approach than RJ, which may simply reflect a greater experience with statistical analysis. In general, RS's results were the same as for RJ, with one exception: RS's regression of net sales on total expenses revealed a potential problem, which upon investigation with the manager of corporate accounting turned out to be an error in a journal adjustment. This error was noted and corrected. In light of the findings of the other tests, and given no indication of problems, RS concluded that no extensive testing of total expenses would be necessary. RS budgeted 16 hours for the statistical analysis, whereas RJ budgeted 24 hours.

8.4 SUMMARY AND CONCLUSIONS REGARDING STATISTICAL ANALYTICAL REVIEW

Table 21 summarizes the results of the statistical analytical review, and compares the findings of the experienced and inexperienced auditors, within each of the research questions.

While the conclusions reached by RJ and RS were the same, the experience factor is clearly evident in the richness of the analysis (corollary tests for RS and no corollary tests for RJ) and in the identification of potential error by RS. Here, in contrast to the concurrent protocols presented in Chapters 5 and 6, the intent of both auditors was to use the statistical analytical review to identify areas for more in-depth substantive testing, and to have comfort with those areas where substantive testing could be reduced (there was practically no evidence of the auditors reducing audit work in the Pacific Electronics case). Since this was in accordance with established accounting firm policy, the two auditors were simply utilizing the statistical techniques in accordance with the guidelines specified by their training.

TABLE 21

Comparison of Statistical Analytical Review Performance

Research Question 6 -A

What was the nature of the auditors' evaluations and decisions during the analytical review phase of the task?

	Experienced Auditor		**Less Experienced Auditor**
(1)	Relatively comprehensive analysis.	(1)	Relatively limited analysis.
(2)	Used corollary tests to cross-validate results.	(2)	Did not use corollary tests for validation.
(3)	Evidence of judgment in support of audit firm policies for ARP.	(3)	Relied almost exclusively on firm policies. Little evidence of judgment or reasoning.
(4)	Directed, well-focused process through the case analysis.	(4)	Something of a "fishing trip", especially on expense account.

TABLE 21 (Continued)
Comparison of Statistical Analytical Review Performance

Research Question 6 -B

What decisions did auditors make while adjusting the planned audit program, and on what basis?

	Experienced Auditor		Less Experienced Auditor
(1)	Detected error in an account using the regression model.	(1)	Did not detect an error in any account.
(2)	Followed up with client, and accepted client's explanation of an error in adjusting a journal entry.	(2)	Not applicable.
(3)	Did not subdivide the three accounts selected for analysis.	(3)	Broke one account into subsections for further analysis.
(4)	Did not recommend detailed testing, but reduced tests of details.	(4)	Recommended detailed testing on the compensation expense account. Reduced tests of detail on other accounts.

Research Question 6 -C

What decision errors were made, if any, and what were their apparent causes?

	Experienced Auditor		Less Experienced Auditor
(1)	None noted, unless accepting client's explanation without further investigation was inappropriate.	(1)	No major errors.
(2)	Experienced with statistical methods.	(2)	Naiveté with respect to statistical methods.

8.5 JUDGMENTAL ANALYTICAL REVIEW

Judgmental analytical review for the real audit client consisted of traditional ratio, trend, and other scanning techniques. There was no reliance on statistical models, except as a means of corroborating the judgmental analysis in selected situations.

Less experienced auditor

RJ began by contrasting statistical and judgmental ARP, stating that with the judgmental approach, "the basic premise that we have is (that) we want to be able to try and estimate what we think certain amounts are going to be." He went on to articulate firm policy on materiality standards, which focused fluctuations in excess of 20 percent of a materiality limit. For this audit, based on income and equity accounts, the materiality limit is $1.8 million.

RJ selected net sales, cost of sales and total expenses for review, and broke sales into two components: drug company and medical/surgical. For both accounts, he took net sales figures from the general ledger accounts, talked to people in each division to obtain estimates of percentage sales increases for the audit year, and then came up with an estimate of sales for comparison to actual sales. For the drug company, RJ obtained a wide range of estimates from the various division managers, which did not agree with the actual book values. Since the fluctuations were outside the materiality limit ($360,000), they were deemed to require further investigation, which RJ conducted by talking to key personnel to obtain a reasonable explanation for the differences.

Given the answers, RJ stated that normal audit procedure would call for more detailed substantiation, such as evaluation of invoices for reasonableness. (This was not done, since the statistical approach had already been used and RJ was satisfied that this was sufficient. Recall that the judgmental ARP was being performed at the request of the authors, and was not standard procedure for this client.) The medical/surgical division had similar fluctuations, and RJ applied the same reasoning as he did for the drug company.

The next item RJ analyzed was cost of sales. He calculated a cost-of-sales percentage on an historical basis, then applied it to monthly net sales data for the current fiscal year to arrive at an estimated cost of sales. This value was compared to the actual amount in the corporate general ledger and differences were identified for explanation. Since all differences were negative in this case, meaning that the estimate was always lower than the actual figure, RJ concluded that gross margin was shrinking and the cost of sales was increasing. To verify this reasoning, RJ talked with the manager of corporate accounting, who concurred with the analysis. RJ stated that he would normally go and select inventory relief items to see if the cost of sales figure was accurate, but did not do so here because of the corroborating statistical analysis.

For total expenses, RJ calculated the total as a percentage of net sales and other revenues. He applied this percentage to monthly net sales for the current fiscal year to come up with an estimate, and compared the estimate to actual values. In this case, the estimates were higher than the actual values, indicating a positive variance which required investigation. RJ discussed the variances with the manager of corporate accounting and conducted a more detailed evaluation by judgmentally selecting five expense items for each of the months that required explanation. He determined that net sales were increasing faster than fixed costs, for two reasons. The reasons are not of special interest here, but the process shows that RJ did a more detailed analysis to explain the variance, rather than simply asking one of the client's staff. Based on his analysis, RJ assigned 40 hours for the detailed testing to complete the audit objective. His rationale is based on the time required for follow-up with client personnel, to obtain satisfactory explanations for variances between the estimated and actual account balances.

Experienced auditor

RS began the judgmental ARP by providing some background and justification for the use of a judgmental approach. The objectives were to determine base data, calculate monthly balances, compare actual and calculated balances, explain differences exceeding 20 percent of a $1.8 million materiality factor, and identify judgmental results that will affect the detailed testing.

For this client, RS attempted to calculate a base that was meaningful. Audit firm policy specified that the base should be independent and, if possible, relevant. Thus, RS looked at various accounts to determine whether a base could be found that would satisfy these requirements. For net sales, since the company had a trend of increasing sales dollars, RS determined that prior years' figures could be used for the base if they were adjusted for inflation and estimated real growth. RS determined that the company had experienced normal growth of 20 to 30 percent in recent years, including 10 percent in price increases, which was considered to be lower than the rate of inflation. The balance of the increase was the result of volume increases. Based on this analysis, RS decided to use prior years' figures as the base. (Although RS did not perform this step, he argued that he should substantiate the volume increase by evaluating inventory records on the flow of input by quantity, and compare sales prices and sales invoices for the base and audit years to verify the price increase.)

RS then conducted a similar analysis on a second division of the client company. This analysis was kept separate because the division had different customers and products, the procedures described for the first division were followed. For the newly-acquired division, there existed no historical information to establish trends that might be useful for determining a base. Thus, the normal maximum detailed testing would be undertaken, and no reduction in tests of detail would be recommended for this division. RS then proceeded to analyze the remaining accounts.

For the cost of sales account, RS used the prior year's average gross profit margin to estimate the current year's cost of sales. Given a slightly decreasing gross profit margin trend, he was confident using the prior year's data as the base. RS initially tried to break out selling, general, and administrative expenses, but found that he could not do so because the data had been summarized and aggregated, excluding compensation expense. Even though it was technically possible to obtain the detail underlying the aggregate amount, RS deemed that the benefit did not justify the cost. Therefore, he used the historical ratio of selling, general, and administrative to sales as a base. Since compensation expense was deemed to be semi-fixed, the prior year's balance was incorporated in the base. RS also looked at the board of directors' minutes to learn the magnitude of annual raises. The resulting base was composed of prior year's value, plus annual raises, and calculations to incorporate other raises and new employees, less officers' salaries.

After establishing the base period, RS began evaluating variances between base and estimated account values. For monthly net sales, he noted some values that exceeded the 20 percent materiality factor and flagged them for further explanation. For some monthly variances, he was able to provide some reasoning as to probable causes, and noted these hypotheses for further investigation.

For cost of sales, RS applied the percentage he had established earlier to see if significant variances were present, and noted several variances. After providing detailed explanations, RS concluded that none of the variances fell outside of the materiality standard, and that they need not be the subject of further evaluation. For selling, general, and administrative expenses, RS did a detailed monthly analysis and noted very low variances except for two months. As with net sales, he hypothesized a cutoff problem and suggested further investigation, although he commented that the variances were probably immaterial from the client's point of view. RS also evaluated compensation expense, and identified several monthly variances. For three of the four months, he hypothesized that the variances were due to the client's method of accruing. RS suggested further investigation of the one apparent error, and then went on to hypothesize some plausible reasons.

RS concluded that if the differences noted could be adequately explained, and if the actual account balances appeared to be reasonable, the detailed testing could be reduced by one-half (based on audit firm guidelines) for divisions one and two. Division three would be subject to normal testing procedures as noted above. He specified a budget of 16 hours to complete the audit objectives.

8.6 COMPARISON OF SUBJECTS AND SUMMARY FOR JUDGMENTAL ANALYTICAL REVIEW

Table 22 summarizes major findings for the two auditors performing judgmental analytical review on an actual client. The summary is categorized within each of the research questions presented earlier.

Several differences are noted between the experienced and less experienced auditor's analytical review. RJ had a very narrow perspective and could apparently provide no rationale when variances were identified. He contacted various accounting personnel within the client firm to obtain explanations, and then proposed more detailed testing to evaluate the veracity of the explanations. This is potentially troublesome, since RJ could potentially be subject to undue influence by the client. RS, on the other hand, identified the same accounts for analysis, but was able to provide much deeper rationale and formulate hypotheses as to why the variances existed. These hypotheses were evidently based on incidents recorded in memory (part of the overall schema described in Chapter 3), and allowed RS to postulate plausible explanations for identified variances.

RS did not suggest follow-up interviews with the client staff or more detailed testing, as did RJ. In addition, RS conducted much more extensive and detailed calculations on the accounts, using monthly data and the relationships between months and to historical data. There is no evidence that RJ conducted as extensive an analysis.

RJ's budget recommendation was 40 hours, whereas RS's recommendation was 16 hours. Thus, the experienced auditor seems able to perform a much more comprehensive, directed analysis, with formulation and some testing of reasonable hypotheses, with a proposed budget of 16 hours. The inexperienced auditor, on the other hand, carries out a very structured analysis with little or no hypotheses formulation and recommends a budget of 40 hours, largely based on his rationale of following up variances with key client firm personnel, and additional testing to verify explanations.

These differences clearly relate to experience factors. The inexperienced auditor relies on a structured, guided approach to ARP. When this guidance is weak or non-existent, his judgment is naive and poorly grounded. The experienced auditor is able to perform at a much higher level and deal with abstractions (exceptions) more effectively because of his past familiarity with the client and general experience in performing analytical review. Accounting firm policy may have had an impact on RS's decisions, since both RS and RJ came from a firm that had a general policy of reducing detailed tests based on appropriate findings from analytical review. But the difference in recommendations was most likely due to experience. These patterns of behaviour are similar to those observed in the Pacific Electronics case, where the inexperienced auditors relied more heavily on firm standards and procedures and failed to exhibit the richness of reasoning and analysis performed by the experienced auditors.

TABLE 22

Comparison of Judgmental Analytical Review Performance

Research Question 6 -A

What was the nature of the auditors' evaluations and decisions during the analytical review phase of the task?

	Experienced Auditor		Less Experienced Auditor
(1)	Deep reasoning and rationale.	(1)	Narrow reasoning and perspective.
(2)	Ability to formulate hypotheses as to why various variances existed.	(2)	Could not provide rationale for variances.
(3)	Did more extensive analysis on selected account items, for example, detailed comparison of monthly sales data.	(3)	No evidence of more extensive analysis.
(4)	Analysis reflected some sophistication and expertise.	(4)	No evidence of sophisticated analysis.

Research Question 6 -B

What decisions did auditors make while adjusting the planned audit program, and on what basis?

	Experienced Auditor		Less Experienced Auditor
(1)	Did not suggest follow-up client interviews.	(1)	Proposed detailed testing based on conversations with client personnel.
(2)	Estimated audit budget at 16 hours.	(2)	Estimated audit budget at 40 hours.
(3)	Recommended reduced tests of detail (reduction of up to one-half).	(3)	Recommended increased tests of detail.

Research question 6 -C

What decision errors were made, if any, and what were their apparent causes?

	Experienced Auditor		Less Experienced Auditor
(1)	No explicit errors noted. Did not interview clients, could miss relevant details; judgment call — not error.	(1)	No explicit errors noted. Spoke with clients and made judgments based on additional information.

Although a dense trace of the information search and decision process is not provided in the retrospective analysis, insights are gained regarding the performance level of the two auditors and the ability to generate and analyze hypotheses suggested by the analysis. This result is consistent with other studies in medical decision-making and other judgment fields. What is of interest, in contrast to the concurrent protocols, is RJ's desire to seek additional information to verify his hypotheses regarding the quality of various account balances.

As noted above, RS did not seek additional information, relying instead on judgments based on experience in resolving discrepancies in account balances. While RS could likely make correct decisions based on this strategy, the strategy could also lead to erroneous conclusions, particularly if the initial diagnoses were in error. RJ's strategy of seeking additional information to verify his prior diagnosis might yield better conclusions regarding account balances, provided that the gathering and evaluation of this evidence was not biased.

Chapter 9

SUMMARY, CONCLUSIONS AND IMPLICATIONS FOR FUTURE RESEARCH

9.1 INTRODUCTION

The purpose of this monograph was to conduct a broadly-based, comprehensive study of analytical review. In so doing, we have included:

(1) A review of the authoritative, professional, and academic literature on analytical review;
(2) A process model of analytical review;
(3) A cognitive model of auditor judgment in analytical review;
(4) Descriptive investigations of experienced and inexperienced auditors planning and conducting statistical and judgmental analytical reviews, and using this evidence to recommend adjustments to audit programs; and
(5) A multi-dimensional scaling study of auditors' perceptions of the use of information in analytical review.

The implications of this study for audit practice and research are significant. We begin this concluding chapter by summarizing the results of the literature review and judgment framework developed in the first two chapters, and presenting the limitations and implications of the descriptive studies of auditor judgment. There were several primary conclusions from the literature review, which was largely complete prior to the design and data collection phases of this study. At that time, the authoritative and professional literature was just starting to fully address analytical review. SAS 23 was issued in 1978, and the Smith monograph appeared in 1983. Thus, there were only broad guidelines and definitions available to help the auditor conduct analytical review and make use of its results.

The study was also launched at a time when the academic literature had concentrated heavily on the development of statistical techniques. While we agreed that statistical techniques could be very useful, our review indicated that they did not eliminate the need for auditor judgment. Moreover, recent surveys had indicated that analytical review techniques that relied most heavily on judgment (e.g. ratio analysis) were being used more frequently in practice than the statistical techniques. Our conclusion from reviewing the literature was that a descriptive, exploratory study of auditor judgment could yield important benefits for auditing research and practice.

With this in mind, we set out to develop an initial model of auditor judgment to guide this and future research. The model was based on the premise that auditor judgment takes place in a complex environment and that the study of auditor judgment should take place in a setting that could replicate at least some of this complexity. The resulting process model attempted to do this. A study of judgment must also reflect the fact that auditors conduct analytical review in an environment that is practically devoid of authoritative guidelines and relevant theory, and must therefore rely on their own experience and expertise to guide their judgment. Studying experience-based judgment in complex environments requires studying the cognitive processes involved [Gibbins and Wolf (1982); Gibbins (1984)]. Thus, in Chapter 3, we proposed two models that provide the basic elements for studying cognitive processes in judgment.

The purpose of the empirical portion of this monograph was to present detailed descriptive evidence of the way auditors use analytical review in realistic audit settings. The research attempted to provide systematic observation of a relatively substantial portion of an audit in two task settings. One setting was an extensive, 100-page case based on an actual client. The second setting was an actual audit, in which two auditors utilized both statistical and judgmental analytical review.

While the effects of one audit procedure on decisions concerning other procedures are often discussed in the literature [see Felix and Kinney (1982)], this was one of the first studies that actually attempted to document such interactions. Even though previous research was quite extensive, it provided only a cursory understanding of interactive effects in an audit.

9.2 LIMITATIONS

Given that this study utilized several methods of collecting evidence, limitations need to be considered for each approach. It is also difficult to draw inferences across methods which are based on different data collection and observation techniques, utilize different subjects, and are based on different tasks.

There are several limitations regarding the concurrent protocol study (the Pacific Electronics case). While the case was based on an actual audit, it is uncertain whether the same findings could be obtained in another task situation. As indicated above, the case did not completely duplicate the complexity of an actual audit situation. Thus, while some of the trade-offs between different audit procedures could be observed, many others might be present in actual auditing situations. It is impossible to know how this limitation might have affected the subject auditors' judgments.

The study of analytical review in an actual audit (the retrospective protocol) presented other limitations. Because of the way in which analytical review is planned and conducted in the study firm, it was not possible to conduct a concurrent protocol study of analytical review audit planning. As a result, the data analyzed in Chapter 8 consisted of a retrospective discussion, explanation, and interpretation of data gathered using statistical and judgmental analytical review methods.

A further limitation is that the retrospective study involved subjects from a firm different than the two firms involved in the concurrent protocol study. Since this particular firm places greater emphasis on the use of analytical review and statistical methods than the other two firms, the differences that occurred could simply reflect differences in firm training or audit approach.

The limitations of retrospective verbal reports were discussed in Chapter 4. Most important, we cannot be sure that the auditors' accounts of their decision processes during the discussion sessions matched their decisions during the actual audit [Ericsson and Simon (1984)]. To at least partially overcome possible gaps of memory, the auditors had access to their work papers. But it is difficult to know how or if this factor affected the auditors' retrospective analysis.

Additional limitations that apply to the concurrent verbal protocol methods utilized for the Pacific Electronics case have been discussed at length in the literature [see Ericsson and Simon (1984, 1980); Payne, Braunstein and Carroll (1978); and Biggs and Mock (1983)]. Nevertheless, a few bear repeating.

Due to the time-consuming methods involved in verbal protocol analysis (and the length of the case), the research involved only four auditors. It is difficult to know whether other auditors would have made the same or similar judgments, or would have exhibited similar decision processes.

Verbal protocols may not capture all of a subject's decision processes, since people think faster than they talk. However, the protocols provide a relatively dense trace of decision processes, and there is no reason to doubt the validity of the protocols that were verbalized.

There is also an element of subjectivity in the coding of protocols. We attempted to minimize these effects by establishing coding rules before analyzing the bulk of the protocols, and by using more than one coder. The latter allowed the measurement of agreement, and reconciliation of differences.

Research involves trade-offs, and we were willing to accept the limitations of verbal protocol analysis in order to obtain more details about auditors' decision processes.

Two criteria were established to evaluate the auditors' decisions during the Pacific Electronics case, and both had limitations. First, the case was based on an actual company where an audit problem had been discovered. The fact that an audit adjustment was made in a real world situation does not mean that the adjustment was correct, and that a problem in accounts receivable actually existed. Nevertheless, a real world criterion is better than no criterion, so it was used recognizing the associated limitations.

Second, decisions were evaluated based upon a comparison of managers and seniors. While it is possible that seniors may have had more expertise than managers on certain aspects of the audit, the managers would be expected to exhibit more expertise in most of the task that was evaluated. In the absence of independent, normative performance standards, manager/senior comparisons seem preferable to having no basis for evaluating the effects of expertise or experience on decisions and decision processes.

The use of multi-dimensional scaling (MDS) and multiple-methods present additional possible limitations. The MDS results are limited by the set of analytical review data actually requested by the auditors which varied somewhat between auditors. In addition, there is no objective way to describe or label the dimensions generated by MDS, and the particular analysis algorithms are subject to choice. Finally, as noted above, comparisons across methods are limited by the different audit settings, and possible differences in the training of the auditors involved.

Taken as a whole, the above limitations suggest caution in generalizing the results of this study to audit practice or theory. On the other hand, the results are sufficiently valid and reliable to suggest preliminary conclusions concerning auditor analytical review, and indicate directions for future research.

9.3 MAJOR FINDINGS AND IMPLICATIONS FOR FUTURE RESEARCH

Our major findings may be conveniently discussed in three areas. First, there are a number of findings that relate directly to our understanding of auditor analytical review. Second, the research has generated a number of observations that should be relevant to cognitive science, especially to those interested in decision behaviour. Finally, there are findings that relate to the use and usefulness of multiple-methods in audit research, and in research in general.

Evidence about auditor analytical review decision behaviour

All three methods used in this study provide evidence concerning one or more aspects of auditors' analytical review decisions and decision processes. The important research questions and details of this evidence have been provided in Chapters 5, 6, 7, and 9, and in the Appendices.

Even as a part of audit planning, it is clear that analytical review involves complex, interrelated information search, evaluation, and decision-making functions. In audit (and analytical review) planning, auditors select numerous analytical review tests, and base many of their audit planning judgments, at least in part, on analysis of financial data. Their decisions are characterized by numerous evaluation judgments, many of which are tentative in nature and involve reasoning by assumption. Their decision processes are largely sequential, although some variation was observed.

For the most part, both managers and seniors performing the Pacific Electronics case made decisions that were quite satisfactory. They all identified the major problems embedded in the case (potential overstatement of accounts receivable), and their adjustments to the audit program were consistent with the problems they identified.

When auditors are not explicitly performing statistical analytical review, the process seems to be used primarily as a means of directing attention, rather than a type of competent evidence that may be relied on to control audit risk and reduce the need for other audit evidence.

Auditor problem identification during analytical review

Smith (1983) and SAS 23 [AICPA (1978)] suggest that analytical review be used to identify both problems and opportunities. But the subjects in the Pacific Electronics case did not use analytical review to identify opportunities to reduce other audit tests, even though there are accounts that showed no unusual fluctuations or that showed improvement in key ratios, so that a reduction in audit work might have been justified. Further research should be conducted to investigate this finding. If auditors need more "solid" evidence to reduce other audit tests, analytical review may not provide the increased audit efficiency that has been expected.

There was an interesting contrast between the auditors performing the Pacific Electronics case and the subjects involved in the actual audit. While there was no evidence of the Pacific Electronics auditors reducing tests of detail based on analytical review, the auditors in the actual audit case (Chapter 8) specifically used statistical analytical review to reduce further tests of detail. However, when the auditors performing the actual audit used judgmental analytical review, their behaviour was similar to that of the auditors who completed the Pacific Electronics case: their judgmental analysis of the actual audit data led to further audit investigations, not reductions in auditing. It should be noted that the firm policy for statistical analytical review indicated that a maximum audit would be performed, except for accounts that were found to be within materiality bounds. This evidence may suggest overconfidence with statistical procedures and underconfidence with judgmental procedures. A resolution of this issue could lead to important audit efficiencies.

Manager/Senior differences: information acquisition

There were several important differences in information acquisition between the managers and seniors who completed the Pacific Electronics case. First, managers' information acquisition was more comprehensive than seniors'. This difference can be related to the underlying goals of information acquisition. Managers saw themselves (particularly during Phase I) as gathering information, not only with a view to adjusting the planned audit program, but also to become thoroughly familiar with the client. Managers evidently wanted to know as much as possible about the client, to consider making recommendations to management in the form of management letter suggestions. By contrast, the seniors' information acquisition was directed primarily at performing the specified task of adjusting the audit program. The difference was reflected in the smaller number of management letter recommendations made by seniors.

A second difference in information acquisition between managers and seniors concerned the sequence of information search. The managers' search was strictly sequential, while one of the seniors (S1) had a search pattern that was not strictly sequential. S1's frequent reference to the case instructions is consistent with a working backward strategy found in physics novices' problem-solving strategies. The sequential search is consistent with physics experts' problem-solving behaviour.

A third difference between managers and seniors was in the emphasis of their information acquisition activities. The seniors concentrated far more of their information acquisition than the managers on the introductory materials in the case. This is also consistent with differences between physics experts and novices, and may be attributed to the managers' richer mental schemata, which may help them assimilate information without relying on task instructions and audit planning information present in the introductory materials. These memory schemata may be based upon past performance of similar tasks, suggesting that analytical review skills are built up in memory primarily through experience. Experience allows auditors to evaluate information about clients through reasoning by analogy [Gick and Holyoak (1983)], an ability that becomes very important in situations like auditing, where there are few normative standards to guide decision-making. This finding also provides evidence for Gibbins' (1984) proposition that auditor templates are developed through experience.

The three categories of difference between managers and seniors are significant for future research. The consistency of our results with other studies of experts and novices suggests some general psychological phenomena that must be better understood if theories of auditor decision behaviour are to be developed. It suggests that expert decision-making is primarily based on knowledge, including task domain information and methods of application of that information. These are based primarily on skills developed through experience, and are represented as memory structures. To understand auditor decision-making, we need more research that can capture the substance of the auditor's experience, as represented in memory structures.

Manager/Senior differences: decisions

For the most part, both managers and seniors made decisions that were quite satisfactory. They all identified the major problems embedded in the case, and their adjustments to the audit program were consistent with the problems they identified.

However, there was a significant difference between managers and seniors in adjustments to the revenue cycle program. The seniors, after finding a problem with accounts receivable during their analytical review, increased the audit work throughout the revenue cycle, but the managers were much more selective in the procedures they increased. While the seniors increased the number of confirmations, the managers did not. The reasoning was clearly stated by one manager, who noted that confirmations related to propriety, and the problem with accounts receivable related to collectability. This somewhat subtle difference in decisions may be attributed to a richer schemata on the part of the managers. While the seniors appeared to be responding to the surface features of the problem (there is a problem with accounts receivable, therefore we should increase all audit work relating to accounts receivable), the managers made more subtle distinctions, based perhaps on a deeper understanding of the problem. This finding is also consistent with differences between physics experts and novices.

The evidence of differences between managers and seniors underscores the importance of further research to identify the decision processes of auditors with different levels of experience. In future research, we plan to evaluate the types of knowledge representation of each auditor, especially on the basis of experience. We hope to be able to identify different types of knowledge that the auditor may retain in memory, such as procedural knowledge (based on firm policy, FASB policy and so on), domain knowledge (knowledge of the particular client or type of business in which the client is engaged), system knowledge (general rules for the conduct of an audit), and prototypic knowledge (knowledge of a "typically good audit situation" based on experience with past clients and audit situations). It is our belief that identification of auditors' knowledge states, coupled with the information acquisition and decision processes identified in this study, will enable us to begin to differentiate between expert and novice decision-making, and provide new insights into the audit decision process in analytical review. These insights should provide the basis for an improved model of the analytical review judgment process. Such a model may be a useful decision tool, providing for more consistent and reliable judgments in analytical review tasks and thus allowing analytical review to become a true substitute for tests of detail rather than the simple "red flag" procedure that emerged in much of our research.

Evidence about general and cognitive theories of decision behaviour

The monograph described auditors' decision processes at various levels of detail. At the most aggregate level, decision flowcharts were developed; at the most detailed level, the auditors' elementary information processes (operator and knowledge states) were identified. Between those levels of detail, episode abstracts were developed that described decision processes as sequences of goal-directed behaviours.

This descriptive evidence is important for two reasons. First, the descriptions of the auditors' decision processes are consistent with general theories of human information processing. Thus, this research provides support for theories that depict decision-making as the application of elementary information-processing operations to states of knowledge [Newell and Simon (1972)], where the elementary operations are related to information acquisition, evaluation and action/choice [Einhorn and Hogarth (1981)]. Support for such general theories may not be too surprising, but neither should it be dismissed as irrelevant. These theories provided a general framework within which more detailed analysis took place. For example, numerous types of information evaluation operators were identified, suggesting decision processes that are consistent with more detailed theories.

Second, the descriptive evidence is important to the development of detailed computer models of auditor analytical review decision processes, particularly expert systems. The development of computerized expert systems for tasks like those performed in this study is extremely time-consuming, requiring up to five person-years [Davis (1982)]. While it is unreasonable to expect one research project to result in an expert system, the descriptive evidence provides a beginning.

An attempt was made to use a current expert system shell, to model the protocols collected from one subject into a prototype expert system. Professor Paul Steinbart attempted to use Emycin to model the protocols from subject M2 in the Pacific Electronics case. Although Steinbart has built other expert systems using Emycin [Steinbart (1984)], he was unable to do so in this case, mainly because Emycin uses a backward chaining logic, and M2's protocols were based largely on a forward chaining logic. Thus, M2 appeared to be following an inductive process that represented knowledge in a form that Emycin could not handle. This is, of course, a problem with expert system shells that depend on one knowledge representation. In the future, other systems that are not limited to one representational form could be used to model the protocols [Biggs and Selfridge (1986)].

Such a computer model of analytical review would be extremely useful. From a research perspective, it would provide the basis for a cognitive science theory of auditor analytical review. In a practical sense, it might serve as a red flag for problem accounts, so that the auditor could efficiently verify them and indicate those with plausible explanations, thus increasing audit efficiency.

The fact that an expert system was not developed on the basis of the protocols collected should not be interpreted as a severe limitation of this study. Research that results in knowledge of expert decision-making behaviour that is not computerized in the form of an expert system should not be considered valueless. One prominent artificial intelligence researcher has recommended that more research be conducted on decision processes before computer-based expert systems are developed. He argues that computer-based tools for knowledge representation often inhibit the understanding and modelling of experts' decision processes [Doyle (1984)].

Cognitive reasoning processes: handling uncertainty

The verbal protocols provided considerable insight into the reasoning processes used by the auditors. As in practice, the subjects had to make judgments where there was uncertainty about whether they were correct. The data showed that the auditors never used any type of probabilistic reasoning to manage uncertainty. Yet evidence of uncertainty in their reasoning processes was present in the large number of tentative evaluation operators they used. Thus, the observed judgments concerning uncertainty are more consistent with the reasoning by assumption model proposed by Doyle (1983a and 1983b), or Cohen's model of endorsements (1984), than with a Bayesian or classical probability model.

Our results are also consistent with Gibbins' (1984) Proposition 10 and Corollary 10(ii) which characterizes auditor decision-making as "matching present perception with past learning" rather than "a forward-looking, probabilistic, or expectation process". This evidence is consistent with other descriptive research on auditor judgment [Biggs and Mock (1983); Biggs, Messier and Hansen (1987)].

Given the emphasis in the auditing literature on probabilistic models (e.g. the audit risk model, statistical sampling, and Bayesian models), it is important to understand why these studies have not found evidence of probabilistic reasoning. Is it because auditors are not properly trained to use probabilities? Is it because auditors do not have the background knowledge to properly quantify uncertainty with probabilities? Is it because auditors do not see probabilistic reasoning as an efficient or effective way to make decisions under uncertainty? Are the frequentist and Bayesian concepts over-emphasized in the literature?

Given the evidence discussed here, and the difficulty humans have in dealing with probabilities [Joyce and Biddle (1981); Tversky and Kahneman (1974)], answers to these questions could provide important insights about auditor decision-making. The traditional frequentist and Bayesian concepts underlying probabilistic judgment are coming under more frequent criticism as bases for human decision-making [see Shafer and Tversky, forthcoming; Shafer (1984); Cohen (1984); Doyle (1983a, 1983b, 1984); Gordon and Shortliffe (1985)]. While some critics argue that probabilistic reasoning may not be effective at all, others suggest different ways of dealing with and combining uncertain evidence. Research to determine how uncertainty is (and should be) dealt with would help build a better understanding of auditor decision-making. Such research could lead to the development of new types of decision aids, to help auditors handle uncertainty and interrelate with audit risk models such as the one contained in SAS 47 [AICPA (1983)]. Moreover, since auditors are experienced at making judgments under uncertainty, such research may provide important evidence about decision-making in general.

Cognitive reasoning processes: confirmation bias

Our evidence indicated that auditors used analytical review as a diagnostic tool to identify problems in the Pacific Electronics financial statements, and in several accounts of the actual audit client. For Pacific Electronics, their approach was to conduct a preliminary analytical review to identify problems, request additional information (i.e. financial ratios), evaluate this new information, and finally evaluate and adjust the audit program. Since most of the information requests seemed directed at confirming identified problems, the question of confirmation bias arose. The protocol evidence was somewhat mixed on this question.

There was explicit evidence that the subjects requested additional information that served the primary purpose of confirming problems they had already identified. On the other hand, the auditors evaluated the new information with an open mind. In fact, we cited protocol evidence where subject M1 disconfirmed a previously hypothesized problem on the basis of the new information. Similar evidence was present in the protocols of the other manager (M2). Thus, there may be an important experience effect with respect to the presence of confirmation bias. Managers appear to guard against confirmation bias by evaluating the evidence with a degree of independence from their previously established hypotheses, while seniors showed less tendency to do so.

This outcome is consistent with findings in the medical literature, where more expert doctors tend to have an intuitive feel for the biases to which they may succumb and guard against their occurrence [Johnson, Severance, and Feltovich (1979)]. Nevertheless, the requests for information were largely what one might expect when confirmation bias is present. Future research should assess this issue, paying particular attention to experience.

Given the retrospective nature of the auditors' reporting in the actual audit situation (Chapter 8), it was not possible to evaluate confirmation bias for this part of the research. However, the inexperienced auditor (RJ) typically followed a strategy of discussing identified problems with the client during analytical review. While this practice is not confirmation bias per se, it could lead to many errors if the auditor were unduly influenced by a client who wanted to hide problems.

9.4 MULTI-METHOD FINDINGS

The research for this monograph involved three methods of empirical research: concurrent protocol analysis, retrospective protocol analysis, and multi-dimensional scaling. There are several points of potential convergence among the three methods.

Concurrent protocol analysis and multi-dimensional scaling

The concurrent protocol analysis provided evidence of the auditors' evaluations and decisions in the completion of the Pacific Electronics case, multi-dimensional scaling provided evidence of the underlying perceptual structure that the auditors utilized in performing the case. Thus, a comparison of the results of the two methods provides evidence of their convergence or divergence.

As discussed in Chapter 7, the results of the protocol analysis and the multi-dimensional scaling were consistent on several points. The dimensions identified in the multi-dimensional scaling were consistent with what would be expected from the protocol analysis of the auditors' analytical review. This was particularly true for the more experienced auditors, M1 and M2.

Second, the dimensional structures identified in the multi-dimensional scaling were consistent with the expertise of the auditors, and with the consistency of the decision strategies employed by the managers and seniors. Specifically, the multi-dimensional scaling required three dimensions for the two seniors, indicating less structure and coherence in their understanding of what is involved in performing analytical review. The multi-dimensional scaling on the managers resulted in a uni-dimensional structure for M1 and a two-dimensional structure for M2. The simpler dimensional structures of the managers are consistent with a more coherent understanding of the analytical review task, and a greater amount of expertise. These conclusions were also consistent with protocol evidence that the managers had deeper and more coherent understanding and better decision strategies.

The convergence of these two very different research methods speaks well for both approaches. Both methods do apparently measure elements of cognitive processes. The convergence should also encourage other researchers to use complementary methods in studying cognitive processes.

Effect of experience across methods

All three methods involved subjects with different levels of experience. In each case, auditors with greater experience were shown to perform with greater expertise. The experienced senior performed considerably better than the junior in the retrospective protocol study, and managers in the concurrent protocol study and the multi-dimensional scaling were shown to made decisions that involved greater expertise.

This finding contrasts with many other studies reported in the accounting literature, where experience had little effect on decisions. A possible explanation for the difference is that our tasks were realistic and complex, and therefore required greater expertise to achieve high level performance.

Statistical and judgmental analytical review

In the retrospective protocol study, the auditors performed both statistical and judgmental analytical review. We previously discussed the apparent greater comfort that the auditors felt with statistical analytical review, since they reduced other audit work based on statistical but not judgmental review. Another difference between statistical and judgmental analytical review involved the inexperienced junior, who identified many more problems with the accounts during the judgmental analytical review than with the statistical process. While it was not clear that the problems he identified were meaningful, they did cause him to increase the audit budget he had established through statistical analytical review.

9.5 CONCLUSION

As this study has shown, analytical review is a complex audit tool that has the potential to provide competent evidence in a very efficient manner. However, analytical review, even when statistical models are used, is heavily dependent upon auditor judgment. Thus, it is the judgment process of auditors that requires further study.

We believe that this study is the logical starting point. We have attempted to systematically study analytical review in settings that are as realistic as possible, and determine how analytical review interacted with other components of the audit. We believe we have been successful in identifying some important issues for practice and research in analytical review. However, this study is just the beginning. Much more needs to be done if analytical review is to achieve its potential.

APPENDIX A

OPERATORS AND OPERATOR DEFINITIONS

OPERATOR		NOTATION	BRIEF DEFINITION
Task Structuring Operator			
1)	Set Goal	SG	Assigned when the subject specifies a goal to be accomplished in performing the task.
Information Acquisition Operators			
2)	Information Search	IS	Assigned when the subject searches the case materials for specific pieces of information (directed search) or searches following some systematic pattern (usually sequential search).
3)	Direct Reading	R	Assigned when the subject reads directly from the case materials.
4)	Algebraic Calculation	AC	Assigned when the subject makes a mathematical calculation in order to obtain new information about the task.
5)	Information Retrieval	IR	Assigned when the subject retrieves a previously stored piece of information from external memory (i.e. notes, calculations) or internal memory.
Information Evaluation Operators			
6)	Assumption	AS	Assigned when the subject generates an arbitrary (unspecified) fact about the case.
7)	Conditional Judgment	CJ	Assigned when the subject draws a conclusion (prediction) which is speculative or predictive in nature. Usually has a degree of uncertainty present.
8)	Evaluation	E	Assigned when the subject makes a definite judgment about the task based on some conditional criterion (no uncertainty).
9)	Comparison	CN	Assigned when the subject compares two items, such as a comparison of account balances between years.
10)	Decision Support	DS	Assigned when the subject provides rationale (premise) to support a decision, recommendation or alternative.

11)	Generate Query	GQ	Assigned when the subject raises a question.

Action/Choice Operators

12)	Generate Alternative	GA	Assigned when the subject generates an optional AD or OD to be considered.
13)	Audit Decision	AD	Assigned when the subject reaches a definite decision concerning the specific audit task (e.g. "revise the planned audit program").
14)	Decision Rule	DR	Assigned when the subject specifies a method (including heuristics) of reaching a decision.
15)	Other Decisions	OD	Assigned when the subject reaches a definite decision that is not an AD. OD operators typically involve making management letter comments.

APPENDIX B

EPISODE ABSTRACT FOR SUBJECT M1

PHASE 1

EPISODE 1: Review case overview to become familiar with Pacific Electronics and task requirements.

1.1	Notes that inflation was a concern during the period covered in the case.
1.1.1	Notes that most companies are on LIFO during inflation but PE is on FIFO.
1.2	With high interest, receivables may be questionable during the coming year.
1.3	Concludes that PE's decision to incur long-term debt was not a good thing to do given the economic conditions.
1.4	Comments that receivables and inventory are critical items, not only because they are material amounts within the financial statements, but also because of the economic conditions. Need to look at their valuation.
1.5	Expresses a general rule to never do a rollforward.
1.6	Unchanged credit terms over the past several years imply that there are a lot of bad debts.
1.7	May have to do additional work or write a management letter because of the lack of controls over inventory.
1.8	Since PE is not a labour intensive firm, undocumented calculations on terminations are probably not a major problem.

EPISODE 2: Evaluate 1980 financial statements through a comparative analysis with 1979.

2.1	Checks to see if PE is on LIFO; finds that they are on FIFO.
2.1.1	In an inflationary environment, the company should be on LIFO.
2.1.2	Checks to see if PE has retained earnings, finds that they do, concludes that they have been paying taxes.
2.2	Cash balance is high.
2.3	Searches for 1979 financial statements to conduct comparative analysis.
2.4	Receivables have gone up twice.
2.5	Allowance has only gone up one-third.
2.6	Installations in progress, just wondering what they are installing.
2.7	Property, plant and equipment has gone up substantially.
2.8	Comments on the deferred tax debits, noting that it is quite unusual.
2.9	Payables are going up.
2.10	Inventory is going up, but disproportionately to the increase in payables.

2.10.1	Liquidity may be a problem, but should be looked at.
2.10.2	They are putting a lot of money into inventory but it is not a liquid asset and is susceptible to obsolescence.
2.10.3	It is possible that their inventory is liquid and their receivables are not collectible.
2.10.4	They could be getting into hard times.
2.11	Investigate long-term debt to determine how soon it is going to mature.
2.11.1	It is maturing in about a year and a half.
2.11.2	They are becoming very ill-liquid.
2.11.3	Their debts may have to be renegotiated very soon, probably at higher rates.
2.12	Sales are up, but so is inflation.
2.13	Gross margin in 1979 is 30%, and is actually increasing in 1980 to 35%.
2.13.1	If their gross margin has been consistent in the past, the increase in 1980 may indicate an inventory problem or a change in sales prices.
2.14	Operating expenses are going up disproportionately to sales.
2.15	Other income has gone down. Do not know why.
2.16	Paying too much in taxes. Not using installment sales, LIFO or anything.
2.17	Loss on discontinued operations.
2.17.1	Reads footnote and wonders why it was called a discontinued segment, implying that it was a separate operation.
2.17.2	Somewhere between 1978 and 1979, PE lost two subsidiaries.
2.18	Summarizes observations about PE up to this point.
2.18.1	Typical company in this situation.
2.18.1.1	Poor cash management.
2.18.1.2	Paying too much in taxes.
2.18.1.3	Liquidity is suffering.
2.18.1.4	Not controlling easily controlled areas.
2.18.1.5	Not maximizing assets like inventory and receivables.
2.19	Reads footnotes.
2.19.1	Installations in process.
2.19.1.1	Do not know if laundromats are a good business or not.
2.19.1.2	Returns to balance sheet.
2.19.1.2.1	Are they shown as a current asset because they are up for sale?
2.19.1.2.2	Assume repossessed stores along with new installations.
2.19.1.2.3	The amount has increased.
2.19.2	Pension footnote.

2.19.3	Notes receivables footnote.
2.19.3.1	Implies that PE has some collection problems, put them into notes, and now are not even collecting the interest.
2.19.4	Intangible assets.
2.19.5	Long-term debt.
2.19.5.1	Debt appears to be unsecured, and does not have compensating balance agreements.
2.19.5.1.1	The lack of collateral indicates that they are not maximizing their debt (in terms of lower interest?).
2.19.5.1.2	Would normally have to examine compensating balance agreements.
2.19.5.1.3	The revolving line of credit that expires soon should be classified as current, not long-term.
2.19.6	Commitments.
2.19.7	Contingent liabilities.
2.19.7.1	The collectibility of discounted notes should be examined, but the amount is not material.
2.19.8	Income taxes.
2.19.9	Discontinued operations.
2.19.9.1	The note is unclear.
2.20	Scans the 1979 footnotes to see if there are any unusual items or major changes.
2.21	Scans 1977/78 financial statements.
2.21.1	Installations in process continued to increase.
2.21.1.1	Scans and reads the footnotes to understand installations in process.
2.21.1.2	There may be capitalized interest considerations, but that would probably be handled elsewhere in the audit rather than analytical review.
2.22	Scans 1976/77 financial statements.
2.22.1	Margin has gone down.
2.22.2	Long-term debt has changed substantially over the years.
2.23	Examines sales analysis schedule.
2.23.1	Sales returns and allowances are up slightly.
2.23.2	Discounts are down slightly.
2.23.3	Bad debt expense is fairly constant.
2.23.4	Purchase returns and allowances are constant.
2.23.5	Nothing unusual in the operating expenses.
2.23.5.1	However, it should be noted that the 1980 statements are unaudited.
2.24	Examines accounts receivable aging analysis.
2.24.1	Over 360 days is an unusual category.
2.24.2	180–360 days indicates a real problem in collection.

2.24.3	30–60 days has gone up.
2.24.4	0–30 days looks fine.
2.24.5	Search for increase in sales for 1980.
2.24.5.1	PE had a significant sales increase during the rollforward period. Would not want to do a rollforward audit on this client.
2.24.6	Needs to do a lot of our analytical procedures on the accounts receivable.
2.25	Examines schedule of operating expenses.
2.25.1	Salaries and wages are up significantly.
2.25.1.1	Suggests that they may have a real lack of control over terminations and overtime.
2.25.1.1.1	If PE accounts for overtime separately, you might want to see that in a comparative analysis.
2.26	Scans quarterly income statements for 1976 to 1979.
2.26.1	Sales increases 2 million in 1980 of which 500,000 occurs in the rollforward period.
2.26.2	Examines earnings for evidence of seasonality but does not find any.
2.27	Examines quarterly balance sheets for 1976 to 1979.
2.27.1	No evidence in protocols of evaluations, apparently just scanned the information.

EPISODE 3: Review objectives of the task and begin listing analytical review program on paper. Identify critical audit areas.

3.1	Accounts receivable.
3.1.1	Growth in accounts receivable is disproportionate to the growth in sales.
3.1.2	Credit policies may be lax.
3.2	Sales returns and allowances may be an area of audit concern.
3.2.1	Rapidly changing product lines in electronic appliances where technological obsolescence is occurring. If a customer has a product and returns it after six months, it could be obsolete.
3.2.2	The percentage of returns is not overly high and has remained constant, there could be a high incidence of a product subject to obsolescence.
3.2.3	Would like an analysis of sales, returns and allowance for two years segregated by product line.
3.3	Digresses to accounts receivable.
3.3.1	Review of aging and days sales in accounts receivable would not be that helpful.
3.3.1.1	It is obvious that there is a problem without looking at the ratios.
3.3.1.2	Primarily, there will have to be more substantive work.

3.4 Doing analytical review at the rollforward and year end would not be cost effective, and there too many sales have taken place during the last 3 months.

3.4.1 There is too much risk since PE has incentives to look better for their refinancing with the bank.

3.4.2 Needs a three-year comparative analysis of cash receipts and accounts receivable by product line and possibly by major division.

3.4.3 Need a two-year analysis of sales returns and allowances also by product line and major division.

3.4.4 It is assumed that the compliance evaluation has been updated.

3.4.5 Needs a comparison of aging as of the interim date, November 30, 1979 versus February 29, 1980.

3.4.5.1 Needs to assess the deterioration.

3.5 Inventory.

3.5.1 Evaluates installations in process and decides that he is not concerned about them.

3.5.2 Subject reviews in his mind the components of inventory.

3.5.2.1 Would like to have inventory turnover by product, but this type of client normally does not have the necessary records.

3.5.3 Subject reconsiders installations in process.

3.5.3.1 Would normally examine the account in terms of repossessed and current.

3.6 Would like to have budgeted information about prospects for sales by product line.

3.7 Accounts payable is a critical audit area.

NOTE: The subject repeats prior decisions (i.e., Episodes 3.1 through 3.7) and discusses general ideas about analytical review and auditing. It is unrelated to the case.

3.8 Reconsiders inventory and stocking policies.

3.8.1 PE has six outlets and one warehouse.

3.8.2 There are descending values in inventory.

3.8.3 Would be interesting to see economic order quantities for inventory to determine if they are overstocking resulting in obsolete inventory.

3.9 Notes receivable are not a material item.

3.9.1 You could do an aging analysis on receivables that have been factored, getting the aging from the bank.

EPISODE 4: Review the audit program to become more familiar with the nature of the required analytical review.

4.1 The subject goes through a general discussion about how expenses are audited through analytical review.

EPISODE 5: Specify the analytical review for critical audit areas.

5.1 Payroll is a relatively significant cost, basically half of the operating expenses, but consistent as a percentage of sales.

5.1.1 Normally, you would not expect that for a retail outlet, unless there is a commission factor.

5.1.2 Needs a comparative analysis of salaries and wages, by department.

5.2 Rent expense.

5.2.1 No capitalizing of rent expense.

5.2.2 Still not sure what PE is doing with repossessed laundromats.

5.2.3 Rent expense has gone up substantially.

5.2.4 Requests a comparative analysis on rent expense.

5.3 Accounts payable.

5.3.1 No major concern, it is overstated.

5.3.2 But should look at accounts payable in relation to inventories, to get insight about liquidity.

5.3.3 Might look at discounts lost, but most companies do not account for them.

5.4 Subject scans the financial statements to see if any significant items were missed.

5.4.1 Would like to see a monthly sales analysis.

5.4.2 Would like to see a comparative analysis of sales.

5.4.3 Would like a comparative analysis of gross profit by product line.

5.4.3.1 This will provide insight on deterioration in particular product lines related to obsolescence.

5.4.4 Sales shipping.

5.4.4.1 Would like to see a backlog comparison by product line.

5.4.5 Trade receivables.

5.4.5.1 Would like a comparison of the rollforward period with year end to look for unusual changes.

5.4.6 Needs to get an understanding of liquidity.

5.4.6.1 Would like to get the current ratio.

5.4.6.2 Would like to get the quick ratio.

5.4.6.3 There could be a going-concern problem.

PHASE 2

EPISODE 1: Sequential search and evaluation of Phase 2 instructions and results of available ARPs requested during Phase 1.

1.1 Sequential search of Phase 2 instructions.

1.1.1 Reads Phase 2 instructions with no additional comment.

1.2 Review and analysis of available ARP results which were requested in Phase 1.

1.2.1 Briefly read and evaluate (selected) ARP results. He explicitly comments on the quick ratio, days sales, AP turnover, days outstanding AP, salaries & wages, insurance, and supplies expense.

EPISODE 2: Review of substantive audit program for nontrade notes and other receivables.

2.1	Read the introductory section of the program for nontrade notes and other receivables which summarizes internal control and audit objectives.
2.2	He reviews financial data and footnotes regarding notes receivable.
2.3	Reads, without comment, audit program for notes and other. (Researcher then reminds M1 of the purpose of Phase 2.)
2.4	Retrieves financial statement data on notes ($73,000 current + $171,000 noncurrent).
2.5	Evaluates balance as "not really much."
2.6	Reviews ARP workpaper.
2.7	"This does not tell you much."
2.8	Reviews Objective B and related steps.
2.9	Suggests that what was done last year may be adequate.
2.10	Tentatively decides not to modify.
2.11	Concerning Step 1, Objective B generates several assumptions concerning possible contingencies, evaluates nature, extent, timing and tentatively decides for status quo.
2.12	Scans financial data again looking at 1979 (vs. 1980) trends.
2.13	Considers a change in extent regarding possible collectibility problems.
2.14	Decides on no change contingent on looking at what they normally do.

EPISODE 3: Review of substantive audit program for revenue cycle: sales, shipping, trade receivable, cash receipts.

3.1	Reads or scans introduction page of revenue cycle which includes approach, internal control, and audit objectives.
3.2	Reviews several sources for cues regarding revenue cycle including the ARP WORKPAPER, 1980 financials, and planning memo.
3.3	Evaluates the items in the ARP WORKPAPER that relate to revenue cycle.
3.4	Begins to consider whether they should confirm at year end. (Refers later to a concern as to liquidity possibly inferred from ARP data above.)
3.5	Decides to do so, which he feels is consistent with audit program.
3.6	Reads Objectives A, B, C, and D with very brief comments and evaluation basically concluding for no changes.
3.7	Reads Objective E (re proper sales cutoff) and related audit steps.
3.8	Begins to evaluate Procedure 3, Objective E which is an ARP.
3.9	He is concerned with the availability and quality of data and with the relevance of the procedure to the objective.

3.10	Repeats previous analysis reconfirming at year end, not relying on internal control, etc. He does decide that a reduction is possible for Step 1, Objective E.
3.11	Reads Objectives F and G (re proper cash receipts cutoff) and Step G1.
3.12	Evaluates procedure as of marginal value (and write DELETE on audit program).
3.13	Reads Step G2 regarding review of subsequent cash receipts.
3.14	Evaluates G2 as not relating to much exposure and decides also to delete.
3.15	Reviews instructions again.
3.16	Reconsiders confirming at year end and doing "collectibility analysis."

EPISODE 4: Review of substantive audit program for production costs and inventory.

4.1	Goes on to "inventory" part of program.
4.2	Reads through the introduction page for inventory, scans some of the financial data and case study, and Objective A.
4.3	Decides on no change in Steps in A.
4.4	Reads Objective B regarding inventory costing.
4.5	Reviews situation and eliminates costing steps as not applicable.
4.6	Reads Objective C and eliminates steps dealing with standard costing.
4.7	Reads Objective D and reviews footnote 8 regarding Laundromats.
4.8	Reads Objective E regarding cutoff of purchases and sales and scans procedures.
4.9	Questions appropriateness of procedures regarding LIFO. (This seems to relate back to previous Objective D.)
4.10	Scans case again and planning section; concludes that he would probably go back to revenue cycle and increase extent regarding doubtful accounts because of potential credit risks.
4.11	Contains mostly a long "aside" to researchers.

EPISODE 5: Review of substantive audit program for purchasing cycle.

5.1	Reads primary objectives of purchasing cycle.
5.2	Scans case study.
5.3	Reads Objective A regarding valid and properly classified AP.
5.4	Searches through ARP workpaper, specifically payable turnover and days outstanding.
5.5	Concludes it is difficult to conclude regarding possible liquidity problem from data.
5.6	Considers lowering scope (threshold) in searching for unrecorded liabilities.
5.7	Decides not to.
5.8	Provide rationale for previous decision.

5.9 Reads Objective B regarding insuring all liabilities for goods or services are recorded.

5.10 Decides to lower scope for Steps 1 and 2 contingent on good confirmation response.

5.11 Reads Step 3 regarding searching for unrecorded liabilities.

5.12 Scans ahead to check for redundancy .

5.13 Evaluates and rereads Step b3 again which deals with propriety of year end accruals for AP and accrued liabilities.

5.14 He notes that his approach here would be a comparison with prior years for reasonableness.

5.15 Scans the ARP workpaper again.

5.16 Evaluates several items on workpaper and concludes that nothing needs to be expanded above normal.

5.17 However, the data re-cues on a possible liquidity problem and footnote 8 on contingent liabilities.

5.18 Reads Objective C regarding purchased goods which he normally does not do much on.

5.19 Notes that he normally relies more on ARPs here and scans and evaluates ARP workpaper.

5.20 Tentatively decides not to do proposed steps but instead a "comparative analysis."

5.21 Scans salaries and wages which "are up significantly."

5.22 This leads to a review of internal control workpaper regarding payroll and query regarding reason for increased payroll.

5.23 On Objective D (cash disbursements are valid and properly recorded), he considers eliminating all steps and definitely Step 2.

5.24 Recalls that normal procedure here is to look at a comparative analysis of big expenses.

5.25 Subepisode concerned with salary and wage expense "problem" identified in ARPs and scan of other materials.

5.25.1 Having completed the program review, he comments that "We are down to salaries and wages, which are a problem."

5.25.2 Based on the recollections that there are poor internal controls and a yet unexplained increase in payroll expenses, he suggests specifically keying in on salaries and wages.

5.25.3 Goes into great detail as to how he would audit this area mostly using "a step-audit procedure" (contingency based) ". . . where I would not put it all in writing."

5.25.4 He completes this evaluation by noting again that this is a significant expense and increase in cash.

5.26 Subepisode concerned with a final review and evaluation of ARP workpaper.

5.26.1 Review of ARP workpaper again.

5.26.2	Identifies two items on ARP workpaper that require further analysis: supplies expense (63% change) and rent expense (102% change).
5.26.3	For supplies he generates several follow-up procedures, primarily inquiry seeking an explanation.
5.26.4	For rent expenses he suggests a similar approach, first reviewing existing data to generate possible explanations and then using inquiry.
5.27	Subepisode concerned with contingent liability.
5.27.1	As a final analysis, he reconsiders contingencies and reviews footnote 8 and related parts of audit program.
5.27.2	After considering some alternatives, he decides to augment Objective B of revenue cycle to include "Examine the collectibility of your off balance sheet receivables."

EPISODE 6: Provide (retrospective) rationale for changes made in audit program.

(In a response to questions from the researchers, provides some additional rationale for his changes and notations on the audit program.)

EPISODE ABSTRACT FOR SUBJECT M2

PHASE 1

EPISODE 1: Read case overview to become familiar with Pacific Electronics and task requirements.

EPISODE 2: Evaluate 1980 financial statements.

2.1	Balance sheet.
2.1.1	Sequential search of all information in balance sheet.
2.1.2	Calculates several key ratios (current ratio, receivable allowance percentage, and debt/equity).
2.1.3	Identifies various accounts that may require audit attention based upon an intrinsic materiality standard.
2.2	Income statement.
2.2.1	Sequential search of all information in income statement.
2.2.2	Calculates gross profit and net income percentages.
2.3	Statement of retained earnings.
2.3.1	Sequential search of all information.
2.4	Statement of changes in financial position.
2.4.1	Sequential search of all information.
2.4.2	Conducts causal analysis by comparing changes in cash, receivables and inventory with changes in sales.
2.5	Evaluate footnotes.
2.5.1	Sequential search of footnotes.
2.5.2	Offers advice to management about financial management.
2.5.3	Identifies potential audit concerns regarding classification of accounts (e.g., long-term versus short-term debt and receivables).

EPISODE 3: Comparative analysis of 1979 and 1980 financial statements to determine significant changes in accounts.

3.1	Notes that accounts receivable allowance is smaller in 1980 than in 1979 and examines aging and bad debt history.
3.2	Investigates major acquisitions due to weak controls and recent large purchases.
3.3	Confirms all debts are due to the increase in prime rate.
3.4	Compares changes in various accounts with changes in sales.
3.5	Makes a sequential search of all information in 1979 financial statements including footnotes and compares with 1980 financial statements to determine changes.

EPISODE 4: Comparative analysis of 1977 and 1978 financial statements to identify significant trends. If a significant change in an account is found, it is compared to 1979 and 1980 amounts.

4.1	Sequential search of all information in 1977 and 1978 financial statements.
4.2	The primary goal of this episode is to gain a more detailed understanding of the company's history and to identify major fluctuations and to determine if fluctuations identified in 1979/1980 show similar patterns in 1977/1978 comparisons.

EPISODE 5: Comparative analysis of 1976 and 1977 financial statements.

5.1	Sequential search of all information in 1976/1977 financial statements.
5.2	Purpose of the search of financial statements is to identify significant fluctuations in accounts to direct audit attention.

NOTE: Subject read and evaluated all pieces of information contained in all five years of financial statements (1976-1980) including all footnotes. The primary purpose of this thorough search was to obtain an understanding of the financial performance of the company. In addition, numerous audit related conclusions were formed.

EPISODE 6: Read and evaluate supplemental schedules.

6.1	Sales analysis schedule.
6.1.1	Notes bad debt as percent of sales went down.
6.1.2	Calculates bad debt expense as percent of allowance for doubtful accounts. Notes that it is about 4%.
6.1.3	Expresses a concern that the allowance for doubtful accounts is not adequate.
6.1.4	Concludes that none of the trends in the sales analysis schedule indicate serious enough problems that would require altering the audit program.
6.2	Accounts receivable aging schedule.
6.2.1	Notes that the aging has gotten worse in 1980.
6.2.2	Due to deterioration in aging, looks very closely at accounts receivable collection.
6.3	Operating expenses schedule.
6.3.1	Compares expense percentages across 1979 and 1980.
6.3.2	Notes that insurance expense has gone down even though there has been an increase in property plant and equipment leaseholds. Because of this, confirms insurance carriers to determine if they mind that PE may be under-insured.
6.3.3	Wants a schedule of supplies expense to determine if there are any unusual items.
6.4	Quarterly income statement.
6.4.1	Concludes the company does not appear to be seasonal.
6.4.2	Because sales, gross profit and operating expenses are going up, would like a comparison of gross profit and before-tax percentages.

6.5 Quarterly balance sheet.

6.5.1 Because receivables went up faster than sales, concludes that there has been an increase in credit sales.

6.5.2 Notes that accounts payable and inventory are changing in the same direction during the period.

EPISODE 7: Specify analytical review program.

7.1 Requests ratios for 1976 through 1980 for current ratio
liquidity ratio (i.e., quick ratio),
days accounts receivable, and
inventory turnover,
accounts payable turnover,
gross profit percentage,
operating income percentage,
effective tax rate,
earnings from continuing operations as a percent of sales, and
accounts receivable turnover.

7.2 Requests aging of accounts receivable percentages.

7.3 Indicates that the major items in analytical review are receivables and inventory.

7.4 Income statement percentages will provide insight about operating inefficiencies.

PHASE 2

EPISODE 1: Review and evaluate analytical review information requested during Phase 1.

1.1 Current ratio is unchanged over the four years.

1.2 Acid test ratio has increased over the four years.

1.3 Debt/equity basically the same over the four years.

1.4 Inventory turnover has decreased consistently over the four years, which is something to consider in the audit.

1.5 Gross profit percentage has stayed the same except for a big increase in 1980.

1.6 Operating income to sales has gone down in the past three years.

1.6.1 Gross profit percentage has stayed the same.

1.6.2 The cause of the decline in operating income to sales is non-direct costs.

1.7 Effective tax rate has increased in 1979 and 1980 during a time when the statutory rate was decreasing.

1.7.1 Probably due to the lack of ITC.

1.8 Earnings from continuing operations as percent of sales has gone down the last three years in the same relation as operating income to sales.

1.9 Days outstanding on accounts receivable has consistently gone up.

1.9.1 Receivables and bad debts could be a problem.

1.10 Accounts payable turnover is flat except for the last two years.

1.11	Accounts receivable turnover in 1979 was bad, but flat the other years.
1.11.1	Aging of accounts receivable is definitely a problem.
1.12	Aging of accounts receivable in 1980 is significantly worse in the 90–180 and 180–360 categories, and the gradual decline in all the categories.

EPISODE 2: Review 1980 balance sheet to "refresh memory."

2.1	Balance sheet primarily consists of accounts receivable and inventory.
2.2	Installations in process are significant.
2.3	Large increase in total assets.
2.3.1	Current assets increased by $2 million.
2.3.1.1	Accounts receivable increased by $700,000.
2.3.1.2	Inventory increased by $550,000.
2.3.1.3	Installations in process increased by $300,000.
2.3.2	Property has increased by $1.3 million.
2.3.2.1	Large increase may cause ITC which should reduce effective tax rates.
2.3.2.2	Examines footnote to determine what was acquired.
2.3.2.2.1	Bought automobiles, furniture shop equipment and leaseholds, most of which would not be eligible for ITC, which indicates the reason for no decrease in the effective tax rate.

EPISODE 3: Review of substantive audit program for nontrade notes and other receivables.

3.1	Deletes the "Approach Section" because it does not add anything and is covered in other parts of the audit.
3.2	Deletes the internal audit section because it is obvious.
3.3	Reads audit objectives and says they are fine.
3.4	Step on internal accounting control is adequate.
3.5	Objective A, Step 1.
3.5.1	NATURE: Have client prepare reconciliation and check it.
3.5.1.1	If schedules are manually prepared, checks the total column and tests for aging.
3.5.1.2	If it is an automated system and our compliance tests show that the system has not been updated and we have checked arithmetical accuracy in prior years, then I would consider reducing scope.
3.5.1.3	But it is probably a manual system.
3.5.1.4	So it is a good step.
3.5.2	TIMING: Should be done at preliminary.
3.5.3	Determines that he is getting ahead of himself and decides to go back and read all the steps under Objective A and search case to determine if the client has an EDP system before making any decisions.

3.5.4 NATURE: Checks the arithmetical accuracy of the detailed schedules and reviews the reconciliation with the general ledger requesting the client to the reconciliation. Reviews support for significant reconciling items to the general ledger.

3.5.5 TIMING: Should be done at preliminary.

3.6 Objective A, Step 2.

3.6.1 Changes Step 2 to read "for new notes in excess of $25,000 originating in fiscal 1980." (Performed at preliminary.)

3.6.2 Adds the following new step: "Inquire whether notes outstanding, which were on hand at February 28, 1979, have been amended and review related amendments if significant." (Performed at preliminary.)

3.7 Objective A, Step 3.

3.7.1 Determines that notes receivable has an immaterial Step 2 using a materiality of $25,000 (the materiality amount is based upon a consideration of 9 million in assets and 600,000 net income) so that too much audit attention is not directed at an insignificant account. (See 3.6.1.)

3.7.2 Adds Step 3A which reads: "Scope of confirmations would be balances greater than $25,000, and all new notes. (Performed at preliminary.)

3.8 Objective A, Step 4 is fine. (Performed at preliminary.)

3.9 Objective A, Step 5.

3.9.1 Adds "have client investigate . . ." (Performed at preliminary.)

3.9.2 Adds Step 5A which reads: "Ascertain whether payments are timely and review cash receipts for last payment received at November 30. (Performed at preliminary.)

3.10 Objective A, Step 6.

3.10.1 Adds "have client . . ." (Performed at preliminary.)

3.11 Objective A adds the following steps to be performed at Final:

1. Have client prepare rollforward schedule indicating payments received and new notes extended in the rollforward period.
2. Perform preliminary Step 2 per notes over scope.
3. Review reconciliation to general ledger at February 28, and review support for reconciling items if significant and tie to general ledger.
4. Consider confirming large new notes.

3.12 Objective B, Step 1.

3.12.1 Adds the following: "Have the company prepare a listing of notes and other receivables with balances greater than 5,000 and in arrears at November 30." (Performed at preliminary.)

3.12.2 Changes remaining part of Step 2 to only ascertain the collectibility of the balances that are listed.

3.13 Objective B, Step 2.

3.13.1 Deletes the following: "Review delinquent balances."

3.14 Objective B, Step 3.

3.14.1 Determines that Step 3 is redundant with Objective A and alters Step 3 as follows: "For those accounts listed in the schedule in Step 1, examine supporting documents for significant payments and retirements." (Performed at preliminary.)

3.15 Objective B, Step 4 is fine as is. (Performed at preliminary.)

3.16 Objective B, Step 5 is fine as is. (Performed at preliminary.)

3.17 Objective B, Step 6 is fine as is. (Performed at preliminary.)

3.18 The following steps would be added to Objective B to be performed at Final:

1. Have client update the preliminary schedule.
2. Examine supporting documents for additions to the schedule of payments and retirements, including those after balance sheet date.
3. Perform preliminary steps 4-6 for update of their rollforward activity.

3.19 Objective C: Do not perform any of Objective C at preliminary, change all steps to be performed at Final.

3.19.1 Changes Step 1 to read as follows:"Test the client's computation of current/noncurrent classification by reviewing payment terms for all new notes over 25,000 in the current year and large notes outstanding from prior year."

3.19.2 Step 2 is fine as is.

3.20 Objective D.

3.20.1 Reviews footnote 3 in 1980 financial statements.

3.20.2 Step 1 is fine as is.

3.20.3 Adds the following to Step 2: "by performing an overall test of interest income based on average note balance outstanding."

EPISODE 4: Review of substantive audit program for revenue cycle—sales, shipping, trade receivables, cash receipts.

4.1 Deletes the "Approach" and "Internal Accounting Control" sections because they should be considered when drafting a program and should not be included in the program itself.

4.2 Objective A, Step 1.

4.2.1 Concludes that the controls are not adequate to do preliminary work.

4.2.1.1 Looks back through the case to determine if controls are adequate. Concludes that the controls are adequate based on an evaluation of the accounting systems. Thus changes mind.

4.2.2 Adds the following to Step 1: "Have the client reconcile the balance with the general ledger."

4.2.3 Deletes the last sentence in Step 1.

4.3 Adds the following to Objective A, Step 2: "using the following scope: (a) all balances in excess of $(blank), (b) (blank) other accounts selected judgmentally with a desired coverage 30-40%, (c) for accounts selected for confirmation agrees balance to detailed records, and (d) Step 3 of Objective B.

4.3.1 No change in scope.

4.4 Objective A, Step 3 is changed to read as follows: "Check replies to confirmations and have client investigate exceptions. Review exceptions. Support all exceptions over (blank). See senior for scope."

4.4.1 No change in scope.

4.5 Objective A, Step 4 is fine as is. No change in scope.

4.6 Objective A Step 5 is fine as is.

4.7 Adds the following to Objective A, Step 6: "for invoices in excess of $(– blank). See senior for scope."

4.8 Objective A, Step 7 is fine as is.

4.9 Objective A, Step 8 is fine as is.

4.10 Objective A, Step 9 is changed to read as follows: "Have the client foot all credit balances and consider reclassification."

4.11 Objective B, Step 1 is fine as is.

4.12 Adds the following to Objective B, Step 2: "to ascertain that controller approval for write-offs was obtained in writing."

4.13 Objective B, Step 3 is performed under Objective A, Step 2.

4.14 Objective B, Step 4 is fine as is.

4.15 Objective B, Step 5.

4.15.1 Notes that the comparison of the ratio of days in accounts receivable with others in the industry is very difficult to do since the comparison groups within the industry are often not comparable. Thus Step 5 is probably not worth the effort.

4.15.2 Since the step was performed in the program last the prior auditors must have had confidence in the comparison and so the step should be left in.

4.16 Objective B, Step 6.

4.16.1 Subject recalls that aging of accounts receivable has deteriorated significantly and the reserve for bad debt has gone up slightly and given the size of the company's receivables, he decides to make changes in Step 6.

4.16.2 Step 6 is changed to read as follows: "Have the client prepare a schedule for all accounts with balances over 90 days old, over $10,000. Discuss collectibility of receivables with appropriate officials, check for subsequent receipts, have client indicate subsequent receipts and review applicable correspondence. Have the client indicate their estimate of reserve required."

4.16.3 Scope decision.

4.16.3.1 Since there has been a deterioration of accounts receivable, should look closer at accounts receivable.

4.16.3.2 Accounts receivable are twice the size as the prior year. May not want to change scope since materiality is going up.

4.16.3.3 Days outstanding of accounts receivable are significantly higher than prior years.

4.16.3.4 Receivable turnover is down from previous years.

4.16.3.5 Using the same dollar scope will result in a greater number of accounts reviewed since the balance has almost doubled. The increased number of accounts is appropriate due to the deterioration of accounts receivable.

4.17 Objective B, Step 7 is fine as is.

4.18 Objective B, Step 8 is fine as is.

4.19 Objective C, Step 1: Not necessary to do monthly. It should be adequate to perform the step on an annual basis by product line.

4.20 Objective C, Step 2.

4.20.1 Adds: "Inquire whether there are any changes from the prior year, and determine their acceptability."

4.20.2 Could be combined with revenue test.

4.20 Objective C is fine as is, but could be combined with Step 2.

4.21 Objective D, Step 1 is fine as is.

4.22 Objective D, Step 2.

4.22.1 This is a good procedure that needs to be done, but the client should do it since it is too expensive to have the auditor footing the sales register.

4.23 Objective D, Step 3 is fine as is.

4.24 Objective D, Step 4.

4.24.1 Sales have increased slightly even in face of a discontinued operation.

4.24.2 Subject decides to delete Step 4 but adds a review of unusual items to Step 1 when the sales register is initially reviewed.

4.25 Objective D, Step 5 is fine and uses the same scope as last year.

4.26 Objective D, Step 6 is fine and uses the same scope as last year.

4.27 Objective D, Step 7.

4.27.1 Adds the following: "Ascertain whether the number of credit memos is comparative to prior year."

4.28 Objective E, Step 1 is fine and uses the same scope as last year.

4.29 Objective E, Step 2 is adequate.

4.30 Objective F.

4.30.1 Objective F should be performed in connection with compliance test in Objective D.

4.30.2 Step 1 is fine, same scope.

4.30.3 Step 2 changes to indicate that a comptometer operator should check the footings. No change in scope.

4.30.4 Step 3 is fine, no change in scope.

4.31 Objective G, Step 1.

4.31.1 Since there are C.O.D. sales, definitely needs to ensure that cash receipts are recorded in the proper period.

4.31.2 There could be a duplication of effort unless the cutoff includes both cash and trade sales. Therefore, it should be changed to say "review cash sales cash receipts to differentiate it from cash receipts on receivables."

4.31.3 Same scope as last year since this does not have anything to do with receivable deterioration.

4.32 Objective G, Step 2.

4.32.1 Should make sure there is no duplication of effort.

4.32.2 This step should be covered on the interbank/intercompany cutoff schedule. Thus the work is probably duplicated in this step.

4.33 The conclusion is fine.

EPISODE 5: Review of substantive audit program for production costs and inventories.

5.1 Deletes the "Approach" and "Internal Accounting Control" sections following a consistent rationale used in eliminating these sections on all prior programs.

5.2 Internal accounting control.

5.2.1 Good step since inventory has gone up $600,000.

5.3 Objective A, Step 1.

5.3.1 Modifies Step 1 to indicate that the client's procedures for inventory should be ascertained and evaluated before the physical inventory is taken, and if any are deficient, they should be corrected.

5.4 Objective A, Step 2.

5.4.1 Inventory turnover has decreased and gross profit percentage has increased a small amount.

5.4.2 Step 2a should be changed by adding the following: "... compare to tags and record (blank number) of test counts for comparison with listing."

5.4.3 Step 2b is not necessary and should be eliminated. It is partially redundant with Step 2a.

5.4.4 Replaces Step 2c with the following: "Obtain client's tag control listing. Examine all unused and voided tags. Select (blank number) of tags and locate merchandise items and the tag."

5.4.4.1 This is a population test of the tags that checks floor to tag and tag to floor.

5.4.4.2 The scope would be the same as prior year.

5.4.5 Adds the following to Step 2d: "and slow moving items including inquiries with warehouse production personnel."

5.4.5.1 Due to the decrease in inventory turnover, there should be an increased scope.

5.4.6	Step 2e is fine.
5.4.7	Step 2f is fine.
5.5	Objective A, Step 3a.
5.5.1	Insert at the beginning of the step: "Have comptometer operator check the arithmetical accuracy?"
5.6	Objective A, Step 3b is fine.
5.7	Objective A, Step 3c.
5.7.1	Adds: "do a physical inventory tag control listing."
5.8	Objective A, Step 3d is fine.
5.9	Adds the following to Objective A, Step 3e: "have client reconcile total and review."
5.10	Adds the following to Objective A, Step 3f: "and audit as necessary."
5.11	Objective A, Step 3g is fine.
5.12	Objective A, Step 3h is fine.
5.13	Objective B, Step 2.
5.13.1	The step is fine.
5.13.2	Due to the lower inventory turnover, would want to increase scope with the express purpose of identifying slow moving goods.
5.14	Objective B, Step 2.
5.14.1	This step should be eliminated since it is not relevant to a retail firm.
5.15	Objective B, Step 3.
5.15.1	This step should be eliminated since it is not relevant to a retail firm.
5.16	Objective B, Step 4.
5.16.1	This step should be eliminated since it is not relevant to a retail firm.
5.17	Objective B, Step 5.
5.17.1	This step should be eliminated since it is not relevant to a retail firm.
5.18	Objective C, Step 1.
5.18.1	Deletes "raw materials and work-in-process" since these inventories are not relevant to a retail firm.
5.19	Objective C, Step 2 is fine.
5.20	Objective C, Step 3.
5.20.1	Deletes this step since any adjustment should go to cost of sales.
5.21	Objective C, Step 4 is fine.
5.22	Objective C, Step 5.
5.22.1	This step should be deleted since it is not relevant to a retail firm.
5.23	Objective C, Step 6.
5.23.1	If this were an SEC client, Step 6 would be performed, but since it is not the step does not need to be performed. Also, Step 2 should identify any unusual fluctuations. Therefore delete this step.

5.24 Objective D, Step 1.

5.24.1 Deletes Step 1 since it is covered in Step 2.

5.25 Objective D, Step 2 is fine.

5.26 Objective D, Step 3.

5.26.1 The subject does not think replacement cost is necessary.

5.26.2 Scope should be increased due to the decrease in inventory turnover.

5.27 Objective D, Step 4.

5.27.1 Step 4 is basically the same as Step 3, a NRV test. Therefore, the two steps should be combined.

5.28 Adds new steps in the program.

5.28.1 The new Step 5 would read as follows: "Review gross profit by product line schedule received in Step 2."

5.28.2 Comments on new Step 5: However, the gross profit has increased so the declining inventory turnover is probably a case of slow moving inventory rather than an actual net realizable value problem.

5.28.3 The new Step 6 reads as follows: "Perform usage test by reviewing historical usage of products and inventory on hand and budgeted sales. Ascertain the company's slow moving reserve policy. Consider purchase commitments and open sales orders. (i.e., write down 50% if there is more than one year usage, or that portion that is over one year worth of usage; write down 75% on two years; and 100% on three years.)"

5.28.4 The new Step 7 reads as follows: "Based on NRV usage tests consider reserve needed."

5.28.5 The usage tests (Steps 6 and 7) are similar to Step 4, but they may be mixing the usage test with the NRV tests.

5.29 Scopes on NRV tests and usage tests (all steps in Objective D) should remain the same since gross profit is fine.

5.30 Objective E.

5.30.1 Deletes Step 6 since it is not applicable to retail firms.

5.30.2 Steps 1 through 5 are fine and scopes should be the same as prior year.

EPISODE 6: Review of substantive audit program for purchasing cycle—purchasing, receiving, accounts payable, cash disbursements.

6.1 Deletes "Approach" and "Internal Accounting Control" sections.

6.2 Reads objectives.

6.2.1 Objective C totally interfaces with inventory.

6.3 Objective A.

6.3.1 Changes Step 1 to indicate that the comptometer operator would perform the step.

6.3.2 Step 2 is great, leave scope the same.

6.3.2.1	Adds the following to the end of Step 2: "for those accounts that were selected for confirmation, compare them to the individual accounts payable records."
6.3.3	Step 3 is fine, no change in scope.
6.3.4	Step 4 is fine, no change in scope.
6.3.5	Changes Step 5 to read as follows: "Have client foot all debit balances and consider reclassification and reasons for debit balances for duplicate payment implications."
6.3.6	Step 6 is fine, no change in scope.
6.3.7	Step 7 is redundant with the receiving cutoff in the inventory area.
6.4	Objective B.
6.4.1	Step 1 is fine, no change in scope.
6.4.2	Step 1 is fine, no change in scope.
6.4.3	Step 3 is fine, no change in scope.
6.4.4	Step 4 is fine, no change in scope.
6.4.5	Adds new Step 5: "Separate test for payroll accrual."
6.4.5.1	For a company of this type, it should have a separate payroll test.
6.4.6	Adds new Step 6: "Perform property tax accrual test."
6.4.6.1	In California, you must have a separate step for property tax accrual.
6.4.7	Adds new Step 7: "Confirm insurance coverage adequacy and accrual."
6.5	Objective C.
6.5.1	Changes Step 1 to read as follows: "Have comptometer operator check footings . . ." No change in scope.
6.5.2	Step 2 is fine, no change in scope.
6.5.3	Adds the following to Step 3: "and examine supporting documents indicating that all cash discounts were received and inventory stock status was properly updated. Relate to cancelled checks."
6.5.3.1	This is part of the compliance disbursements tests.
6.5.3.2	Scope should not change since there have been no significant changes in the system.
6.5.4	Step 4 is fine.
6.5.4.1	This is part of the compliance disbursements tests.
6.5.4.2	Scope should not change since there have been no significant changes in the system.
6.6	Objective D.
6.6.1	Step 1 is fine, no change in scope.
6.6.1.1	This step is really part of the compliance tests but it is also fine under Objective D.
6.6.2	Step 2 is great, no change in scope.
6.6.3	Step 3.

6.6.3.1	Have comptometer operator perform this test.
6.6.3.2	No change in scope.
6.6.4	Step 4 is fine, no change in scope.
6.6.4.1	Initially thinks this step is only appropriate if the cash balance is valid. However he notes that other steps would determine if the cash balance was valid, so concludes that this step is valid regardless of the validity of the cash balance.
6.6.5	Conclusion is fine. Sales by product line.

EPISODE ABSTRACTS FOR SUBJECT S1

PHASE 1

EPISODE 1: Sequential search and evaluation of the planning memo.

1.1 Reads case study, Part I (Case Study Overview).

1.1.1 Concludes some additional internal control work may need to be done based on evaluation of fact that previous in-charge auditor, who did internal control, just left audit.

1.2 Reads case study, Part II (Planning Workpaper). Generates a few queries and general audit decisions (e.g., something to follow-up on).

1.2.1 Concludes that obsolescence is a concern.

1.2.2 Concludes that he will have to watch the credit reviews based on the fact that client maintains own credit department.

1.2.3 Identifies covenant agreements and fixed assets as areas "to look at".

1.2.4 Repeats credit review concern.

1.2.5 Based on cue that client has some EDP files, considers using firm audit software.

1.2.6 Considers using sampling if client is using LIFO.

1.2.7 Concludes that client's staff is "fairly well educated" and audit time budget is one month.

1.2.8 It is "great" that client's internal auditor's work may be relied on.

1.2.9 Considers using internal auditor for other areas.

1.2.10 Concludes that planned timing of audit program (specifically the interim work with one or two months rollforward) is inappropriate.

1.2.11 Suggests that cost of rollforward work exceeds value of interim work.

1.2.12 Generates some alternatives to general planned audit approach in planning memo.

1.3 Reads (sequential search) case study, Part 3 (Summary of Compliance Tests). Generates a number of audit decisions concerning internal accounting control evaluation weaknesses.

1.3.1 Suggests that a substantive rather than reliance audit may be more efficient.

1.3.2 Feels that reliance is not necessary regarding equipment audit.

1.3.3 Rationale for previous decision.

1.3.4 Generates alternative possible audit tests to counteract control weakness.

1.3.5 Reiterates audit decision to do detailed credit procedures regarding identified weakness in client's credit policy.

1.3.6 Identifies possible rollforward problem based on weakness in shipping log.

1.3.7 Generates possible management letter comment and use of EDP regarding shipping weakness.

1.3.8	Concludes parts manager weakness is definitely a problem.
1.3.9	Suggests an inventory will address problem.
1.3.10	Suggests payroll weakness may lead to inventory valuation problem.
1.3.11	Decides if inventory needed.

EPISODE 2: Comparative analysis and general analytical review of unaudited (1980) and audited (1979) financials.

2.1	Comparative analysis of financials with some implications to audit program.
2.1.1	Comparison and evaluation of significant 79 and 80 accounts regarding amount and relevance of change.
2.1.2	Reiteration of need to confirm A/P at year end and take physical inventory based on "dramatic" change in accounts payable.
2.1.3	Decides that decrease in interest will be audited through confirmations and that discontinued operations must be addressed.
2.2	Directed evaluation of audit approach based upon unclear search process. Seems to focus on 1) material accounts and 2) a balance sheet approach. Puts a great deal of emphasis on the staff time budget related to suggested changes.
2.2.1	Decides to start with receivables.
2.2.2	Suggests and concludes on a number of alternatives for auditing A/R including the use of statistical specialists, computer-aided auditing, and changes in timing.
2.2.3	Specifies estimated time budget requirements.
2.2.4	Decides to use an analytical review of monthly sales primarily to assist in establishing sampling criteria.
2.2.5	Selects cash side of receivables to analyze next.
2.2.6	Selects and evaluates tracing of cash receipts as appropriate procedure.
2.2.7	Decides to emphasize collectibility of AR "for credit side".
2.2.8	Specifies several audit steps to assess collectibility of AR.
2.2.9	Selects inventory to evaluate next (using materiality search criterion).
2.2.10	Based on IR concerning several weaknesses in internal control relating to inventory, decides to change timing of taking inventory to year end.
2.2.11	Reviews available details on inventory and suggests several audit steps and possible ways of using a computer to be more efficient.
2.2.12	Specifies a number of ARPs that would be useful in inventory area (most based on monthly data). Interruption from researcher noting some quarterly, but no monthly data are available.
2.2.13	Considers other inventory ARPs, but again researcher notes data is not available.
2.3	Turns his attention to specifying a staff time budget (including audit timing considerations).
2.3.1	Sets goal to timing and time table.

2.3.2	Considers and evaluates various timing issues.
2.3.3	Generates query regarding existence of"any detailed information". Researcher interrupts and directs him to supplemental schedules at end of case.

EPISODE 3: Review supplemental, quarterly data at end of case.

3.1	Evaluation of supplemental schedule of sales analysis and AR aging.
3.1.1	Evaluates changes in schedule and draws a few audit implications.
3.1.2	Decides to definitely look at AR allowance, the aging, and some ratios relating to sales and AR.
3.2	Evaluation of supplemental operating expense schedule.
3.2.1	Evaluates schedule, finds little which effects audit.
3.2.2	Suggests "reasonableness tests" for ARP of depreciation.
3.3	Evaluation of supplemental quarterly financial statements for 1976 through 1979.
3.3.1	Search through and evaluation of condensed statements.
3.3.2	Specifies a number of alternatives and decisions for ARPs: Gross margin as a % by quarter, 4-year percentage income statements, 4-year aging with percents, bad debts as a % of sales, and 4 years current ratio.
3.4	Explains substantive audit approach to researcher.
3.5	Final review of Phase 1 by going down balance sheet and considering his Phase 1 decisions.

PHASE 2

EPISODE 1: Review of analytical review results requested during Phase 1.

1.1	Evaluation of ARP results.
1.2.1	Evaluation of ARP results regarding significance to audit.
1.2.2	Identifies cutoff and obsolescence and variance in gross profit percent as areas of concern.

EPISODE 2: Evaluate audit program for revenue cycle.

2.1	Brief review of case study.
2.2	Decides to do revenue cycle first based on materiality evaluation.
2.3	Reviews or retrieves cues concerning revenue cycle control weaknesses.
2.4	Decides to take a substantive approach to auditing receivables. (No direct link to ARP results).
2.5	Begins evaluating audit objectives and procedures in revenue cycle.
2.6	Decides to change timing of confirmations to May 31, but writes 1/31 on audit program. Also, specifies 5/31, 1/31, and 2/28 as dates to evaluate aged listing.

2.7	Suggests use of computer audit software.
2.8	Decides to set sample sizes next.
2.9	Decides that sample sizes "definitely" are going to increase.
2.10	Discusses logic in arriving at a sample size including setting materiality (gauge) and making internal control reliance judgment.
2.11	Calculates sample at 95, but evaluates this as "way out of line".
2.12	Generates and considers alternatives to sample size including gratification, DUS, and interpreting "firm guidelines are just used as a guideline".
2.13	Guesses that sample size for confirmations would be around 40 to 50 under revised approach.
2.14	Begins to look at other objectives. Ends up evaluating last objective in this section of audit program (proper cash cutoff).
2.15	Decides to make some adjustments to audit program in this section: e.g., adding rollforward steps (but again no explicit tie to ARP information).
2.16	Read objective F (note reverse sequential search).
2.17	Following INTERRUPTION, goes back to Objective A and begins evaluation of confirmations.
2.18	Evaluates and considers fine tuning to confirmation, specifically sampling considerations. (No obvious tie results.)
2.19	Begins reading and evaluation of Objective B: collectibility and valuation of trade receivables.
2.20	Decides to look into any post year-end credits.
2.21	Sets timing for all related tests at 2/28 (year end).
2.22	Adds analysis of aging for 3-4 years.
2.23	Reads Audit Step 2, (note sequential search through steps under each objective) and on to Step 3 (test aging of AR).
2.24	Generates and considers a number of alternatives regarding step. (Researcher "reminds" him to specify increases or decreases.) Decides to test 20 items from 2/28 aging using computer and to review, say, all AR balances greater than 60 and greater than $10,000.
2.25	Reads Step 5 (Compute days sales and compare to previous years.)
2.26	Evaluates this as appropriate.
2.27	Reads Step 6 (Discuss collectibility with officials, check subsequent receipts, . . .).
2.28	Evaluates significance of aging problem referring partly to ARP results. (Seems to always use 60 days rule of thumb when evaluating aging and bad debt allowance).
2.29	Decides that scope would definitely be increased.
2.30	Reads Step 7 (...scan material charge-offs and unusual transactions).
2.31	Specifies materiality at $30,000-$50,000.
2.32	Reviews and evaluates Objective B as appropriate.

2.33	Reads Objective C, revenue cycle. (Evaluate method of recognizing revenue and related cost...)
2.34	Reads Step 1. (Obtain and check arithmetic fluctuations.)
2.35	Evaluates this as a "great analytical tool" and one which could reduce sample sizes "in 1 and 2". (Not clear what procedures could be reduced.)
2.36	Reads Objective 2.
2.37	Refers to previous financial statement review as not indicating anything significant.
2.38	Reads Step 3. (Investigate any large sales, contracts, etc.)
2.39	Considers and decides on alternatives concerning timing.
2.40	Evaluates this ARP as a "good tool".
2.41	Reads Objective D regarding proper recording of sales.
2.42	Evaluates steps as appropriate.
2.43	Reads Objective E (proper sales cutoff).
2.44	Step 1.
2.45	Expands upon Step 1 by specifying timing and sampling approach (judgment sample: traces 5 each of greater than $5,000 for both populations).
2.46	Reads Step 2 regarding review of subsequent credit memos. (Researcher then interrupts regarding query concerning whether the preceding decision was an increase or decrease. He remarks that he does not have previous scopes, but "bets" that they did not do as many and thus he is increasing.)
2.47	Decides that review of credit memos (also) needs to be increased.
2.48	Selects $10,000 as threshold to use in looking at credit memos.
2.49	Reads Step 3. (Ascertain that there is adequate provision for returns and warranties.)
2.50	Scans case for further data.
2.51	Decides that scope would need to be increased if this turns out to be a significant area.
2.52	Reads Objective F. (Proper recording and application of cash receipts.)
2.53	Evaluates both debit and credit side of transaction and generates a number of alternatives (tentative) including sampling. No explicit use of ARPs is evident.
2.54	Details how he should accomplish objective.

EPISODE 3: Review of substantive audit program for nontrade notes and other receivables.

3.1	Selects first area of audit program to evaluate next.
3.2	Searches and reads relevant parts of financials and introduction to this section of audit program.
3.3	Reads Objective A regarding physical existence and propriety of notes and other receivables.

3.4	Makes general decision that he would confirm.
3.5	Agrees with Step 1 to obtain schedule of notes and other receivables and reconcile.
3.6	Reads Step 2 (no explicit comments).
3.7	Decides that the first thing he would do is send confirmation and agree replies. (Step 3)
3.8	Based on calculation of total account balance, gauge, prior reliance decision, etc. Estimates necessary scope and specifies some contingent audit work depending on actual results.
3.9	Reads and agrees with Step 4, then specifies timing.
3.10	Reads Step 6 regarding employee receivables.
3.11	Concludes not much work likely is needed. [Researcher requests changes (increases).]
3.12	Specifies scope changes in Steps 3 and 6.
3.13	Reads Objective B (Collectibility and valuation of balances) and Step 1 (Ascertain collectibility through various approaches).
3.14	Conclusion on this is clear, except that timing should be year end.
3.15	Agrees that Step 2 needs to be done, and sets "scope" at $10,000, maybe $5,000. Concludes that "review process" and "steps" would have to be increased, but "scopes" would decrease.
3.16	Reads Step 3 regarding examining supporting documents for additions, etc., after balance sheet date.
3.17	Concludes step not needed unless certain contingencies occur. Specifies steps to be taken if they occur.
3.18	Reads Step 4 regarding reasonableness of interest rates.
3.19	Decides that an ARP would do using a reasonableness test comparing to previous years. (Notes that in addition to the ARPs, the auditors specified in Phase 1 many "substantive" ARPs are imbedded in substantive audit program.)
3.20	Step 5 regarding employee advances is deemed likely to be immaterial and thus NCN (not considered necessary).
3.21	Reads Objective C regarding proper classification as current/noncurrent.
3.22	Agrees with objective and gives some limited detail on his approach.
3.23	Reads Objective D regarding proper recognition or interest income.
3.24	Evaluates Step 1 as immaterial, but feels that an ARP directed at reasonableness is appropriate.

EPISODE 4: Review of substantive audit program for purchasing cycle.

4.1	Purchasing cycle audit program.
4.2	Reads all objectives, then Objective A.
4.3	Specifies all payable work for year end (timing).

4.4	Specifies computer-assisted approach for Step 1 (checking arithmetic accuracy, reconciliation with general ledger, etc.).
4.5	Read Step 2 regarding requesting statements from suppliers.
4.6	Concludes that understatement is a concern.
4.7	Generates alternative of confirming 7-10 largest balances rather than a sample.
4.8	Notes that this is an increase over last year.
4.9	Notes Step 4 regarding sending second requests.
4.10	Reads Step 5 regarding investigating material debit balances.
4.11	Specifies $10,000 as material.
4.12	Decides that ARP would be sufficient for step 6 (investigate employee, officer, payables) and evaluates as "usually not material".
4.13	Reads Step 7 regarding determining any payables that should be classed as non-current.
4.14	Lists other procedures and an alternate for accomplishing this objective.
4.15	Specifies materiality here as $30,000.
4.16	Evaluates Objective B (All for goods or services received are recorded) as a "big thing".
4.17	Decides that "scope" (probably meaning "precision" or size of threshold) must decrease for this objective.
4.18	Reads Step 1 regarding checking proper cutoff by reviewing vendors invoices pre and post balance sheet date.
4.19	Specifies details of procedure: materiality ($10,000), sample size (5), and decides scope would be increased.
4.20	Reads Step 2 regarding checking post balance sheet debit memos.
4.21	Decides that scope would increase, and to look at items greater than $10,000.
4.22	Reads Step 3 regarding search for unrecorded liabilities using a number of possible procedures.
4.23	Evaluates this as "my critical procedure".
4.24	S1 specifies in detail his approach for the AP part of this. Decisions include answering materiality scope to $5,000, etc.
4.25	For accruals, specifies "a more detailed analytical review", and goes on to suggest what that might entail.
4.26	Reads Step 4 regarding unfilled purchase orders.
4.27	Decides this step is something that must be addressed.
4.28	Generates two alternatives to specified procedure.
4.29	Scans Objective C regarding proper accounting for purchased goods.
4.30	Specifies a number of alternate procedures, including a detailed analytical review of all operating expenses, and concludes Objective C would be accomplished by these other procedures.

EPISODE 5: Review of substantive audit program for inventory.

5.1	Begins review of final portion of audit program.
5.2	Reviews, scans relevant parts of financial and planning workpapers regarding inventory.
5.3	Concludes internal control weakness is definitely a management letter comment, but of no additional concern at this time.
5.4	Returns to audit program, begins reading internal control section of inventory program.
5.5	Reiterates that internal control problems can be mitigated by the fact that substantive procedures will be performed at year end.
5.6	Recollects nature of warehouses.
5.7	Generates alternative on whether all warehouses need to be tested.
5.8	Decides to next calculate a sample size and distribution strategy.
5.9	Based on some previous data and evaluations, calculates a sample size of 126.
5.10	However, this is evaluated as being "a little high".
5.11	Searches for some alternative which would allow him to reduce sample size (e.g., segregating the high-ticket items). As in some other places, he is bothered by the lack of detail knowledge here.
5.12	Concludes this subepisode by restating that the sample size is too large, and suggesting 60-80 would be more typical for the given parameters for this case.
5.13	Reads Step 2c regarding checking accountability of inventory tags.
5.14	Suggests using computer assistance for this step.
5.15	Suggests other details for procedure.
5.16	States the possibility of obsolete inventory regarding Step 2d.
5.17	Conjectures on greater possibility of obsolescence based on analytical review cues.
5.18	Decides on a memo to senior if anything of this nature comes to his attention.
5.19	Reads Step 2e regarding determining whether all goods are counted.
5.20	Details appropriate audit procedures.
5.21	Reads Step 2f regarding listings of latest shipments, etc. for subsequent cutoff tests.
5.22	Conjectures that scopes are definitely going to increase and decides that two warehouses "would be fine".
5.23	Reads Step 3 regarding client's final extended inventory.
5.24	Suggests using computer-assisted techniques to do the footings, etc.
5.25	Concludes that these procedures within Step 3 would all have to be increased in lieu of (increased) amount of test work.
5.26	Reads Step 3f regarding client explanation of differences.
5.27	Details this procedure and some alternatives.

5.28	Concludes these steps do not apply to detailing.
5.29	Spends a lot of time considering the problem of overhead costs for this detailing firm. He states at one point that he has no experience in a retail environment! He assumes that if there are any overhead costs which are allocated to inventory, they are immaterial.
5.30	Reads Objective C regarding proper recording of cost of sales.
5.31	Notes, in an implicit reference to Step 1, that the part relating to work in process is not applicable.
5.32	Generates query regarding cost of sales analyses.
5.33	Searches out ARP results.
5.34	Evaluates gross margins, identifies some changes worth considering, conjectures product mix or pricing may have changed, decides it should be looked into.
5.35	Reads Step C2 regarding turnover and other ratios.
5.36	Concludes this is a "good item".
5.37	Specifies timing at year end.
5.38	Reads Step C3 regarding unusual entries.
5.39	Uses $10,000 again for materiality.
5.40	Reads Step C4 regarding unusual relations between inventory and other financial statement items.
5.41	Makes several general statements regarding this ARP.
5.42	Evaluates Steps C5 and C6 as basically not necessary.
5.43	Reads Objective D regarding reasonable inventory valuation.
5.44	Reads Step D1 regarding determining pricing methods.
5.45	Specifies several procedures to accomplish this: FIFO testing, a sample size of 20, computer-assisted techniques.
5.46	Reads Procedures D2, D3 and D4, valuates each briefly, and suggests the use of computer-assistance for D4.
5.47	Concludes again that these procedures should be increased over last year. (Note that S1 assumes last year was a limited scope audit and this year is a full scope audit.)
5.48	Reads Objective E regarding proper cutoff of purchases and sales.
5.49	Reads Steps E2 through E6 and briefly evaluates them and specifies a few more details.
5.50	Generates a query regarding dealer reserve and suggests this may need to be addressed and generates an alternative.
5.51	Concludes that with the above exception, "we can perform a substantive audit", covered in a different cycle such as cash disbursements. If not, it should be included.

EPISODE ABSTRACT FOR SUBJECT S2

PHASE 1

EPISODE 1: Review case overview to become familiar with the workpaper materials.

1.1	Assumes that this is his first year on the job.
1.2	Notes no AJEs from last year.
1.3	Attempts to understand company name and product lines.
1.4	Raises several questions including "what did they incur debt for? Are they planning to buy facilities?"
1.5	Indicates desire to know scopes and date for in-house receivables confirmation.
1.6	Raises possibility of testing nine or ten month numbers in order to reduce time in the field.
1.7	Assumes all inventory is held at one location, and that client will count inventory.
1.8	Indicates desire to go through inventory and make test counts looking for high dollar items.
1.9	Indicates desire to talk to people who do various kinds of tasks, e.g., bank deposit clerk to see effect on scope.
1.10	In a fixed asset area, indicates need to set capitalization scope.
1.11	Wants to talk to clerk applying cash receipts and sales and accounts receivable. Has questions regarding separation of duties.
1.12	Has concern over disbursements—need for double signatures.
1.13	Identifies areas where management improvement could be initiated, such as board of directors' approval for certain disbursements and the need for a job description judgmental.
1.14	Cites the need to re-evaluate their credit department policies for granting credit.
1.15	Raises possibility of multiple copy tags for shipping log control and support in detail.
1.16	Cites weaknesses in regard to upcoming merchandise not always being checked; wants to see it checked against purchase order and receiving, shipping reports.
1.17	Wants to know what the policies and procedures are relating to payroll.
1.18	Wants to know total number of employees and breakdown by retail store and warehouse.
1.19	Wants to apply principles of FASB 43 to payroll operation.

EPISODE 2: Evaluate 1980 financial statements.

2.1	Assume that client prepares statements.
2.2	Begins with balance sheet.
2.3	Notes that cash is high.

2.4	Proceeds to evaluate accounts sequentially, comparing to 1979 on occasion.
2.5	Not sure what dealer reserves and installations in process are.
2.6	Notes payroll accrual and wants to see detail on the account.
2.7	In Increases/Decreases in working capital section, indicates the need to know more about the types of equipment and costs per unit.
2.8	As he becomes familiar with the client through the sequential review, he notes that the client is more commercial business-oriented than consumer-oriented.
2.9	Indicates that he should probably test operating versus capital lease determination.

EPISODE 3: Evaluate financial statements of remaining years.

3.1	Decides that since the audit opinion only has two paragraphs, it is a clean opinion.
3.2	Wants a plant tour or warehouse tour, so he can become familiar with operations and the job.
3.3	Requests dividend history.
3.4	Goes through a deductive process of identifying balance sheet and income statement items. For example, he asks "what is equipment?" and then, through a deductive process, answers the question.
3.5	Begins to go through 1978 and older financial statements, but concludes that most of the useful information will be found in 1980 and 1979 statements.
3.6	Tries basically a scanning approach to see if anything makes an impression—a pattern recognition strategy.
3.7	Wants the credit manager to prepare a schedule of accounts receivable greater than $5,000 and 90 days past due.
3.8	Determines that evaluating the bad debt reserve is the major portion of the audit.
3.9	Request percentage total figures of the AR aging.
3.10	For supplies, operating supplies, rent expenses (1980), concludes that they are awfully high. Wants to spend time with credit manager discussing credit policy. Wants knowledge of credit department procedures in evaluating potential costumers.
3.11	Identifies the need to look at industry data for bad debt expense, receivables, and turnover.
3.12	Observes salaries and wages at 50% of total expenses; wants to develop a predictive test and determine extent of vacation accrual.
3.13	Wants more detail on supplies expense.
3.14	Looks at condensed statement of income for 1976-1979; wants to look at gross profit percentages by quarter.
3.15	Looks at 1978-1979 comparisons and asks for more percentages on other financial statement items.

3.16 After going through all financials once, makes requests: more industry information, and development of tests to apply to receivables and related accounts and inventory.

3.17 Wants to know more about the contents of inventory.

3.18 Determines that the major area of audit concern is the receivables, including credit procedures and bad debt expense.

3.19 Identifies debt area as a significant audit area.

3.20 Identifies two major areas of audit risk: inventory and receivables and their related P & L accounts.

3.21 Wants to look into tax requirements and tax workpapers.

3.22 Wants to do more risk analysis.

3.23 Request the following information for Phase 2: Industry statistics, Pacific Electronics history (more detail), number of employees, if there is a union, breakdown of accounts payable and accrued expenses. Also copy of policies, list of suppliers, all standard ratios, (states he wants all available information to have and then discard unimportant, this is consistent with his scanning, exception strategy.)

PHASE 2

EPISODE 1: Review the analytical review material requested.

1.1 Compare financial ratios to industry median.

1.2 Opens up 1980 balance sheet as point of reference.

1.3 Notes that inventory turnover ratio has been on a decline from a high in 1977 to near industry average in 1980.

1.4 Notes that AR turnover is 10 compared to industry average of 18; indicating support for deterioration of PE AR quality.

1.5 Notes lengthening of collection period from 36 to 75 days, compared to industry average of 20; adding to evidence supporting deterioration of AR.

1.6 Notes that PE's acid test is lower than industry, concludes that this is evidence of more debt.

1.7 Notes gross profit percentage is near industry and is stable.

1.8 Evaluates aging of AR as percent of gross AR and goes through an iterative analysis looking for trends; notes evidence of slight deterioration of AR.

1.9 Evaluates gross profit percentages, financial ratios based on annual data.

1.10 Asks for industry information on bad debt expense (is told it is not available so goes to next step).

EPISODE 2: Evaluation of audit program.

2.1 States that considerable time be spent looking at credit function and collectibility of bad debts.

2.2 Expresses concern that total liabilities/assets is considerably higher than the industry.

2.3 Reads through the entire audit program to familiarize himself.

EPISODE 3: Review of substantive audit program for nontrade notes and other receivables.

3.1 First steps he notes are to obtain and check the accuracy of the schedules.

3.1.1 Assumes that PE generates all schedules by computer, and that they have proper controls and therefore the numbers on the schedules are accurate and need no verification.

3.1.2 If computerized, tie only to G/L.

3.2 First audit step is to tie balances to general ledger or to lead schedules (depending on how audit was set up).

3.3 Next audit step is to inspect notes and other agreements and examine related collateral on hand for agreements added during the current year.

3.3.1 Also wants to inquire as to changes in existing notes.

3.4 Combines Audit Steps 3, 4, 5 on the current audit program into one audit step.

3.4.1 Comments that undelivered requests for confirmations would be treated as non-replies.

3.5 Changes last step in Audit Objective A to exclude obtaining a schedule of notes to officers and employees based on assumption of immateriality. Perhaps should comment or make a note such as employee advances on the lead schedule. Key is whether the notes are between related parties. If material, he would consider confirmations to officers/employees.

3.6 Audit Objective B.

3.7 No change on Step 1.

3.8 Makes Step 2 a subset of Step 1 labeled 1A (relates to the review of delinquent balances).

3.8.1 Offers some rationale to the effect that any collectibility problems would likely come up with discussions with the client.

3.9 Eliminates Step 3, since he combined the intent into Objective A1.

3.10 For Step 4, he would compare interest rates between years. For new notes, he would trace rates to agreements.

3.11 Step 5: If advances are not material, he would not do anything; if material, he would confirm amounts or selected amounts.

3.12 Would combine Step 6 with Step B2.

3.13 Audit Objective C.

3.14 Scans the balance sheet and note 3, and concludes that the way to accomplish Step 1 is to look at the agreements for a span of time and require the client to generate a schedule listing each individual note repayment date. Would then test it using a couple of agreements.

3.15 Not comfortable with Step C2; confused by its meaning and would talk to the audit manager about it.

3.16 Objective D.

3.17 If the client has a large number of similar type sales, then should address Objective D with one overall predictive test of interest income.

3.17.1 Rationale is because we know the rate, the beginning and ending balances, the test could be refined down to month-end balance which could be divided by 13 and then apply the average interest rate.

3.17.2 If interests are all over the board, prepare a schedule listing interest rates and payments received.

3.18 For Step D2, compares interest between years and go for predictive tests.

3.19 Makes no changes to the conclusion section.

3.19.1 Notes that now he has gone through the key risks, believes the two areas of concern are classification of current and long-term collectibility. Also, advocates the use of one big predictive test to lay to rest interest income.

EPISODE 4: Revenue of substantive audit program for revenue cycle.

4.1 Goes through list of procedures under approach and eliminates those which do not apply to PE.

4.1.1 Retains for consideration special discounts and rebates, long-term contracts and installment sales.

4.2 Audit objectives for revenue cycle.

4.2.1 Again notes problems in PE with collectibility, aging and credit policies on receivables.

4.3 Objective A, Trade receivables.

4.4 Eliminates the need to foot listing of receivables, will scan for any material noticeable problems; will tie listing to G/L.

4.4.1 Does not know what to do with portion of step dealing with selected individual accounts with detail trade receivable records. Would prefer to look for high dollar accounts in the listing, but would not do a specific revenue test, other than confirmation.

4.5 For Step 2, confirmation, would increase the scope in 1980 because of the $600,000 increase in the AR balance.

4.6 Would combine Steps 2 through 7 into one step.

4.6.1 As part of the current Step 7, would summarize results by both dollars and number of responses, and then look at percentages. Would provides examples of how he would calculate these items.

4.6.2 Rationale for Step 7 is to make conclusions based on the whole population of receivables.

4.7 Step 8. Not sure about this step and would therfore have some detailed discussions with the controller as to the nature and procedures.

4.8 Likes Step 9, and would request a computerized report to evaluate total with respect to materiality.

4.9 Objective B.

4.10 Feels this is a most important area and adds several steps different than the original audit program.

4.10.1 Wants to review computerized listing.

4.10.2 Wants to look at aging totals (from supplemental schedules).

4.10.3 Will then select some scope-like accounts over $10,000 and over 90 days past due, and have the credit manager prepare a schedule listing over the account; will sit down with him and do a specific account-by-account collectibility analysis.

4.10.3.1 Will then begin to determine if his bad debt reserve was adequate.

4.11 Returns to Step 2 and wants to look at what was written off during the year. For significant items, would talk to the credit manager. Would not spend much time with accounting people because he feels they would not know enough.

4.12 Would combine Step 3 and Step 1. Would compare between years and be done.

4.13 Does not comment on Step 4.

4.14 Regarding Step 5, would talk with both the credit manager and the controller (defined as top financial person under VP level).

4.15 Step 6 would be part of his step under 4.10, where he has the credit manager prepare a listing. He would want to see aging for 90, 120, and 180, and even further (even 360). He would add a column to the schedule titled "Subsequent payments", and would test those payments. For subsequent payment accounts, he is not concerned about collectibility, but would still look at it.

4.16 Would not do first part of Step 7 here, but would do it in connection with subsequent review work. Would retain the phase of the step involved with scanning of general ledger for unusual items. Would include discussions with the client, particularly in the area of unusual write-offs.

4.17 Would basically retain Step 8 and spend a fair amount of time looking at the reserve. Would utilize his specific review in Step 1, and have the client identify problems. Would then discuss these problems with the controller or credit manager. To summarize: he would go through, perform calculations of specific review, add client's identified problems and a general reserve, which would be aged between years. One percent of credit sales for the last twenty years is what would be called general reserve. Rationale for calculating general reserve is based on increases in receivables. Would calculate his reserve and compare it to the client's reserve and determine if an adjustment is needed.

4.18 Objective C.

4.19 For Step 1, would probably obtain the schedule, but does not think he would do much more than review and tie it in. Would catch the items that are significant variations and explain them in the review.

4.20 Step 2 does not seem to be a really big problem area; would compare between years, and discuss with the client.

4.21 For Step 3, assumes many customers and will rely on his confirmations.

4.22 Audit Objective D.

4.22.1 Generally feels that much of the work could be done in connection with some of the inventory procedures, and thus not much of the work would be done here.

4.23 Step 1 is fine, no change.

4.24 Step 2, would test on some type of scope basis, providing sales have been compared between years.

4.25 No change on Step 3.

4.26 Modifies Step 4 to either page through the listing or ask client if he is aware of any large items.

4.27 Notes that Step 5 is a type of revenue test and that the key is to make sure invoices are picked and then determine sales and accounts receivable. Also notes that we may want to look at inventory relief, but that would be done later.

4.28 For Step 6, depending on the environment, he may skip this step.

4.29 Might combine Step 7 and Step 5 and just pick a couple of credit memos. Would not spend a lot of time in this area.

4.30 Audit Objective E.

4.30.1 Feels that, to a degree, this objective will be done in the inventory work. Does not know if he would do much here, but would want to get a little more familiar with their inventory procedures. Should consider closing down for a few days to take inventory. Notes that he would not change the scope on invoices.

4.31 Step 1. Determines that he may want to test, but in connection with inventory, not in revenue cycle.

4.32 For Step 2, he comments that any material credit memos would be detected in the subsequent review but he would basically do this step here.

4.33 Would delete Step 3, depending on what is done in the inventory audit area.

4.34 Objective F.

4.34.1 Goes through a process of considering whether or not he could simply extend procedures under Step D5 by adding a column on the trade receivable records for subsequent payments and tracing it to the cash receipts book. Suggests that we probably get this information in the compliance work which is done at preliminary, whereas more of these steps seem to suggest final work. He would feel better about confirming receivables at year end.

4.35 Proceeds to steps 1, 2, 3, and jointly considers them. He concludes that the application of cash receipts would be done with the testing of invoices which is B5. One reason for not wanting to do a lot of work on the application of cash is that there is a built-in check against the misapplication of cash, e.g., customers who have paid and who get a statement showing they have not. He would lean toward a compliance test in the whole area of objective F at preliminary.

4.36 Audit Objective G. Considers Steps 1 and 2 together.

4.36.1 Concludes he would not do a specific testing in the revenue cycle of this, as much as would be done in the treasury cycle. Gives some rationale regarding cutoff bank statements and schedules of interbank transfers which would allow detection of undeposited accounts and shifts between accounts; so no work in the revenue cycle on cash. Does not comment on the conclusion.

EPISODE 5: Review of substantive audit program for production costs and inventory.

5.1.1 Goes through list of items under approach and identifies those relevant to PE: perhaps inventories billed to customers but stored on premises (check with client), and others as follows.

5.1.2 For goods stored in public warehouses, he would probably amend to make sure that the goods are counted in the retail units, would eliminate the need for cycle counts for perpetual inventories—does not apply to PE, since we take year-end physical. For contract work in progress, looks at this as installations in process and suggests that some testing be done. Inquires if there is any pledged inventory or debt that was not listed. Concludes that intercompany, intracompany profits are not appropriate for PE.

5.1.3 Audit objectives summary.

5.2 Eliminates Objective B, because the inventory would have no labour or overhead components since there is no manufacturing going on.

5.3 Makes summary statement that cutoff (Objective E) has already been looked at in the revenue section.

5.4 Audit Objective A.

5.4.1 Hopes that the client will give a copy of the inventory instructions and will invite auditors to sit in on the inventory meeting.

5.4.2 The inventory instructions should cover all locations where inventory is stored. Assumes ongoing engagement and thus does not expect surprises in taking the physical inventory.

5.4.3 Would request (if they have it) some type of detailed computer run of each type of inventory item, by part number.

5.4.4 Would also look at balance between years and, if possible, compare that to a forecast of sales to see if there is any obsolescence or slow-moving problem.

5.4.5 Would also address the inventory at the retail outlets: What is the dollar amount? Is it worth counting? Gives some rationale for these substeps, such as technological obsolescence, etc.

5.5 Steps 2a and 2b.

5.6 Would possibly increase test count scope, but basically regards this step as information rather than a step.

5.7 Step 2c.

5.8 Would get tag control and test that. Would also test both tags (but primarily inventory which is not included in this step) by selecting a number of tags from the physical inventory run, and would then go out on the floor and verify that those items exist. This would be in addition to test counts. He would find a number of tags on inventory on the floor and take it back to the physical inventory list and compare the two. He calls this a "tags-to-floor, floor-to-tags" test.

5.9 Step 2d.

5.10 Does not feel this is much of a step, just information.

5.11 Step 2e. Believes he would rely on the client's representation, and may want to stop by retail outlets and take a look.

5.12 Would do Step 2f as is.

5.13 Step 3. Would transfer his tags-to-floor, floor-to-tags" procedure from Step 2c to Step 3 here.

5.14 Step 3a. Does not feel the need to check for accuracy if the listing is computer-generated. He suggests an alternative test which is a master price file test which would price out the inventory for costing purposes. Also, wants to know if client's computer can generate a listing by part number by dollar value to show which part accounts for the highest dollar value portion of inventory. Rationale is that it may be looked at in connection with obsolescence review or he may just want to know what areas to concentrate other testing or even test counts. For example, take the prior years and count more of a particular part to get better coverage of total inventory in the count.

5.15 Would do Step 3b as is.

5.16 Step 3c. Would just sit down and compare the tags to the listing and would also go out to the floor.

5.17 Step 3d would just be part of tag control and we should be able to see the unused tags as part of the test to that.

5.18 Steps 3e and 3f. No comment on Step 3e. Would get a separate schedule, perhaps a descending dollar type, to find out what part had the biggest booked physical and inquire why. Would sit down with the client to determine what the difference was. He would expect a small booked physical, because everything coming in is finished, and he feels the client should be able to identify it from the time it is in the door until the time it is out the door; theft would not happen.

5.19 No change on Step 3g.

5.20 Step 3h. Would look for large extensions with small quantities and vice versa.

5.21 Audit Objective B.

5.22 Step 1. Crosses out the last sentence dealing with manufacturing processes, since it is not applicable to PE. Would extend test to deal with purchased items. Proposes some kind of test, just based on comparing the cost to the invoice.

5.23 Step 2 is not applicable to PE since merchandising firm.

5.24 Steps 3, 4, 5 are not applicable for same reason as 5.2.3.

5.25 Audit Objective C.

5.26	Step 1. Feels that this is covered in Step 1b.
5.27	Step 2. Feels that this step was already accomplished in the revenue cycle; the product line extension may be appropriate.
5.28	Steps 3 and 4. Believes these could be looked at in connection with gross.
5.29	Step 5 is not applicable since PE has no standard cost system.
5.30	Step 6 is dependent on previous findings; if he had cost of goods sold, he could test that by just looking at the invoices.
5.31	Objective D.
5.32	States that we already know the basis of pricing, LCM, but do not know the basis of determining market—would ask client.
5.33	Steps 2 and 3 are, for the most part, not applicable. Rationale is type of product line.
5.34	Step 4. Would do as previously recommended: obtain computerized listing by part between year, and compare to sales forecast.
5.35	Audit Objective E.
5.35.1	Under this heading, would like to have a copy of their inventory procedures in the workpapers, which would say "we are not receiving anything after 7 a.m. on Monday the 9th", as an example, so they would have something to test. Also, would like to see a memo from the individual(s) who took the physical inventory, on what they noted: any disturbances of inventory.
5.36	Steps 1 and 2, the general statement in 5.35.1 applies.
5.37	Step 3. Would confirm and test.
5.38	Step 4. Would add a time dimension, such as the time outstanding.
5.39	Step 5. Agrees with step as it stands.
5.40	Step 6. He feels it is not applicable to PE.
5.41	Conclusion: No specific comments about the conclusion, but states that he is bothered by the $600,000 increase between years in inventory, and wants to get a thorough coverage, especially in the high dollar areas. He (as previously stated in A2a) would increase the account scope because of the inventory increase. Would expand on the reasons in more detail. Would like to know their procedures for damaged goods, and feels key is existence in valuation, so they can beat the debt cutoffs in inventory, revenue or expenditure.

EPISODE 6: Review of substantive audit program for purchasing cycle—accounts payable and cash disbursements.

6.1	The general observation is that PE may not have consignments and intercompany transfers.
6.2	Audit objectives summary.
6.2.1	Adds another objective: Test the approval procedures over purchases. Rationale is he wants control over purchases.

6.2.2 Would compliance test the approval procedures and requisition procedures? Heavy compliance testing in this area can reduce substantive scope.

6.3 Audit Objective A, Step 1. Would only tie to G/L unless unusual items were noted per review. Would eliminate portion of step that says "compare a select number of individual accounts with detailed subsidiary accounts payable records." Rationale for tying to G/L only is he wants to do a disbursement test which he will explain later.

6.4 At this point, raises the question concerning the accounts payable balance, and provides further rationale for the decision in 6.3.

6.5 Steps 2, 3, and 4. Decides that these steps are not appropriate for PE. Rationale is that work in other areas would probably compensate for these steps and that confirming A/P is of little value.

6.6 Step 5. Agrees with step; would not modify.

6.7 Step 6. Only comments that he would not expect a lot of transactions to employees. The utilization of this step would depend on materiality.

6.8 Step 7. Simply comments that this issue would be resolved in discussions with the client.

6.9 Objective B, Step 1. Comments that he would only do this procedures in inventory if he sees some problems.

6.10 Step 2. Not concerned with this step because it is a cutoff problem, and would be done in connection with inventory.

6.11 Step 3. Would look at cash disbursements, backed up with cash receipts in any other journals. Notes that attorney's letters are usually included with the attorney's confirmation.

6.12 Step 4. Suggests that this might be done in connection with the obsolescence review when comparing balances between years and sales forecasts.

6.13 Audit Objective C. Here is where he would add his disbursements test. He would define his disbursement test as picking a scope number (would not change the scope between years, but would have the client prepare a schedule which lists date, cheque number, payee, and account).

6.14 Rereads Objective C and scans forward; reads Objective D, and suggests that all these things can be done together.

6.15 Goes back to Objective C, Step 1. Would not do this step, since his disbursement test would cover this. He might trace a couple of postings to the general ledger, but not into the subsidiary ledger.

6.16 Step 2. Would utilize this step, by having a tick mark that says traced and agreed to voucher register distribution, noting agreement and reasonableness of distribution. But again, feels disbursements test would cover this.

6.17 Step 3. Would do this with a tick mark with the check number and amount columns, saying that they traced to vendor invoice noting prices in accordance with current catalog.

6.18 Step 4. Would do this step.

6.19 Audit Objective D.

6.20 This step would be done in connection with his proposed disbursements test. He gives some examples and rationale and states that he is not eliminating these steps but consolidating them into one test.

6.21 Step 2. Suggests his disbursements test is a worksheet to accomplish this step.

6.22 Step 3. Says this was accomplished when the footings of the voucher register were accomplished.

6.23 Step 4. Again, this step is subsumed in his disbursements test.

APPENDIX C

REVENUE CYCLE PORTION OF AUDIT PROGRAM USED IN PACIFIC ELECTRONICS CASE

REVENUE CYCLE—SALES, SHIPPING, TRADE RECEIVABLES, CASH RECEIPTS

Approach

This transaction cycle represents the principal revenue-generating process, and is of prime concern to the auditor. The audit objectives and procedures contained in this section should be reviewed and, where appropriate, tailored to meet the specific needs of the engagement. In addition, other matters that may give rise to amended or additional detailed audit objectives and/or procedures are:

— Significant cash sales;

— Consignment sales;

— Intercompany sales or sales to related parties;

— Export sales;

— Trade notes receivable;

— Goods delivered direct to customer by a supplier;

— Significant scrap sales;

— Special discounts or rebates;

— Long-term contracts and installment sales;

— Returnable containers; and

— Lease, rental, or other financing-type transactions.

Internal Accounting Control

Evaluation and documentation of the company's system of internal accounting control is required. Such evaluation and documentation should adhere to firm standards as set forth in the audit manual. To effectively tailor the audit program to meet the needs of the engagement, the auditor must understand the system of internal accounting control in each audit area. The auditor may want to confirm his understanding of the system and ascertain the completeness of the documentation by walking one or more transactions through the system prior to tailoring the audit program.

Audit Objectives

Primary audit objectives normally include obtaining reasonable assurance that:

A) Trade receivables exist and balances are properly recorded;

B) Trade receivable balances are collectible and properly valued;

C) The method of recognizing revenue and related costs is acceptable and consistently applied;

D) Items shipped or services rendered are recorded as sales;

E) Sales cut-off is proper;

F) Recording and application of cash receipts is proper; and

G) Cash receipts cut-off is proper.

Item No.	Auditing Procedure	Period and Extent	Done By
	Internal Accounting Control		
1	Prior to performing the audit procedures, (a) review the documentation of the system of internal accounting control, and (b) ascertain that the audit program is appropriate in the circumstances.		
	Audit Objective A *Trade receivables exist and balances are properly recorded*		
1	Obtain and check the arithmetical accuracy of an aged listing of trade receivables as of the balance sheet date. Reconcile the balance with the general ledger and compare a selected number of individual accounts on the listing with the detailed subsidiary trade receivable records.		
2	Obtain confirmation of account balances from customers.		
3	Check replies to confirmations and investigate exceptions.		

Item No.	Auditing Procedure	Period and Extent	Done By
	Internal Accounting Control		
4	Send second request where replies to positive requests are not received. (Exceptions to sending second requests for non-responding positive confirmations should be rare, and the reasons for not sending them should be fully documented.)		
5	Investigate undelivered requests returned by post office. If possible, obtain better addresses and remail.		
6	Where replies are not received to positive requests for confirmation, apply alternative auditing procedures (e.g., check to subsequent remittance advices, shipping documents, billing records, customer orders, and correspondence files).		
7	Summarize results of confirmation requests and alternative procedures.		
8	Ascertain amount of any receivables that are non-current, and consider reclassification.		
9	Investigate material credit balances, and consider reclassification.		
	Audit Objective B		
	Trade receivables balances are collectible and properly valued		
1	Obtain and check the arithmetical accuracy of an analysis of allowance for doubtful trade receivables, and reconcile with related bad debt expense and general ledger.		
2	Examine supporting documents for material charge-offs during the year.		
3	Test aging of receivable balances.		
4	Compare aging summary with that of preceding year and investigate reasons for significant changes.		
5	Compute the number of days' sales in receivables, and compare with prior periods and others. Investigate reasons for significant changes.		

Item No.	Auditing Procedure	Period and Extent	Done By
	Internal Accounting Control		
6	Discuss collectibility of receivables with appropriate officials, check for subsequent receipts, and review applicable correspondence.		
7	For period of examination and period following balance sheet date, scan general ledger control and investigate material charge-offs and unusual transactions.		
8	In the light of findings from preceding steps, determine whether the allowance for doubtful receivables as of the balance sheet date is adequate.		
	Audit Objective C		
	The method of recognizing revenue and related costs is acceptable and consistently applied		
1	Obtain and check arithmetical accuracy of a summary of monthly sales and deductions from sales (by product lines, if possible) and cost of goods sold in comparative form with preceding year, and reconcile with general ledger. Investigate reasons for material or unusual fluctuations.		
2	Determine the acceptability and consistent application of the accounting methods used to recognize revenue and related cost, by reviewing the accounting principles involved and considering authoritative literature and current practice.		
3	Ascertain if sales are confined to relatively few large customers, whether any large sales contracts are about to expire, and the impact these may have on the financial statements and future operations.		
	Audit Objective D		
	Items shipped or services rendered are recorded as sales		
1	Review sales register for period and investigate posting to accounts other than cash or trade receivables.		

Item No.	Auditing Procedure	Period and Extent	Done By
	Internal Accounting Control		
2	Check footings of sales register and trace selected postings to general ledger.		
3	Ascertain whether the numerical sequence of sales-related documents (sales invoices, shipping reports, bills of lading, etc.) is accounted for properly.		
4	Scrutinize sales records and examine supporting documents for material or unusual items.		
5	For sales invoices selected throughout the year, examine supporting documents and trace postings to sales register and trade receivable records.		
6	For shipping records selected throughout the year, examine sales invoices and trace to postings in the sales register.		
7	For credit memos selected throughout the year, examine supporting documents and trace postings to sales register.		
	Audit Objective E		
	Sales cut-off is proper		
1	For the period before and after balance sheet date, check sales billed to and from shipping records to ascertain that a proper cut-off was made.		
2	Review credit memos issued subsequent to the balance sheet date for returned merchandise, discounts, allowances, etc., and ascertain whether any significant amounts relate to sales for the period under review.		
3	Ascertain whether adequate provision has been made for returns and product warranties, through a review and analysis of historical data, etc.		
Note:	Care should be taken not to duplicate procedures performed in connection with the production costs and inventories audit.		

Item No.	Auditing Procedure	Period and Extent	Done By
	Internal Accounting Control		
	Audit Objective F		
	Recording and application of cash receipts is proper		
1	Investigate significant postings from cash receipts book to accounts other than sales or trade receivables.		
2	Check footings of cash receipts journal and trace selected postings to the general ledger.		
3	Reconcile selected initial listings of cash receipts with total postings to trade receivables (or cash sales), compare with amount deposited in bank, and trace postings to individual customer account records.		
	Audit Objective G		
	Cash receipts cut-off is proper		
1	Review cash receipts recorded before and after the balance sheet date, to ensure that they are recorded in the correct period.		
2	Review cash receipts appearing on the bank statement subsequent to the balance sheet date and not appearing on the bank reconciliation, and ascertain that they were in fact receipts after the balance sheet date.		
Note:	Care should be taken not to duplicate procedures performed in the cash balances Audit. Consider performing these procedures before returning cut-off statements to the client.		

Conclusion

After performing the audit procedures, state your conclusion with respect to the work performed. If the auditor performing the procedures does not believe that they attained the audit objectives, the auditor should immediately inform the in-charge accountant, and appropriate action should be taken.

APPENDIX D

SUPPORTING MATERIALS FOR THE MULTI-DIMENSIONAL SCALING ANALYSIS OF CHAPTER 7

TABLE D-1

Stimulus Coordinate from MDS for the Four Auditors

Figure 7

M1's Final Stimulus Coordinates
Derived Stimulus Configuration

1 Dimension

1	-.385
2	.852
3	-.685
4	.416
5	.940
6	-1.138

Figure 8

S1'S Final Stimulus Coordinates
Derived Stimulus Configuration

3 Dimensions

1	.140	-.020	-.024
2	.378	.250	.072
3	.200	.414	.002
4	-.881	-.063	.241
5	-.540	-.227	-.313
6	.033	-.033	.381
7	.130	-.934	-.650
8	-.419	-.713	.135
9	-.159	.148	-.966
10	-.698	.866	1.421
11	-.747	.624	-.050
12	.937	-.519	-.013
13	.246	.204	-.217
14	.772	-.176	-.051
15	.607	.179	.031

Figure 9

M2's Final Stimulus Coordinates
Derived Stimulus Configuration

2 Dimensions

1	-.735	.450
2	-.846	.304
3	-.499	1.735
4	.253	.199
5	.772	-.116
6	.780	-.102
7	.864	.145
8	.781	-.102
9	-.701	-.447
10	.058	-.328
11	-.060	-.907
12	-.667	-.830

Figure 10

S2's Final Stimulus Coordinates
Derived Stimulus Configuration

3 Dimensions

1	.456	.665	-.379
2	-.346	-.382	.137
3	-.161	-.551	.359
4	.400	-.368	-.469
5	.528	-.527	-.651
6	-.902	.483	-.041
7	1.311	1.070	1.268
8	-.328	-.752	.185
9	-.958	.364	-.408

TABLE D-2
Summary Statistics for Subject M1

The Effective number of parameters is	5
The -2*log-likelihood is	14.7144
The value of the AIC statistic is	24.7144
The value of the BIC statistic is	30.6046

Standard Errors of Estimated Stimulus Coordinates

Stimulus	Dimension	Active parameters	Estimate	Standard error
1	1	1	-.385	.276
2	1	2	.852	.411
3	1	3	-.685	.355
4	1	4	.416	.211
5	1	5	.940	.570
6	1	6	-1.138	.520

Estimates of Dispersion Parameter(s)

Replication	Active parameters	Estimate	Standard error	Variance equivalent (in normal distribution)
All	Fixed	5.00000		.13159

TABLE D-3
Summary Statistics for Subject S1

The effective number of parameters is	39
The -2*log-likelihood is	312.6989
The value of the AIC statistic is	390.6989
The value of the BIC statistic is	518.3459

Standard Errors of Estimated Stimulus Coordinates

Stimulus	Dimension	Active parameters	Estimate	Standard error
1	1	1	.140	.249
2	1	2	.378	.216
3	1	3	.200	.227
4	1	4	-.881	.431
5	1	5	-.540	.384
6	1	6	.033	.194
7	1	7	.130	.558
8	1	8	-.419	.342
9	1	9	-.159	.298
10	1	10	-.698	.475
11	1	11	-.747	.339
12	1	12	.937	.362
13	1	13	.246	.192
14	1	14	.772	.291
15	1	15	.607	.220
1	2	16	-.020	.258
2	2	17	.250	.269
3	2	18	.414	.263
4	2	19	-.063	.241
5	2	20	-.227	.229
6	2	21	-.033	.257
7	2	22	-.934	.444
8	2	23	-.713	.297
9	2	24	.148	.325
10	2	25	.866	.562
11	2	26	.624	.339
12	2	27	-.519	.503
13	2	28	.204	.271
14	2	29	-.176	.245
15	2	30	.179	.247

Standard Errors of Estimated Stimulus Coordinates (cont.)

Stimulus	Dimension	Active parameters	Estimate	Standard error
1	3	31	-.024	.275
2	3	32	.072	.315
3	3	33	.002	.337
4	3	34	.241	.291
5	3	35	-.313	.205
6	3	36	.381	.309
7	3	37	-.650	.560
8	3	38	.135	.310
9	3	39	-.966	.397
10	3	40	1.421	.538
11	3	41	-.050	.210
12	3	42	-.013	1.394
13	3	43	-.217	.240
14	3	44	-.051	.501
15	3	45	.031	.395

Estimates of Dispersion Parameter(s)

Replication	Active parameters	Estimate	Standard error	Variance equivalent (in normal distribution)
All	Fixed	5.00000		.13159

TABLE D-4
Summary Statistics for Subject M2

The effective number of parameters is	21
The -2*log-likelihood is	109.6233
The value of the AIC statistic is	151.6233
The value of the BIC statistic is	210.1607

Standard Errors of Estimated Stimulus Coordinates

Stimulus	Dimension	Active parameters	Estimate	Standard error
1	1	1	-.735	.404
2	1	2	-.846	1.110
3	1	3	-.499	.348
4	1	4	.253	.331
5	1	5	.772	.304
6	1	6	.780	.330
7	1	7	.864	.412
8	1	8	.781	.319
9	1	9	-.701	.325
10	1	10	.058	.255
11	1	11	-.060	.300
12	1	12	-.667	.460
1	2	13	.450	.271
2	2	14	.304	.277
3	2	15	1.735	.843
4	2	16	.199	.285
5	2	17	-.116	.227
6	2	18	-.102	.223
7	2	19	.145	.268
8	2	20	-.102	.221
9	2	21	-.447	.195
10	2	22	-.328	.211
11	2	23	-.907	.406
12	2	24	-.830	.391

Estimates of Dispersion Parameter(s)

Replication	Active parameters	Estimate	Standard error	Variance equivalent (in normal distribution)
All	Fixed	5.00000		.13159

TABLE D-5
Summary Statistics for Subject S2

The effective number of parameters is	7
The -2*log-likelihood is	39.2707
The value of the AIC statistic is	53.2707
The value of the BIC statistic is	68.2727

Standard Errors of Estimated Stimulus Coordinates

Stimulus	Dimension	Active parameters	Estimate	Standard error
1	1	1	.456	.040
2	1	2	-.346	.018
3	1	3	-.161	.030
4	1	4	.400	.028
5	1	5	.528	.018
6	1	6	-.902	.074
7	1	7	1.311	.027
8	1	8	-.328	.041
9	1	9	-.958	.030
1	2	10	.665	.044
2	2	11	-.382	.023
3	2	12	-.551	.048
4	2	13	-.368	.036
5	2	14	-.527	.035
6	2	15	.483	.030
7	2	16	1.070	.057
8	2	17	-.752	.051
9	2	18	.364	.031
1	3	19	-.379	.032
2	3	20	.137	.013
3	3	21	.359	.018
4	3	22	-.469	.040
5	3	23	-.651	.038
6	3	24	-.041	.055
7	3	25	1.268	.058
8	3	26	.185	.031
9	3	27	-.408	.023

Estimates of Dispersion Parameter(s)

Replication	Active parameters	Estimate	Standard error	Variance equivalent (in normal distribution)
All	28	29.93131	.00026	.00367

In the case of MAXSCAL4, error terms can be measured in two ways: through an additivity assumption or a multiplicative assumption (technical details may be found in Takane, [1982]). The use of AIC and BIC statistics in these tables allows selection of the "best" model for the data. Details are shown for the "best" models selected; the statistics are provided for completeness. The standard errors of the estimated stimulus coordinates show the precision with which the points are being fitted in multi-dimensional space. Large standard errors indicate noisy data and imprecise estimation. For most subjects, the standard errors are relatively small, showing good estimation of the points.

Bibliography

Abdel Kahlik, A. R., and K. M. El Sheshai. **Information Choice and Utilization in an Experiment on Default Prediction.** *Journal of Accounting Research,* Autumn 1980: 325-342.

Abelson, R.P., and J.B. Black. **Introduction to Knowledge Structures.** In *Knowledge Structures,* ed. J.A. Galambos, R.P. Abelson and J.B. Black, Hillsdale, NJ: Lawrence Erlbaum Associates, 1986: 1-19.

Alba, J., and L. Hasher. **Is Memory Schematic?** *Psychological Bulletin,* Vol. 93, 1983: 203-231.

Albrecht, W., and J. McKeown. **Toward an Extended Use of Statistical Analytical Reviews in the Audit.** *Symposium on Audit Research II,* University of Illinois, 1977: 53-69.

Altman, E. I., and T. P. McGough. **Evaluation of a Company as a Going Concern.** *Journal of Accountancy,* Vol. 138, December 1974: 50-57.

American Institute of Certified Public Accountants. *Statement on Auditing Standards No. 23: Analytical Review Procedures,* 1978.

American Institute of Certified Public Accountants. *Statement on Auditing Standard No. 36: Review of Interim Financial Information,* 1981.

American Institute of Certified Public Accountants. *Statement on Standards for Accounting and Review Services 1,* 1979.

American Institute of Certified Public Accountants. *Proposed Statement on Auditing Standards: Analytical Procedures,* 1987.

American Institute of Certified Public Accountants. *Statement on Auditing Standards No. 47: Audit Risk and Materiality in Conducting an Audit,* 1983.

Arens, A. A., and J. K. Loebbecke. *Auditing: An Integrated Approach.* 2nd ed., Englewood Cliffs, NJ: Prentice-Hall, 1980.

Arrington, C. E., W. Hillison, and R. C. Icerman. **Research in Analytical Review: The State of the Art.** *Journal of Accounting Literature,* Vol. 2, Spring 1983: 151-185.

Ashton, R. H. *Research in Audit Decision Making: Rationale, Evidence and Implications.* Research Monograph No. 6. Vancouver, Canada: Canadian Certified General Accountants' Research Foundation, 1983.

Biggs, S. F. **Improving Auditor Judgment Through Research: A Problem and Some Potential Solutions.** *Advances in Accounting,* Vol. 2, 1985: 169-183.

Biggs, S. F. **An Empirical Investigation of the Information Processes Underlying Four Models of Choice Behavior.** In *Behavioral Experiments in Accounting II,* ed. T. J. Burns. Ohio State University, 1979.

Biggs, S. F., W. F. Messier, and J. V. Hansen. **A Descriptive Analysis of Computer Audit Specialists' Decision-Making Behavior in Advanced Computer Environments.** *Auditing: A Journal of Practice and Theory,* Vol. 6, No. 2, Spring 1987: 1-21.

Biggs, S.F., and T. J. Mock. **An Investigation of Auditor Decision Processes in the Evaluation of Internal Controls and Audit Scope Decisions.** *Journal of Accounting Research,* Spring 1983: 234-255.

Biggs, S. F., T. J. Mock and P.R. Watkins. **A Survey of ARPs in Auditing.** Working Paper, University of Southern California, 1984.

Biggs, S. F., T. J. Mock and P.R. Watkins. **Auditors' Use of Analytical Review in Audit Program Design.** *The Accounting Review*, January 1988.

Biggs, S. F., and M. Selfridge. **Combining Rule-Based Logic and Network-Based Logic in Expert Systems in Accounting.** *Collected Abstracts of the National Meeting of the American Accounting Association.* New York, August 1986.

Biggs, S.F., and J. J. Wild. **A Note on the Practice of Analytical Review.** *Auditing: A Journal of Practice and Theory*, Spring 1984: 68-79.

Biggs, S.F., and J. J. Wild. **An Investigation of Auditor Judgment in Analytical Review.** *The Accounting Review*, October 1985: 607-633.

Blocher, E., R. Esposito and J. J. Willingham. **Auditors' Analytical Review Judgments for Payroll Expense.** *Auditing: A Journal of Practice and Theory*, Fall 1983: 75-91.

Chi, M.T.H., R. Glaser and E. Rees. **Expertise in Problem Solving.** In *Advances in the Psychology of Human Intelligence*, Vol. 1, R.J. Sternberg, ed. Hillsdale, N.J: Lawrence Erlbaum Associates, 1982: 7-75.

Chi, M.T.H., P. J. Feltovich and R. Glaser. **Categorization and Representation of Physics Problems by Experts and Novices.** *Cognitive Science*, 1981: 121-152.

Canadian Institute of Chartered Accountants. **Extent of Audit Testing.** *CICA Handbook*, Toronto: The Canadian Institute of Chartered Accountants, 1980.

Carroll, J.D., and P. Arabie. **Multi-dimensional scaling.** *Annual Review of Psychology*, 1980: 607-649.

Cohen, P.R. *Heuristic Reasoning about Uncertainty: An Artificial Intelligence Approach.* Unpublished Doctoral Dissertation, Stanford University, 1984.

Collins, D.J. **Analytical Review: The Problem of Model Validity.** Paper presented at the Fourth Duke University Symposium, April 28-29, 1980.

Davis, R. **Expert Systems: Where are We? And Where Do We Go From Here?** *AI Magazine*, Spring 1982: 3-22.

Dawes, R. M., and B. Corrigan. **Linear Models in Decision Making.** *Psychological Bulletin*, Vol. 81, 1974: 95-106.

Doyle, J. **Methodological Simplicity in Expert System Construction: The Case of Judgments and Reasoned Assumptions.** *AI Magazine*, Summer 1983a: 39-43.

Doyle, J. **Some Theories of Reasoned Assumptions: An Essay in Rational Psychology.** Unpublished Working Paper CS-83-125, Computer Science Department, Carnegie-Mellon University, May 1983b.

Doyle, J. **Expert Systems Without Computers or Theory and Trust in Artificial Intelligence.** *AI Magazine*, Summer 1984: 59-63.

Dugan, M., J. Gentry and K. Shriver. **The X-11 Model: A New Analytical Review Technique for the Auditor.** *Auditing: A Journal of Practice and Theory*, Spring 1985: 11-21.

Einhorn, H., and R. Hogarth. **Behavioral Decision Theory: Processes of Judgment and Choice.** *Journal of Accounting Research,* Spring 1981: 1-41.

Einhorn, H., and R. Hogarth. **Prediction, Diagnosis, and Causal Thinking in Forecasting.** *Journal of Forecasting,* January-March 1982: 23-36.

Einhorn, H., and R. Hogarth. **Probable Cause: A Decision Making Framework.** Unpublished Working Paper, Center for Decision Research, Graduate School of Business, University of Chicago, January 1985.

Elstein, A.S., L. S. Shulman and S. A. Sprafka. *Medical Problem Solving: An Analysis of Clinical Reasoning.* Harvard University Press, 1978.

Ericsson, K., and H. Simon. **Verbal Reports as Data.** *Psychological Review,* Vol. 87, 1980: 215-51.

Ericsson, K., and H. Simon. **Thinking-Aloud Protocols as Data.** *Psychological Review,* 1980: 215-51.

Ericsson, K., and H. Simon. *Protocol Analysis: Verbal Reports as Data.* Cambridge, MA: MIT Press, 1984.

Esposito, R. *Analytical Review Procedures: Discussion Paper.* Unpublished manuscript, Peat, Marwick, Mitchell & Co., September 10, 1980.

Feigenbaum, E., and P. McCorduck. *The Fifth Generation Artificial Intelligence and Japan's Computer Challenge to the World.* Addison-Wesley, 1983.

Felix, W., and W. Kinney. **Research in the Auditor's Opinion Formulation Process: State of the Art.** *The Accounting Review,* April 1982: 245-271.

Gibbins, M. **Propositions About the Psychology of Professional Judgment in Public Accounting.** *Journal of Accounting Research,* Spring 1984: 103-125.

Gibbins, M., and F. M. Wolf. **Auditors' Subjective Decision Environment - The Case of a Normal External Audit.** *The Accounting Review,* Vol. 57, January 1982: 105-124.

Gick, M., and K. Holyoak. **Schema Induction and Analogical Transfer.** *Cognitive Psychology,* Vol. 15, 1983: 1-38.

Gordon, J., and E. Shortliffe. **A Method for Managing Evidential Reasoning in a Hierarchical Hypothesis Space.** *Artifical Intelligence,* July 1985: 323-357.

Hayes-Roth, F., D. Waterman and D. Lenat. *Building Expert Systems.* Addison-Wesley, 1983.

Heintz, J., and G. White. *Auditor Judgment in Analytical Review: Some Further Evidence.* Unpublished manuscript, Indiana University, 1986a.

Heintz, J., and G. White. *Effects of Context and Trend in Analytical Review Judgments.* Unpublished manuscript, Indiana University, 1986b.

Hogarth, R. *Judgment and Choice: The Psychology of Decision.* New York: Wiley, 1980.

Hogarth, R., and S. Makridakis. **Forecasting and Planning: An Evaluation.** *Management Science,* Vol. 27, 1981: 115-138.

Hopwood, A. G. **Editorial.** *Accounting, Organizations, and Society,* Vol. 5, No. 2, 1980.

Hylas, R., and R. Ashton. **Audit Detection of Financial Statement Errors.** *The Accounting Review,* October 1982: 751-765.

Johnson, P. **The Expert Mind: A New Challenge for the Information Scientist.** In *Beyond Productivity: Information Systems Development for Organizational Effectiveness*, ed. Th. M. A. Bemelman, Elsevier Science Publishers B.V. Amsterdam: The Netherlands 1984: 367-384.

Johnson, P. A. **Cognitive Models of Expertise.** Paper presented at the USC/DH&S Audit Judgment Symposium, February 1986.

Johnson, P., D. Severance and P. Feltovich. **Design of Decision Support Systems in Medicine: Rationale and Principles from Analysis of Physician Expertise.** In *Proceedings of the Twelfth Hawaii International Conference on System Sciences: Selected Papers in Medical Information Processing*, ed. B. Shriver, T. Walker and R. Sprague, Western Periodical Company, 1979.

Johnson, P., A. Duran, F. Hassebrock, J. Moller, M. Prietula, P. Feltovich, and D. Swanson. **Expertise and Error in Diagnostic Reasoning.** *Cognitive Science* Vol. 5, 1981: 235-283.

Johnson, P., F. Hassebrock, A. Duran, and J. Moller. **Multimethod Study of Clinical Judgment.** *Organizational Behavior and Human Performance*, Vol. 30, 1982: 201-230.

Joyce, E. **Expert Judgment in Audit Program Planning.** *Supplement to Journal of Accounting Research*, 1976: 29-60.

Joyce, E., and G. Biddle. **Anchoring and Adjustment in Probabilistic Inference in Auditing.** *Journal of Accounting Research*, Spring 1981: 120-145.

Kaplan, R. **Developing a Financial Planning Model for Analytical Review: A Feasibility Study.** Symposium III, University of Illinois, 1979: 3-30.

Kinney, W. R. **ARIMA and Regression in Analytical Review: An Empirical Test.** *The Accounting Review*, January 1978: 48-60.

Kinney, W. R. **Integrating Audit Tests: Regression Analysis and Partitioned Dollar-Unit Sampling.** *Journal of Accounting Research* Vol. 17, Autumn 1979: 456-475.

Kinney, W. R. **The Predictive Power of Limited Information in Preliminary Analytical Review: An Empirical Study.** *Supplement to the Journal of Accounting Research*, 1979: 148-165.

Kinney, W. **Predicting Auditor-Initiated Adjustments Using Paired-Balance Method.** *Accounting, Auditing and Finance*, Fall 1981: 5-17.

Kinney, W. R. **Quantitative Applications in Auditing.** *Journal of Accounting*, Vol. 2, Spring 1983: 187-204.

Kinney, W. R., and G. Salamon. **The Effect of Measurement Error on Regression Results in Analytical Review.** Symposium III, University of Illinois, 1979: 49-64.

Kinney, W., and W. Uecker. **Mitigating the Consequences of Anchoring in Auditor Judgments.** *The Accounting Review*, January 1982: 55-69.

Klersey, G. F., and T. J. Mock. *Common Coding of Verbal Protocols in Accounting and Auditing.* Working Paper No. 93, Center for Accounting Research, University of Southern California, January 1986.

Kolodner, J.L., and R.L. Simpson, Jr. **Problem Solving and Dynamic Memory.** In *Experience, Memory, and Reasoning*, ed. J.L. Kolodner and C.K. Riesbeck, Hillsdale, NJ: Lawrence Erlbaum Associates, 1986: 99-114.

Kuhn, T.S. *The Structure of Scientific Revolutions, International Encyclopedia of Unified Science*, 2nd enlarged edition, Chicago: University of Chicago Press, 1970.

Kuhn, T.S. **Logic of Discovery or Psychology of Research?** In *Criticism and the Growth of Knowledge*, I. Lakatos and A. Musgrave, Cambridge University Press, 1974.

Lachman, R., J.L. Lachman, and E. C. Butterfield. *Cognitive Psychology and Information Processing: An Introduction*, Hillsdale, NJ: Lawrence Erlbaum Associates, 1979.

Larkin, J., D. McDermott, D. Simon and H. Simon. **Expert and Novice Performance in Solving Physics Problems.** *Science*, June 1980: 1335-1342.

Lev, B. **On the Use of Index Models in Analytical Reviews by Auditors.** *Journal of Accounting Research*, Vol. 18, Autumn 1980: 524-550.

Libby, R. **Availability and the Generation of Hypotheses in Analytical Review.** *Journal of Accounting Research*, Vol. 23, Autumn 1985: 648-667.

Luce, R. D. *Individual Choice Behavior*, New York: Wiley, 1959.

McCloskey, D. *The Rhetoric of Economics*, Madison: University of Wisconsin Press, 1985.

Minsky, M. **A Framework for Representing Knowledge.** In *The Psychology of Computer Vision*, P. Winston, ed., New York: McGraw-Hill, 1975.

Mitroff, I.I., and R. H. Kilmann. *Methodological Approaches to Social Science*. San Francisco: Jossey-Bass, Inc., Publishers, 1978.

Mock, T., and J. Turner. **Internal Accounting Control Evaluation and Auditor Judgment**. Audit Research Monograph No. 3, AICPA, 1981.

Newell, A., and H. Simon. *Human Problem Solving*, Englewood Cliffs, NJ: Prentice-Hall, 1972.

Nisbett, R., and L. Ross. *Human Inference: Strategies and Shortcomings of Social Judgment*, Englewood Cliffs, NJ: Prentice-Hall, 1980.

Norman, D., and D. Bobrow. **On Data-Limited and Resource-Limited Processes.** *Cognitive Psychology*, Vol. 7, 1975: 44-64.

Payne, J., M. Braunstein and J. Carroll. **Exploring Predecisional Behavior: An Alternative Approach to Decision Research.** *Organizational Behavior and Human Performance*, 1978: 17-44.

Pylyshyn, S. *Computation and Cognition: Toward a Foundation for Cognitive Science*, Cambridge, MA: MIT Press, 1984.

Reinharz, S. *On Becoming a Social Scientist*, San Francisco: Jossey-Bass, Inc., Publishers, 1979.

Reiser, Brian J. **Knowledge-Directed Retrieval of Autobiographical Memories.** In *Experience, Memory, and Reasoning*, eds. J.L. Kolodner and C.K. Riesbeck, Hillsdale, NJ: Lawrence Erlbaum Associates, 1986: 75-98.

Reynolds, Schiffman and Young. *Applied Multi-dimensional Scaling*, New York: Academic Press, 1980.

Roshi, S. *Arity Expert Development Manual*, Preface, 1986.

Rosnow, R. L. *Paradigms in Transition: The Methodology of Social Inquiry*, Oxford, England: Oxford University Press, 1981.

Schank, R., and R. Abelson. *Scripts, Plans, Goals and Understanding: An Inquiry into Human Knowledge Structures*, Hillsdale, NJ: Lawrence Erlbaum Associates, 1977.

Shafer, G. **Probability Judgment in Artificial Intelligence and Expert Systems.** Unpublished Working Paper No. 165, School of Business, The University of Kansas, December 1984.

Shafer, G., and A. Tversky. **Languages and Designs for Probability Judgment.** *Cognitive Science* (forthcoming).

Shanteau, J. Paper presented at the 1987 USC/DH&S Audit Judgment Symposium, 1987. (forthcoming, Accounting, Organizations and Society)

Shepard, R. N. **Representation of Structure in Similarity Data: Problems and Prospects.** *Psychometrika,* December 1974: 373-417.

Shields, M., I. Solomon, and W. Waller. **Unaudited Book Values and the Accuracy of Auditors Pre-Sampling Judgments and Decisions.** Unpublished manuscript, University of Arizona, 1986.

Simon, H. *The New Science of Management Decision,* Englewood Cliffs, NJ: Prentice-Hall, 1977.

Slovic, P., D. Fleissner, and W. S. Bauman. **Analyzing the Use of Information in Investment Decision Making: A Methodological Proposal.** *Journal of Business,* April 1972: 283-301.

Smith, D. *Analytical Review: A Research Study,* Canadian Institute of Chartered Accountants, 1983.

Steinbart, P. *The Construction of an Expert System to Make Materiality Judgments.* Ph.D. Dissertation, Michigan State University, 1984.

Stringer, K. **A Statistical Technique for Analytical Review.** *Supplement to the Journal of Accounting Research,* 1975: 1-9.

Stringer, K., and T. Stewart. *Statistical Techniques for Analytical Review,* New York: Wiley, 1986.

Swieringa, R., M. Gibbins, L. Larsson, and J. Sweeney. **Experiments in the Heuristics of Human Information Processing.** *Supplement to the Journal of Accounting Research,* 1976: 159-187.

Tabor, R. H., and J. T. Willis. **Empirical Evidence on the Changing Role of Analytical Review Procedures.** *Auditing: A Journal of Practice and Theory,* Vol. 4, Spring 1985: 93-109.

Takane, Y. **Multi-dimensional Successive Category Scaling: Maximum Likelihood Method.** *Psychometrika,* Vol. 46, 1981a: 9-28.

Takane, Y., and J. D. Carroll. **Nonmetric Maximum Likelihood Multi-dimensional Scaling from Directional Rankings of Similarities.** *Psychometrika,* Vol. 46., 1981b: 389-405.

Tversky, A., and I. Gati. **Studies of Similarity.** In *Cognition and Categorization,* ed. E. Rosch and B.B. Lloyd. Hillsdale, NJ: Lawrence Erlbaum Associates, 1978.

Tversky, A., and D. Kahneman. **Judgment Under Uncertainty: Heuristics and Biases.** *Science,* September 1974: 1124-1131.

University of Georgia. **Identification of Audit Research Issues.** *Audit Research Newsletter,* Vol. 2, No. 1, Spring 1981.

Wallace, W. A. **Analytical Review: Misconceptions, Applications and Experience.** Part 2, *CPA Journal,* Vol. 53, February 1983: 18-27.

Watkins, P. R. **Internal Auditors' and Financial Executives' Perceptions of Internal Accounting Controls.** Working Paper CAR, University of Southern California, 1980.

Watkins, P. R. **Multi-dimensional Scaling in Accounting.** *Journal of Accounting Research*, Spring 1984.

Wild, J., and S. Biggs. **Strategic Considerations for Unaudited Account Values in Analytical Review.** Unpublished manuscript, University of Connecticut, 1986.

Willingham, J. Presentation at USC Symposium on Audit Risk, February 1985.